RULE AND ENERGY

GEORGE ELLISTON, well-known Cincinnati journalist and poet, in her will established the GEORGE ELLISTON POETRY FOUNDATION at the University of Cincinnati. A programme of public lectures by distinguished poets has been presented on this foundation annually since 1951.

1951	ROBERT P. TRISTRAM COFFIN
1952	JOHN BERRYMAN
1953	STEPHEN SPENDER
1954	ROBERT LOWELL
1955	ROBERT FROST
1956	PETER VIERECK
1957	JOHN BETJEMAN
1958	RANDALL JARRELL
1959	KARL SHAPIRO
1960	DAVID DAICHES
1961	RICHARD EBERHART
1962	JOHN PRESS

RULE AND ENERGY

TRENDS IN BRITISH POETRY SINCE
THE SECOND WORLD WAR

The George Elliston Poetry Foundation Lectures
University of Cincinnati, 1962

JOHN PRESS

London
OXFORD UNIVERSITY PRESS
NEW YORK   TORONTO
1963

Oxford University Press, Amen House, London E.C.4

GLASGOW NEW YORK TORONTO MELBOURNE WELLINGTON
BOMBAY CALCUTTA MADRAS KARACHI LAHORE DACCA
CAPE TOWN SALISBURY NAIROBI IBADAN ACCRA
KUALA LUMPUR HONG KONG

Printed in Great Britain

To
Bill and Gladys Clark

and to my other friends
in Cincinnati

PREFACE

WHEN the University of Cincinnati honoured me with its invitation to give the George Elliston Poetry Foundation Lectures for 1962, it suggested that I should take as my theme Trends in British Poetry since the Second World War. Anybody rash enough to write about trends, movements, schools, or tendencies in poetry must run the risk of being haunted and mocked by William Empson's sardonic lines:

> Waiting for the end, boys, waiting for the end.
> Not a chance of blend, boys, things have got to tend.
> Think of those who vend, boys, think of how we wend,
> Waiting for the end, boys, waiting for the end.[1]

Yet I have given this book its somewhat cumbrous sub-title in order to remind myself and my readers that the field of my survey is strictly limited. I have not considered verse written by Americans or by poets of other English-speaking lands outside Britain, and I have disregarded the work of poets who enjoyed a substantial reputation before 1939: although it is not easy to determine which poets fall into this category, I have judged that, for example, the poetry of W. H. Auden, Ronald Bottrall, Norman Cameron, Roy Campbell, C. Day Lewis, Patrick Kavanagh, Louis MacNeice, Kathleen Raine, Stephen Spender, and Dylan Thomas lies beyond the confines of this study. I have discussed only those poets who had not published a collection of poems before 1939, or who, in that year, were under the age of thirty. I am aware that I have omitted several poets who come under these headings, and who would deserve to be mentioned in any comprehensive history of the period under review.

This book was designed for an American audience: the dedication which it bears acknowledges a debt of gratitude that I constantly remember but cannot hope to repay.

J.P.

[1] 'Just a Smack at Auden'.

ACKNOWLEDGEMENTS

For permission to quote copyright passages grateful acknowledgement is made to the following:

the author, Macmillan & Co. Ltd., London, St. Martin's Press, Inc., New York, and The Macmillan Company of Canada for John Wain's 'A Song for Major Eatherley' from *Weep Before God*;

John Murray Ltd. and Houghton Mifflin Co., Boston, Mass. for John Betjeman's 'Middlesex' from *Collected Poems*;

The Times Literary Supplement for Terence Tiller's 'Prothalamion';

Mrs. W. B. Yeats, Macmillan & Co. Ltd., London, and The Macmillan Company, New York for lines by W. B. Yeats from *Collected Poems* (Definitive Edn. © 1956 by The Macmillan Company);

Routledge & Kegan Paul Ltd. for lines by D. J. Enright from *The Laughing Hyena*, by John Wain from *A Word Carved on a Sill*, and by Donald Davie from *A Winter Talent*;

Victor Gollancz Ltd. for lines by Kingsley Amis from *A Case of Samples*;

The Hand and Flower Press for Thomas Blackburn's 'The Journey' from *The Outer Darkness* and 'The Margin', 'Intimations', and 'Orpheus' from *The Holy Stone*;

J. M. Dent & Sons Ltd. and New Directions, Publishers (U.S.A.) for Dylan Thomas's 'A Refusal to Mourn the Death, by Fire, of a Child in London' from *The Collected Poems of Dylan Thomas* (© 1957 by New Directions);

Macmillan & Co. Ltd. for Donald Davie's 'Too Late for Satire' from *New Lines*, edited by Robert Conquest;

Rupert Hart-Davis Ltd. for lines by R. S. Thomas from *Song at the Year's Turning*, *Poetry for Supper*, and *Tares*, and for Charles Causley's 'Innocent's Song' from *Johnny Alleluia*;

Hamish Hamilton Ltd. for Kathleen Raine's 'Invocation' from *Collected Poems*;

Methuen & Co. Ltd. for lines by J. R. Clemo from *The Map of Clay* and by John Heath-Stubbs from *A Charm Against the Toothache*;

Chatto & Windus Ltd. and Harcourt, Brace & World, Inc., New York for William Empson's 'This Last Pain' from *Collected Poems*;

Martin Secker & Warburg Ltd. for lines by D. J. Enright from *Bread Rather than Blossoms*;

the authors and the University of Reading for Kingsley Amis's 'Sonnet from Orpheus' from *A Frame of Mind*, lines by Bernard Spencer from *The Twist in the Plotting*, and lines by Gordon Wharton from *Errors of Observation*;

the author for Philip Larkins's 'At First';

The Marvell Press for lines by Philip Larkin from *The Less Deceived*, for Anthony Thwaite's 'Oedipus' from *Home Truths*, and lines by Donald Davie from *A Sequence for Francis Parkman* and *The Forests of Lithuania*;

the authors and *Listen* for Kingsley Amis's 'After Goliath' and A. Alvarez's 'The Vigil';

André Deutsch Ltd. for lines by Roy Fuller from *Collected Poems*, for Elizabeth Jennings's 'Song at the Beginning of Autumn' from *A Way of Looking*, and David Wright's 'Monologue of a Deaf Man';

The Hogarth Press Ltd. for lines by Terence Tiller from *Unarm, Eros, Reading a Medal*, and *The Inward Animal*; lines by Norman MacCaig from *A Common Grace, The Sinai Sort*, and *Riding Lights*; and for Norman Cameron's 'The Compassionate Fool' from *Collected Poems*;

Putnam & Co. Ltd. for lines by Thomas Blackburn from *In the Fire, The Next Word*, and *A Smell of Burning*;

William Morrow & Co. Inc., New York for lines by Thomas Blackburn from *A Smell of Burning*;

Eyre & Spottiswoode Ltd. and A. Watkins, Inc., New York for lines by John Heath-Stubbs from *The Swarming of the Bees* (U.S. title: *The Charity of the Stars*);

Faber & Faber Ltd. for lines by Vernon Watkins from *Ballad of the Mari Lwyd, The Lady with the Unicorn, The Death Bell*, and *Cypress and Acacia*; for Louis MacNeice's 'Notes for a Biography' from *Solstices*; for lines by W. H. Auden from *Collected Poems;* lines by George Barker from *Collected Poems*; lines by F. T. Prince from *Poems*; lines by Ted Hughes from *The Hawk in the Rain* and *Lupercal*; lines by Thom Gunn from *Fighting Terms, The Sense of Movement*, and *My Sad Captains*; and lines by Lawrence Durrell from *Collected Poems*;

the author for *The True Confession of George Barker;*

David Higham Associates Ltd. for lines by John Heath-Stubbs from *A Charm Against the Toothache* and by D. J. Enright from *Some Men are Brothers;*

Fortune Press Ltd. for lines by F. T. Prince from *Soldiers Bathing*;

Fantasy Press, Oxford, for lines by Donald Davie from *Brides of Reason*;

Oxford University Press, Inc., New York for Louis MacNeice's 'Notes for a Biography' from *Solstices*;

Mr. John Lehmann for Demetrios Capetanakis's 'Abel';

The University of Chicago Press for lines by Thom Gunn from *The Sense of Movement* and *My Sad Captains*;

Harper & Row, Publishers, New York for lines by Ted Hughes from *The Hawk in the Rain* (© 1956, 1957 by Ted Hughes) and *Lupercal* (© 1960 by Ted Hughes);

New Directions, Publishers (U.S.A.) for lines by Vernon Watkins from *The Death Bell* and *Cypress and Acacia*;

Criterion Books, Inc., New York for lines by George Barker from *Collected Poems, 1930–1955* (© 1958 by Criterion Books, Inc.);

E. P. Dutton & Co., Publishers, New York for lines by Lawrence Durrell from *Collected Poems* (© 1956, 1960 by Lawrence Durrell);

Random House, Inc., New York for lines by W. H. Auden from *Collected Poems*.

CONTENTS

I

A NEUTRAL TONE

IT would be a much neater world than it is if great changes in politics always brought about an immediate revolution in the arts, if new ways of living invariably went hand in hand with experiments and discoveries in poetry, painting, and music. The arts, however, moving with a rhythm of their own and responsive to an inner logic, obey laws of their own nature; and whatever their relationship may be with the society in which they flourish or decay, it is one that cannot be reduced to a simple formula. The First World War, for example, which destroyed beyond repair an elaborate and complex civilization, altered the pattern of life in almost every occidental society; yet its direct influence on the arts was negligible. For the radical innovations in the arts of the Western world belong to the years before 1914, when Stravinsky and Schoenberg, Picasso, Kandinsky and the Cubists were fashioning the music and the painting which today we still call modern, although they are already more than half a century old. If we confine ourselves to English poetry we shall find that Pound, Eliot, and Yeats had, by 1914, laid the foundations of the modern movement in poetry which was to flower so abundantly during the next three or four decades. I use the phrase 'English poetry' with some misgivings: we ought always to remember that modern poetry in English was created by two Americans and an Irishman, all of whom took from their study of French Symbolism those elements which they found most congenial, and which it seemed they could most readily exploit in order to enlarge and enrich the development of their own art.

There is, then, no reason to suppose that poetry must necessarily have been transformed by the outbreak of the Second World War, or that verse written since 1945 will inevitably be radically different from pre-war verse. Poets do not group themselves into movements and schools, or alter their habits of composition, in order to justify the labels cherished by so many compilers of literary textbooks and by some tidy-minded, pigeon-holing sociologists. A poet's job at any given moment is to solve certain problems, technical, intellectual, imaginative, and spiritual, knowing that their solution will pose a further set of difficulties and challenges. Only in this solitary exploration of his uniqueness, and not in any flamboyant pursuit of the contemporary, can a poet hope to grasp that elusive and indefinable reality which stamps the work of all major poets — the spirit of the age.

Yet it so happens that the years 1939–41 mark the end of an epoch in English poetry, for reasons only partially connected with the coming of war. In January 1939 the death occurred of W. B. Yeats, whom I take to be the greatest poet in the English language of the present century, although as a technical innovator he ranks below Eliot, and below Ezra Pound, who had helped him to remould his style in middle age and so to remake himself. 'East Coker', the second of the *Four Quartets*, appeared in September 1940, having been designed as a poem for the Easter of that year. The Quartets are the crown and consummation of that phase of Eliot's career which began with 'Ash Wednesday', and, indeed, of all his pre-war poetry. Since 1945, apart from one short, unsatisfactory poem, he has written no verse except in dramatic form. For Ezra Pound also the outbreak of war proved decisive, and (if I may for a moment diverge from my main theme) the deaths of James Joyce and of Virginia Woolf, in their very different ways, confirm the impression that an age was drawing to its close.

The departure of W. H. Auden for America a few months before the coming of war is noteworthy both as a turning-point in his own life and as a landmark in the relationship between English and American poetry. Matthew Arnold derided the notion that any such entity as American literature existed, there being only English literature one and indivisible. When Quiller-Couch compiled the *Oxford Book of English Verse* (1900) he included Poe, Longfellow,

Whittier, Emerson, and Whitman, casually remarking that he had not 'sought in these Islands only, but wheresoever the Muse has followed the tongue which among living tongues she most delights to honour', and not pausing to ask whether in the course of her travels the Muse had acquired any distinctive American accent. It was natural for Pound and Eliot to swoop on London in the early years of the century since only there could the citadel of English poetry be taken by storm, nor was it strange that Robert Frost, unable to find a publisher in his native land, should gain recognition first in the England of 1913. That Henry James and T. S. Eliot should acquire British nationality was flattering to their adopted land, but not an occasion for astonishment.

Auden's decision to cross the Atlantic and to take American citizenship, though less momentous, may well appear in retrospect an indication that the tide has turned. It is significant, and to an Englishman depressing, that, like Robert Frost in his day, the poet Charles Tomlinson, scarcely granted a hearing in his own country, should have achieved success and the publication of his first substantial volume on the far side of the Atlantic. One of the most gifted young poets of the nineteen-fifties, Thom Gunn, has made his home in the States, and although none of his contemporaries has followed his example, a spell of teaching in an American university, or a journey there on a scholarship, has become for a young English post-war poet the equivalent of the spell in Paris so eagerly sought by a young American in the nineteen-twenties.

In 1945 the way was clear for a new generation of poets to practise their art in a Britain where much had been swept away by German bombs, economic change, and a revolution in men's political ideas. Before examining the work of these younger poets, we must first glance at this new society which has been developing its characteristic patterns for the past decade and a half. The physical appearance of Britain has been transformed, and so has the way of life of fifty million people. New housing estates, the proliferation of dormitory suburbs festooned with television aerials, the setting up of a National Health Service, the provision of compulsory free secondary education for all up to the age of fifteen, the Ameri-canization of our culture — these are revolutionary features of a society which, enjoying an unbroken spell of full employment and a greater measure of social security than ever before, has nonetheless been living in the shadow cast by the fear of nuclear annihilation. It is a society which has displayed an increasing aimlessness and boredom, a growing mania for watching commercialized sport, an obsession with violence, a fascinated interest in sexual titillation, and a desire to escape from human responsibility and reality by dwelling upon the dreamworld of space-travel:

> We had fed the heart on fantasies,
> The heart's grown brutal from the fare.

One or two results of the social revolution have already begun to influence the writing of poetry in this country. The burdens of direct taxation, heavy death duties, and steady inflation have removed from the scene the young writer who in the past managed to live in London or in the Mediterranean on a small private income, and have virtually wiped out the leisured, cultivated patrons of literature who still survived between the wars. At the same time, the expansion of the universities and the increasing number of government scholar-ships have made it possible for young men and women of all classes to become university graduates.

In a society such as our own where education is revered as a means of acquiring technical knowledge and power, and where class-barriers have been camouflaged rather than destroyed, a degree, especially from one of the major universities, gives a man prestige and a passport to a comparatively well-paid, interesting job. Some egalitarian thinkers deplore the process of creaming-off, on the grounds that it diverts the cleverest working-class boys to Oxford and Cambridge, infecting them with the ideals of a com-petitive society whose potent, vulgar symbol is the ladder of success, and depriving the working-class of its natural leaders. (Egalitarians are almost the only people who wish to keep in currency so vague and misleading a term as *working-class*.)

Many of the young men in question, divided between admiration for the genuine values and traditions still maintained at the older universities, contempt for the futile superficiality of upper-middle-class culture, and a shamefaced desire for the pickings which it may provide, regard the affluent society that has fostered them with a mixture of disgust, envy, and aloof resentment. Some of these men have been taught English at school by pupils or followers of F. R. Leavis and may themselves become graduates in English, after which they may teach English in schools or in provincial universities. Despising the concept of *belles lettres* as the frivolous pastime of hollow gentlemen, they believe that, like the study of the Classics in the past, the study of English literature might form the centre of a finer, more humane education than anything which our present system has to offer. Many poets who have gone through the same mill write poetry which, explicitly or implicitly, is directed at an audience of such graduates; and since nobody can hope to live on the proceeds of his verse, most poets earn their keep by reviewing or by similar hack-work, by teaching English at a university or grammar-school, or by some form of cultural diffusion.

These shiftings in the contemporary climate of opinion help to account for the current emphasis on strenuous intelligence, moral discrimination, and maturity of judgement, virtues dearest to academic puritans; they have been partially responsible for some of the disfiguring elements which can be detected in recent verse and criticism of verse — a grating tone of arid self-righteousness, of uneasy, rancorous moralizing, a tight-lipped narrowness of response, which are poor substitutes for the finely tempered intelligence of Eliot, the tragic passion of Yeats, or the tender, lyrical humanity of Hardy. It is against this background of change and confusion that we must try to discern the characteristic features of the poetry written by the younger poets since the war.

The most striking of these features is the general retreat from direct comment on or involvement with any political or social doctrine, and this is particularly noticeable if we contrast the verse of the past two decades with that of the nineteen-thirties. From the

B

rise of Hitler to the outbreak of the war English poets were mesmerized and haunted by events in Europe and by the pattern of society at home. Even Yeats composed songs for General O'Duffy's pinchbeck fascist Blueshirts, while T. S. Eliot was moved by the ever-darkening chaos of Western Europe to write 'Triumphal March' and 'Difficulties of a Statesman'. The Spanish Civil War, which inspired the publication of *Poems for Spain*, an anthology of verse by poets who supported the Republicans, lured a number of young writers to their death in battle. Such anthologies as *New Signatures* and *New Country*, both edited by Michael Roberts, were avowedly political, designed to be part of a general assault on the rotting structure of capitalist society, to ease the birth of a new society, and even (although Roberts was never an orthodox communist) 'to prepare the way for an English Lenin'.[1] John Lehmann, while proclaiming his willingness to print creative work from any source in his periodical *New Writing*, drew the line at accepting contributions from sympathizers with fascism. Anybody reading the poems by Auden and his contemporaries would have discovered there an attempt, however crude and melodramatic, to portray the physical and the social landscape of Britain, with its slums, its two million unemployed, its waste of material and of men:

Smokeless chimneys, damaged bridges, rotting wharves and choked canals,
Tramlines buckled, smashed trucks lying on their side across the rails.[2]

In these poems also one could find references to the brutal facts of the contemporary European scene, the recrudescence of barbarism, the systematic use of torture:

There flows in the tide of killers, the whip masters,
Breeches and gaiters camouflage blood,
Gangsters shooting from hips, pathics with rubber truncheons,
Spontaneous joy in the padded cell.[3]

[1] *New Country*, p. 12.
[2] W. H. Auden, *Poems*, XXII. Omitted from his *Collected Shorter Poems 1930–1944*.
[3] Stephen Spender, 'The Uncreating Chaos'.

English poets since the war have scarcely attempted to describe the physical or the mental contours of the new, revolutionary society established here in 1945, nor have they explored the significance of the changes in the world beyond these islands: the establishment of communist rule in China and in Eastern Europe, the ruthless determination of Asians and Africans to drive out their white masters and to gain independence, the succession of bitter civil wars which have broken the peace of every continent, leaving as their most cruel memento the crowds of hopeless refugees who rot away in miserable shanties. It may be argued that no English poet has experienced at first hand what it means to suffer and to struggle in Asia, Africa, or Eastern Europe, and that verse about the Hungarian revolution or the Korean war would be turgid poetical journalism. But almost all English poets of the present day have lived through the birth and the early development of the Welfare State, and poets in the past have, without descending to trivial journalism, recorded most vividly and profoundly the configurations and the hidden meaning of the society in which they were living. This is true not only of satirists such as Dryden and Pope but of so great a visionary poet as Blake, who, himself a man without a mask, depicts with a terrifying insight the realities which lurked behind the façade of eighteenth-century enlightenment and elegance.

That it is possible to convey something of the physical appearance and varied life of post-war England, the poetry of John Betjeman is sufficient proof. I am not referring to his attacks on the Welfare State with its nasty bureaucrats and its idle workers and its superficial courses in progressive citizenship; for there creep into his verse on these occasions a certain thinness and half-hearted petulance never found in his other poems, however much he may laugh at the quirks and snobbishness of his characters. Where Betjeman succeeds is in showing us, with such skilled precision, how his beloved Victorian and Edwardian England has been almost swept away by the new England of coffee bars, television masts, mass-produced goods, and miles of sodium-lit suburbia, a world in which, as one of his friends remarked, regular attendance at the cinema is the ideal preparation for a funeral service at the crematorium. Tenderly, mockingly, and pityingly he portrays for us the lives of lonely business women in Camden Town, the aimless, extravagant existence of

>   shining ones who dwell
>   Safe in the Dorchester Hotel,

the innocent yet empty ritual of Elaine, home from the office in post-war Outer London:

> Gaily into Ruislip Gardens
>   Runs the red electric train,
> With a thousand Ta's and Pardon's
>   Daintily alights Elaine;
> Hurries down the concrete station
> With a frown of concentration,
> Out into the outskirt's edges
> Where a few surviving hedges
> Keep alive our lost Elysium — rural Middlesex again.

> Well-cut Windsmoor flapping lightly,
>   Jacqmar scarf of mauve and green
> Hiding hair which, Friday nightly,
>   Delicately drowns in Drene;
> Fair Elaine the bobby-soxer,
> Fresh-complexioned with Innoxa,
> Gains the garden — father's hobby —
> Hangs her Windsmoor in the lobby,
> Settles down to sandwich supper and the television screen.

Then, in two stanzas almost as poignant in their feeling for the evanescence of things as a Proustian remembrance of childhood, Betjeman takes us back to the outskirts of London as they were in the days before 1914, to the world inhabited by figures from *The Diary of a Nobody*, whose passing is celebrated in the long, resonant, final line:

> Gentle Brent, I used to know you
>   Wandering Wembley-wards at will,

Now what change your waters show you
    In the meadowlands you fill!
Recollect the elm-trees misty
And the footpaths climbing twisty
Under cedar-shaded palings,
Low laburnum-leaned-on railings,
Out of Northolt on and upward to the heights of Harrow hill.

Parish of enormous hayfields
    Perivale stood all alone,
And from Greenford scent of mayfields
    Most enticingly was blown
Over market gardens tidy,
Taverns for the *bona fide*,
Cockney anglers, cockney shooters,
Murray Poshes, Lupin Pooters,
Long in Kensal Green and Highgate silent under soot and stone.[1]

None of the younger poets has emulated John Betjeman in portraying the outer face of post-war Britain, or in conveying the pattern of her inner life. There has been scarcely any serious attempt to fashion poetry out of the problems and aspirations of people who live in the worlds made familiar to us in plays and novels by John Osborne, Arnold Wesker, and Alan Sillitoe.[2] The reader of any representative anthology such as the annual P.E.N. *New Poems* or the *Guinness Book of Poetry* will seldom come across a poem which can be described, even in the broadest sense, as political, or as revealing to us the shape and meaning of our times, nor is this because the compilers of these anthologies are determined to exclude such poems. Why have our younger poets withdrawn from the public world in which, to gain our daily bread, we spend a third of our lives, the only world in which, as political animals, we can satisfy certain of our needs and develop certain of our potentialities?

It is, admittedly, no easy task to discover any principle of coherence or imaginative order in the political and social life of our

[1] 'Middlesex'.
[2] I am aware that Alan Sillitoe has published a long poem called *The Rats*.

day, but has this not been true for three hundred and fifty years? Shakespeare is haunted by the prospect of utter discord in human society, just as Pope sees in the approaching triumph of Dullness a threat to the whole structure of Western civilization, a return to primeval chaos. In the Victorian noon-tide, often regarded as a period of calm assurance, James Smetham acknowledges the magnitude of Tennyson's achievement in subduing the welter of disconnected facts which confronted him, and in turning them into poetry:

The poetic power which can swallow newspapers full of business, bankruptcy courts, sanitary commissions, wars, murders, and medical reports on the adulteration of food, and then reproduce them, as the conjurer brings out his coloured horn from his mouth after a meal of shavings, *is* poetic power.[1]

Eliot has told us how he learned from Baudelaire and from Laforgue

that the sort of material that I had, the sort of experience that an adolescent had had, in an industrial city in America, could be the material for poetry; and that the source of new poetry might be found in what had been regarded hitherto as the impossible, the sterile, the intractably unpoetic.[2]

There is no evidence to suggest that the post-war world has become too formidably complex for any poet to understand, but it is possible to argue that the new Welfare State has proved singularly unrewarding and intractable as a poetic theme, because of its dull, amorphous quality. It is true that the dramatic, glaring political and social injustices of pre-war Britain have ceased to provide material for poetry: the unemployed no longer hunger-march, the ship-building towns on the Tyne have ceased to be derelict and hopeless centres of human misery ('special areas' was the discreet bureaucratic term for them), nor do black-shirted thugs in the streets of our cities remind us of the political bitterness and suffering which Europe has known for so long, and which we have been largely

---

[1] *Letters of James Smetham* (1891). Quoted by G. Grigson, *The Victorians* (Routledge, 1950), p. 84.
[2] T. S. Eliot, 'A Talk on Dante', given at the Italian Institute, London, 4 July 1950. Printed in *The Adelphi*, First Quarter, 1951.

spared. Yet it is absurd to pretend that in our affluent society a poet can find nothing to arouse his compassion or his savage indignation. Although we have tidied away the slums, we have 750,000 houses officially 'condemned as unfit for habitation', two million with no internal lavatory, and four million without a bath. Three million houses are over one hundred years old, this total increasing by 150,000 each year, yet only 60,000 houses are demolished annually in Britain.[1] The mild inflation which scarcely harms men in full employment brings ever-increasing anxiety to the weakest members of society, elderly people scraping along on fixed incomes, and old-age pensioners. We live in a community where thousands of people are employed checking football pools, and where it is impossible to recruit enough nurses to staff the hospitals. In our society the young are reluctant to look after their ageing parents and relatives, although the proportion of old people in need of care and attention grows greater year by year. Auden's sharp insight posed the question in *The Orators*:

What do you think about England, this country of ours where nobody is well?

It has been left to a prose-writer, Muriel Spark, in her terrifying novel *Memento Mori*, to reframe Auden's question and ask what we think of England, a country where no one is young, and where the geriatric ward awaits us all.

Mere fashion and the swing of the pendulum may have played their part in discouraging post-war poets from political commitment, for the desire to distinguish themselves from the writers who dominated the nineteen-thirties seems to have goaded some of the livelier figures of the 'forties and 'fifties. This latent hostility to an earlier generation comes out strongly in a review by John Wain of Philip Toynbee's *Friends Apart*, an account of what it was like to be a young left-wing intellectual in the decade before the Second World War. Speaking of the nineteen-thirties, Wain tartly comments:

[1] I take these figures from an article by Gavin Lyall in the conservative *Sunday Times*, 23 April 1961.

It was the last age, consciously and feverishly the last, in which people had the feeling that if only they took the trouble to *join* something, get a party card, wear a special shirt, organise meetings and bellow slogans, they could influence the course of events. Since 1946 nobody above the Jehovah's Witness level has taken this attitude; are we right or will the Sixties think us as silly as we think the Thirties?[1]

Having cavalierly dismissed the writers of an earlier decade, Wain proceeds to analyse the mood of his contemporaries:

There has been, since 1945, a general feeling that there is no harm in taking one's training and being tough about it; if the way to get a First is to assimilate a certain amount of useless information about Beowulf and Chaucer's analogues, then the thing to do is to assimilate it, without necessarily selling out to the values implied. The only way to make a living is to do something that someone else wants you to do, and the problem of how to do this *and still stay human* has been the dominant problem of the younger intelligentsia since the war.

We may consider that Wain is revealing here a deplorable selfishness, cynicism, and lack of hope in his apparent indifference to the course of public events, or we may find in his comments a refreshing honesty, a welcome absence of the humbug so often displayed by men of letters who assure us that their hearts bleed for the wrongs of the world. His scepticism may recall to us Dr. Johnson's dictum, evoked by Boswell's saying: 'I should be the less happy for being in Parliament. I never would sell my vote, and I should be vexed if things went wrong':

JOHNSON. That's cant, Sir. It would not vex you more in the house, than in the gallery: publick affairs vex no man;[2]

or Leslie Stephen's advice to Cambridge undergraduates a century ago:

Stick to your triposes, grind at your mill, and don't set the universe in order until you have taken your bachelor's degree.[3]

---

[1] *The Spectator*, 19 March 1954. Emmanuel Litvinoff was quick to retort that we did not need to wait until the 'sixties to know what we thought of Mr. Wain.

[2] *Boswell's Life of Johnson* (ed. Hill), iv, 220.

[3] Quoted in Noel Annan, *Leslie Stephen* (MacGibbon and Kee, 1951), p. 39.

In 'Remembering the 'Thirties', Donald Davie, a poet of the 'fifties looking back upon the work of Auden and his coevals, tries to analyse the mixed feelings which his scrutiny has evoked. Some of the writers of the 'thirties, who have detected in this poem a malicious attack by a young poet on his seniors, have taken offence at Davie's satirical backward glance. Such a reading of the poem seems to me unjustifiable and inadequate, for to regard it as a sneer at Davie's elders and a justification of his contemporaries is to misread his argument and to ignore the careful nuances of tone and changes of key which colour and control the poem. It is, primarily, a poem about the impossibility of one generation's understanding the next, about the failure to communicate, the illustrations of his argument being drawn from recent literary history:

> Hearing one saga, we enact the next.
> We please our elders when we sit enthralled;
> But then they're puzzled; and at last they're vexed
> To have their youth so avidly recalled.
>
> It dawns upon the veterans after all
> That what for them were agonies, to us
> Are high-brow thrillers, though historical;
> And all their feats quite strictly fabulous.
>
> This novel written fifteen years ago,
> Set in my boyhood, and my boyhood home,
> These poems about 'abandoned workings', show
> Worlds more remote than Ithaca or Rome.
>
> The Anschluss, Guernica — all the names
> At which those poets thrilled, or were afraid,
> For me mean schools and schoolmasters and games;
> And in the process someone is betrayed.

The next stanza makes it clear that Davie is no less critical of himself than of his elders: the responsibility for the lack of imaginative understanding may rest with those who allow themselves to become the dupes of literary fashion:

> Ourselves perhaps. The Devil for a joke
> Might carve his own initials on our desk,
> And still we'd miss the point, because he spoke
> An idiom too dated, Audenesque.

Why, then, has 'Remembering the 'Thirties' been mistaken for a nasty stab at the poets of that decade? The answer may lie in those stanzas where Davie is poking a little gentle fun at the representative figures of the time, at the schoolboyish, conspiratorial atmosphere which shrouds some of their work:

> Even to them the tales were not so true
> As not to be ridiculous as well:
> The ironmaster met his Waterloo,
> But Rider Haggard rode along the fell.

> 'Leave for Cape Wrath to-night!' They lounged away
> On Fleming's trek or Isherwood's ascent.
> England expected every man that day
> To show his motives were ambivalent.

Yet even in this section of the poem, where Davie lays his finger upon all that is ephemeral and dated in the poets of the 'thirties, he clearly implies that they possessed the sovereign quality of courage, which led some of them, for example, to die in Spain defending what seemed to them a just cause. When the poem was printed in the P.E.N. *New Poems 1954* it bore as an epigraph the following quotation from Paul Tillich:

Courage is an ethical reality, but it is rooted in the whole breadth of human existence and ultimately in the structure of being itself.

The poem's final stanzas unmistakably reveal its true intent, its praise of courage as a reconciling virtue:

> A neutral tone is nowadays preferred.
> And yet it may be better, if we must,
> To find the stance impressive and absurd
> Than not to see the hero for the dust.

For courage is the vegetable king,
The sprig of all ontologies, the weed
That beards the slag-heap with its hectoring,
Whose green adventure is to run to seed.

C. E. Montague wrote an admirable book about the aftermath of the First World War, giving it the title of *Disenchantment*. This word conveys precisely the mood common to most poets who have lived through the years after the end of the Second World War. Almost all the events most ardently desired by the intelligentsia of the 'thirties have come to pass since 1945: the overthrow of Nazism and Fascism in Europe; the defeat of Japan in Asia; the granting of independence to the Indian subcontinent and to most of our colonies; the victory of socialism in Britain as soon as the war was over. Few of those who once envisaged a world free of want, violence, and injustice, and even fewer of their juniors, would deny the bitter truth which Yeats has condensed into that savage quatrain, 'The Great Day':

Hurrah for revolution and more cannon-shot!
A beggar upon horseback lashes a beggar on foot.
Hurrah for revolution and cannon come again!
The beggars have changed places, but the lash goes on

and into the couplet, 'Parnell':

Parnell came down the road, he said to a cheering man:
'Ireland shall get her freedom and you still break stone.'

Scarcely any poets in England turn nowadays to communism as a source of hope, nor do they feel the least enthusiasm for an anti-communist crusade. For them the Soviet Union is not so much a monstrous tyranny as a narrow, rigid, illiberal, dull bureaucracy, remarkably efficient in certain ways, but fundamentally a dreary civilization. The pompous academicism of officially approved Soviet painting, the insistence that the arts should be morally improving, the pressure on artists to conform to the doctrine of social realism as defined by some governmental committee — all these precautions designed to ensure the triumph of mediocrity recall the stuffiest and most ponderous aspects of our own Victorian world, multiplied sevenfold and far more impervious to criticism. For whereas Ruskin, Morris, Arnold, Pater, and Wilde were able, in their several ways, to put to rout, by denunciation or by mockery, the solemn humbug of the Philistines, it is clearly much harder for any dissenter from current Soviet orthodoxy to wage a similar campaign in contemporary Russia. Roy Fuller's 'On Reading a Soviet Novel' delineates with a wry, sardonic wit the unease and the wariness which assail most of our younger poets when they contemplate the Soviet Union:

> Will not the Local Party Secretary
> Prove that his love of men's not innocent:
> The heroine at last be blown off course
> By some base, gusty, female element:
> And the grave hero be eventually torn
> By a disgraceful infantile event?
>
> No, in this world the good works out its course
> Unhindered by the real, irrelevant flaw.
> Our guilty eyes glaze over with ennui
> At so much honest purpose, rigid law.
> This is not life, we say, who ask that art
> Show mainly what the partial butler saw.
>
> And yet with what disquiet we leave the tale!
> The mere appearance of the descending Goth,
> So frightful to a sedentary race,
> Made him invincible. It is not wrath
> That breaks up cultures but the virtue of
> The stupid elephant, the piddling moth.
>
> The threatened empire dreads its rival's arms
> Less than the qualities at which it sneers —
> The slave morality promoted to
> A way of life: naive, old-fashioned tears
> Which once it shed itself by bucketsful
> In nascent, optimistic, long-dead years.

Perhaps a poem of this nature, like the general distaste of our younger poets for political verse, merely reflects our situation in the post-war world: an old, complex society, tolerant, sceptical, a little weary, surveying half enviously, half disdainfully, the enormous power of the U.S.S.R. and of the U.S.A., acutely conscious that its own material resources have dwindled. In much the same spirit, a Venetian grandee or artist of the late eighteenth century might have watched with a fastidious irony the struggle between England and France, the one so coarse, exuberant, and prosperous, the other dedicated to a fanatical revolutionary creed. To savour the dying fall, the sunset glow, the aesthetic of failure — these are the temptations assailing all poets who come to maturity in a civilization where subtlety and mellowness have diluted the brasher, rougher qualities of energy and ambition.

There is another, and more creditable, reason for the reluctance of our younger poets to plunge into the turbulent waters of political strife. W. B. Yeats, who faced almost every problem which has troubled the poets of our century, had laboured for many years before 1914 to rouse his countrymen from their petty bickering and from their mean timidity. In 1913 his bitterness at their ignoble torpor, and at the unprepossessing way in which their calculating materialism went hand in hand with a narrow religious creed, spilled over into his poem, 'September 1913':

> What need you, being come to sense,
> But fumble in a greasy till
> And add the halfpence to the pence
> And prayer to shivering prayer, until
> You have dried the marrow from the bone?
> For men were born to pray and save:
> Romantic Ireland's dead and gone,
> It's with O'Leary in the grave.

Three years later, the Easter Rebellion proved that even MacBride, whom Yeats hated and despised as 'a drunken, vainglorious lout', was capable of heroism. Yeats, who had not so much as been told that there was to be a rising, celebrated this astounding proof of Ireland's capacity to achieve a tragic dignity in his 'Easter 1916', with its refrain

A terrible beauty is born.

Too honest and courageous a man to shrink from unpleasant truths (one of his volumes bears the significant title *Responsibilities*), Yeats continually asked himself whether his poems had spurred men to risk their lives in the streets of Dublin, whether he bore some guilt for the horrors of the civil war:

I lie awake night after night
And never get the answers right.
Did that play of mine send out
Certain men the English shot?
Did words of mine put too great strain
On that woman's reeling brain?
Could my spoken words have checked
That whereby a house lay wrecked?[1]

Since 1939 there has been no excuse for ignorance about the nature of political action. A poem urging men to rise against their oppressors may gratify its author's vanity but do comparatively little harm, provided that nobody takes it seriously. What if its readers should, in fact, rebel against their rulers? Byron dying for Greece, John Cornford and Julian Bell sacrificing their lives for one side in the Spanish Civil War and Roy Campbell fighting for the other — to such men one accords a respect which one withholds from propagandists (however high-minded they may be) who summon men to battle from the snug refuge of a peaceful cottage, a government office, or a university post. Even if a poet shares all the dangers and suffers all the consequences, has he the right to awaken men's political passions, knowing that blood will be shed and innocent lives lost? Those Hungarian poets whose verses encouraged the poorly-armed students and workers of Budapest to fight against tanks and artillery in the rising of 1956 cannot hope (and probably

---

[1] 'The Man and the Echo'.

would not wish) to escape their portion of responsibility for the death of many brave men.

English poets, although they have mercifully not been required to endure the perplexities which must have racked their Hungarian contemporaries, have for the past fifteen years been writing in the shadow of the mushroom cloud that rose above Nagasaki and Hiroshima. I have suggested that a reader of our post-war poetry would find it hard to discover there many of the basic facts about the world in which we live. At least he could hardly fail to discern in this body of verse an awareness of the one brute reality in whose glaring light these facts assume their full meaning — the threat of man's annihilation by nuclear warfare. From Edith Sitwell's 'The Shadow of Cain' down to John Wain's 'A Song About Major Eatherley' the texture of our verse is shot through with the ghastly pink glow of the first two atom bombs to explode over man's cities. D. J. Enright's poem, 'The Laughing Hyena', ostensibly about a Japanese work of art, is suffused with this glow, which illuminates the hidden implications of the poet's theme as they unfold to reveal their significance for us today:

> And the Laughing Hyena, cavalier of evil, as volcanic as the rest:
> Elegant in a flowered gown, a face like a bomb-burst,
> Featured with fangs and built about a rigid laugh,
> Ever moving, like a pond's surface where a corpse has sunk.
> Between the raised talons of the right hand rests an object —
> At rest, like a pale island in a savage sea — a child's head,
> Immobile, authentic, torn and bloody —
> The point of repose in the picture, the point of movement in us.

English poets have not found it easy to convey in words the sense of horror and of guilt aroused in them by the destruction of the two Japanese cities. Louis MacNeice, who has carried over into the post-war years the feelings of political responsibility, the direct concern with public events, characteristic of poets in the nineteen-thirties, has chosen to make his comment on this theme through the lips of a not very intelligent ex-Indian Army officer. This device permits MacNeice to express the groping bewilderment, incredulity, and resignation which assail most of us when we contemplate the prospect before us; and MacNeice heightens the effectiveness of his observation by causing his protagonist to speak in the surging, heroic rhythm of 'Bonnie Dundee':

> '. . . Now follow our pointer; look, here is Japan
> Where man must now make what he chooses of man,
> And these towns are selected to pay for their crime —
> A milestone in history, a gravestone in time.'

> When I first read the news to my shame I was glad;
> When I next read the news I thought man had gone mad,
> And every day since the more news that I read
> I too would plead guilty — but where can I plead?

> For no one will listen, however I rage;
> I am not of their temper and not of this age.
> Outnumbered, outmoded, I only can pray
> Common sense, if not love, will still carry the day.[1]

In 'A Song About Major Eatherley', an American pilot who suffered a mental breakdown through remorse for his part in the raid on Nagasaki, we encounter a similar atmosphere of near despair, a similar groping for words that shall be adequate to carry the burden of the poet's semi-articulate horror. Just as a man cannot look at the glare of an atomic explosion for fear of being blinded, so John Wain averts his glance from the full enormity of the desolation at Nagasaki, taking refuge in an uneasy irony, an oblique, mocking bitterness:

> Good news. It seems he loved them after all.
> His orders were to fry their bones to ash.
> He carried up the bomb and let it fall.
> And then his orders were to take the cash,

> A hero's pension. But he let it lie.

Although the poem lacks the grandeur and the weight to sustain its terrifying theme, it is typical of its epoch in that it both shows

---

[1] 'Notes for a Biography'. In the first of the three stanzas quoted the Lords of Convention are speaking.

how our younger poets are, like Major Eatherley, obsessed by the devastation of the Japanese cities, and also indicates their attitude to the political realities of our day — an attitude in which disgust and disillusion mingle with a wry, stoical acceptance of the fact that we live in barbarous and bloody times. The poem ends with a vale-diction to Major Eatherley, who has been consigned to prison for petty thievery, and whom we cannot even venerate as a scapegoat for our sins:

> Leave him; if he is sleeping, come away.
> But lay a folded paper by his head,
> nothing official or embossed, a page
> torn from your notebook, and the words in pencil.
> Say nothing of love, or thanks, or penitence:
> say only, 'Eatherley, we have your message.'

Donald Davie, another poet who more than once reverts to this theme, draws the moral that, after such a catastrophe, almost any strong emotion is likely to prove dangerous. We have endured a shock so tremendous that, like Creon, we no longer dare yield to any powerful feeling, or take any decisive action:

> Creon, I think, could never kill a mouse
> When once that dangerous girl was put away,
> Shut up unbridled in her rocky house,
> Colossal nerve denied the light of day . . .

> If too much daring brought (he thought) the war,
> When that was over nothing else would serve
> But no one must be daring any more,
> A self-induced and stubborn loss of nerve.[1]

Davie's most explicit statement of this belief occurs in 'Rejoinder to a Critic', which envisages a self-imposed loss of nerve, a negative incapability, as the only means by which poets who have almost succumbed to the disease of living through the horrors of the present time can hope to recuperate:

[1] 'Creon's Mouse'.

C

You may be right: 'How can I dare to feel?'
May be the only question I can pose,
'And haply by abstruse research to steal
From my own nature all the natural man'
My sole resource. And I do not suppose
That others may not have a better plan.

And yet I'll quote again, and gloss it too
(You know by now my liking for *collage*):
Donne could be daring, but he never knew,
When he inquired, 'Who's injured by my love?'
Love's radio-active fall-out on a large
Expanse around the point it bursts above.

'Alas, alas, who's injured by my love?'
And recent history answers: Half Japan!
Not love, but hate? Well, both are versions of
The 'feeling' that you dare me to. Be dumb!
Appear concerned only to make it scan!
How dare we now be anything but numb?

A young poet who wanted to refute my accusation that he and
his contemporaries have evaded the task of embodying in their verse
the hopes, aspirations, and fears of men in society might claim that
he had a full answer to my charge. He might begin his defence by
remarking that the one great issue of our time is the survival of
human life on this planet and that, even on my own admission, our
post-war poets have constantly shown themselves aware of this
sombre truth. Propaganda for or against the Welfare State, adulation
or denunciation of communism, heroics about uprisings against
tyranny, hymns of praise in honour of the emergent Asian and
African states, or laments for the passing of Britain's imperial destiny — all such peripheral themes belong to the realm of journalism
rather than of poetry. Going one stage further, he might then
advance the argument which Proust so eloquently pleaded, that we
can never hope to understand society (or ourselves) by studying its
institutions or its political and economic machinery. The artist's
duty is to scrutinize himself and his fellow men, to probe into the

human heart and to discover its innermost secrets: only then will he be able to comprehend the true significance of society and of those forces which govern men's actions.

I am half convinced by this defence and should be wholly convinced if I were satisfied that our younger poets had indeed analysed the most profound movements of the heart and invented an appropriate language to portray what they found there. Unhappily, what I have stigmatized as the withdrawal from the public world has gone hand in hand with another kind of retreat. In order to clarify this assertion I must now turn to consider the most striking developments in poetic technique during the past two decades.

Technical changes in the writing of verse may be introduced for a wide variety of reasons, nor is it always the most gifted poets of an epoch who busy themselves with such innovations. Sometimes a very minor poet discovers a prosodic device, a fresh source of imagery, a new way of organizing the formal structure of a poem, and a much more gifted poet then profits by the lesser man's invention. Even good poets who devote much time to technical experiment may write their best verse when working in a more traditional style.

Poets may become bored with the current mode of poetic composition and hanker for a new way of doing things, much as dress-designers raise or drop the hem-line every year or two. Those who object to the frivolity of this comparison should remember that fashion is an exacting tyrant in every branch of human activity, and that in our modern, sophisticated world the craving for novelty is immensely strong. Moreover, technical innovations may become an emotional necessity when a particular style has been brought to perfection, and when to continue in that vein would be to write according to a stultifying formula. Hopkins recognizes this fact in an essay on 'Health and Decay in Art', written while he was an undergraduate:

Perfection is dangerous because it is deceptive. Art slips back while bearing, in its distribution of tone, or harmony, the look of high civilization towards barbarism. Recovery must be by a breaking up, a violence, such as was the Preraphaelite school.[1]

Finally, poets who have experienced a new imaginative vision of the world may find all the available, ready-made moulds of verse totally inadequate for their purposes, and may be driven to search for new formal devices in order that they may convey truthfully and precisely the pattern of their vision.

All these motives, which had been operating powerfully since the early years of this century, became even more widespread and insistent between 1918 and 1939. Whatever our verdict may be on the poetic achievement of this period, we can hardly deny that the poets of these decades exhibited a remarkable virtuosity and daring in their handling of imagery, of verse-forms, and of diction. A short list of some technical experiments made by English poets between the wars gives a fair idea of the ingenuity and resourcefulness of these poets: the use of sprung rhythm and of other prosodic systems explored by Hopkins; the employment of assonance, consonance, and half-rhymes in the manner of Wilfred Owen; the imitation of Anglo-Saxon models, and the reliance on heavy alliteration; the attempt by Robert Graves to re-introduce Skeltonic rhythms into English verse; the rhyming of stressed with unstressed syllables; the replacement of end rhymes by internal rhymes; the attempt to create a prosody based on syllabic verse, accentual verse, and quantitative verse; Edith Sitwell's investigations into the orchestral properties of language; the reliance upon unrhymed cadence and upon so-called organic rhythm rather than upon regular metrical patterns; an abandonment of normal expository logic and of plain narrative in favour of the logic of images and the intimations of musical suggestiveness foreshadowed by the Symbolists and the Imagists.

In his Introduction to the *Faber Book of Modern Verse* (1936), Michael Roberts explains that his anthology 'represents the most significant poetry of this age', although it 'is not intended to be a

[1] Quoted by W. H. Gardner, *Gerard Manley Hopkins* (Secker and Warburg, 1944), vol. i, p. 9.

comprehensive anthology of the best poems of our age'.[1] Since
Roberts goes on to say that he omitted Sorley, de la Mare, Blunden,
Muir, Plomer and Campbell (presumably Hardy and Edward
Thomas also) because they 'seem to me to have written good poems
without having been compelled to make any notable development
of poetic technique',[2] we must assume that for him significant poets
are those who develop poetic technique, and a later passage expands
this brief hint. Modern poets, we learn, dislike the tendency to over-
emphasize regular metrical patterns, which 'seems to them not to
increase the significance of the poetry, but to diminish it by asserting
an arbitrary music at the expense of meaning, and to read their poems
as songs, and necessarily bad songs, is to misread them completely'.[3]
Roberts then restates Coleridge's distinction between 'organic form'
and 'mechanical regularity' by observing that 'today the auditory
rhetoric of a poem is dictated, not by its own rules, but by the
central impulse of the poem'.[4]

Since 1945, many of our most gifted younger poets have displayed in their poetic technique what Donald Davie has called 'a
rational conservatism'. While feeling at liberty to employ a flexible,
unrhymed verse when to do so appears to them appropriate, they
work with an equal lack of constraint in the most strict, traditional
forms — the sonnet, the *villanelle*, the *sestina* and *terza rima*. Few
of them would accept Sir Herbert Read's contention, advanced in
The True Voice of Feeling, that organic form is in some way more
sincere and less artificial than external form; nor would they agree
with V. de S. Pinto's judgement on organic, or expressive, form:

it is the only kind of poetic form which is really alive in the modern
world. . . . In the twentieth century the poet is more isolated, perhaps,
than he has ever been in the whole of human history. The use of traditional forms in such an age becomes more and more of a pretence, the
pretence that there is a living society that shares the poetic sensibility
embodied in traditional forms.[5]

[1] Michael Roberts, *Faber Book of Modern Verse*, p. 1.
[2] Ibid., p. 1.   [3] Ibid., p. 30.   [4] Ibid., p. 32.
[5] V. de S. Pinto, 'Poet Without a Mask', *Critical Quarterly*, vol. 3, No. 1 (Spring
1961), p. 7.

Donald Davie has explicitly challenged the assumption that all genuine poetry shapes its own organic form, an assumption which, between the wars, gradually hardened into a sacred tenet of orthodox modern poetic theory. For, when Christopher Levenson, the undergraduate editor of the Cambridge periodical *Delta*, announced *ex cathedra* that 'to impose arbitrary and external rules rather than to allow the artist's experience to mould [a poem's] organic form, is merely perverse',[1] Davie made a brisk rejoinder:

The metrical and other habits of English verse seem to me to be in no sense 'arbitrary', but rather to be rooted in the nature of English as a spoken and written language; I see no other explanation of the fact that the rules which, say, Mr. Amis and Mr. Graves observe are the rules which have governed ninety per cent of English poetry for more than 500 years. I think it is of the nature of a rule to be 'external'. And as for that old crotchet of 'organic form', I must admit that I find it only a form of words.[2]

There has, then, been a widespread reaction against certain presuppositions in vogue among the most gifted experimental poets of the period 1918–1939. R. P. Blackmur is speaking for a large number of post-war poets on both sides of the Atlantic when he claims that we are saved in poetry 'by prosody, by expertness, conscious or not',[3] and when he passes these strictures upon a whole generation of writers who practised the art of verse in the second and third decades of this century:

What they did was to make just enough of a prosody to heroize the sensibility and not quite enough to make a heroic statement. Just enough meter to make a patter, just enough rhyme to make a noise, just enough reason to make an argument; never enough of anything to bind together what came out of the reservoir of their extraordinary sensibility into possible poetry.[4]

This rational conservatism is, in my judgement, salutary: unceasing experimental ferment is no less futile than perpetual

---

[1] *Delta*, Number 8 (Spring 1956), p. 8. [2] *Delta*, Number 9 (Summer 1956), p. 27.
[3] R. P. Blackmur, *Language as Gesture* (Allen and Unwin, 1954), p. 429.
[4] Ibid., p. 428.

stagnation, nor is poetry obliged always to be, as T. E. Hulme advocated, 'the advance-guard of language'. At certain times, poets need to reject the crust of metrical custom, to experiment restlessly, to make poetic diction draw as close as possible to the rhythms of common speech; at other times their prime concern must be to elaborate and to perfect metrical patterns, to create a subtle, learned, richly orchestrated language, sharply distinguished, although never totally divorced, from the dialect of the tribe.

But much as one may sympathize with the formal conservatism of the past twenty years, none but a complacent bonehead can escape a twinge of disquiet when faced by the imaginative poverty which has accompanied (and maybe sprung from) this technical decorum. We may grant that Yvor Winters[1] and Graham Hough[2] have drawn up a formidable, though not unanswerable, indictment against the theory and practice of the Imagists and the post-Symbolists in general, and against Pound and Eliot in particular. Yet these two poets, like Yeats and D. H. Lawrence, have unflaggingly tried to make sense of the world, employing myth, image, and symbol in the hope of

controlling, of ordering, of giving a shape and a significance to the immense panorama of futility and anarchy which is contemporary history. ... It is, I seriously believe, a step towards making the modern world possible for art, towards order and form.[3]

No attempt comparable in scope or in poetic intensity has been made in the past twenty years; worse still, talented poets now in their late thirties or early forties deprecatingly refer to the daring achievement of these elder masters as though it were a faintly disreputable episode in family history, which the younger generation must try to hush up or to live down by parading their own respectability. Thus Philip Larkin, seeking to discredit the post-Symbolist movement in English poetry, invites us to consider

---

[1] Yvor Winters, *In Defense of Reason* (Routledge, 1960).

[2] Graham Hough, *Idea and Image* (Duckworth, 1960).

[3] T. S. Eliot, 'Ulysses, Order and Myth', *The Dial*, November 1923; reprinted in *James Joyce: Two Decades of Criticism*, ed. Seon Givens. I owe this reference to G. Melchiori, *The Tightrope Walkers* (Routledge, 1956), p. 131.

the inexplicable fact that forty or fifty years ago obscurity suddenly became fun in a way it never had been before. . . . Now it is fun no more. Deserted by the tide of taste, the modern movement awaits combing like some cryptic sea-wrack; obscurity, as the general reader has always known, is its definitive characteristic, an obscurity unlike previous types, in being deliberate and unnecessary.[1]

If Yeats, Pound, Eliot, Lawrence, Stevens, Auden, and Dylan Thomas indeed lie shipwrecked, fine treasure awaits the beach-combers. Measured against their work, the poetry of the past two decades is puny; Yeats's lines on 'Three Movements' are cruelly applicable to the movements and counter-movements which have flickered and guttered out since 1939:

> Shakespearean fish swam the sea, far away from land;
> Romantic fish swam in nets coming to the hand;
> What are all those fish that lie gasping on the strand?

It would be wrong to assume that timidity and smugness invariably go hand in hand with a devotion to technical proficiency, nor are all the good young poets and critics happy about the present state of English poetry. Donald Davie and Charles Tomlinson believe that our post-war poets have shamefully evaded the task of extending and developing the territory explored by the French Symbolists and their Anglo-American successors. Alvarez, while employing different terms, betrays a similar uneasiness about the debility of much post-war verse. Speaking of D. H. Lawrence's poems, he remarks: '. . . their excellence comes from something that is rare at best, and now, in the 1950s, well-nigh lost: a complete truth to feeling'.[2]

W. B. Yeats has proposed a stringent test for all imaginative work, and one that only a handful of poems written since 1939 can hope to survive. Perhaps it is unfair to subject our post-war verse to a scrutiny so rigorous that it would eliminate all but a few poems of any decade. Nevertheless, I propose to end my general survey of the

---

[1] From his review of John Press, *The Chequer'd Shade*, in the *Manchester Guardian*, 18 November 1958.
[2] A. Alvarez, *The Shaping Spirit* (Chatto, 1958), pp. 140–1.

period by quoting the stanza from 'Vacillation' where Yeats makes his exacting demand; it may warn us that we should not abandon or lower our standard of excellence, and may remind us that poetry is something more than relaxation, lively journalism, interesting comment, and technical expertise:

> No longer in Lethean foliage caught
> Begin the preparation for your death
> And from the fortieth winter by that thought
> Test every work of intellect or faith,
> And everything that your own hands have wrought,
> And call those works extravagance of breath
> That are not suited for such men as come
> Proud, open-eyed and laughing to the tomb.

II

ARGUMENT AND INCANTATION

ROBERT GRAVES once toyed with the notion that an established poet should train aspiring practitioners of verse, rather as painters at the time of the Renaissance would take into their workshops young apprentices, allowing them to prepare their materials, to sketch the outline of a cloak, even to paint the hand of a minor figure in a huge composition. Since there is in fact no satisfactory equivalent for writers of a painter's studio, a school of art, or an academy of music, a poet at the start of his career must grasp the rudiments of his craft as best he may. If he has a taste for lively conversation and for alcohol, he will probably drift into the taverns of Soho; more profitably and less expensively, he will study those writers who minister to his particular needs. He may turn to an acknowledged major poet of the past; or he may feel that some partially-neglected figure is, for him, more alive and relevant than any of those whom the literary dictators of the day have proclaimed as the indubitable stalwarts of the English poetic tradition. At certain periods, only an unusually strong-minded novice can resist the influence of a living poet who enjoys a vast fashionable reputation, just as, at other times, a young writer will look for guidance to a slightly older contemporary who has recently begun to acquire a band of disciples.

These facts are distasteful to enthusiastic romantics who demand that a poet should, like a bird, warble unconstrainedly in his own voice or, less ornithologically, look into his heart and write. But to look into one's heart is a difficult surgical operation, and to describe with unwavering precision what one finds there is the task of a lifetime. Moreover, a poet's voice, like that of a singer, attains its unique character and its perfection only after years of training.

Nor is there any question of mere imitation: a young poet who does not know what he wants to say, still less how he can begin to say it, will suddenly find illumination in the work of another poet. He is, as it were, possessed by this poet, by his rhythms, his mental habits, his vision of the world. In this formative period, what the unsympathetic spectator regards as the rankest plagiarism or pastiche will seem to the young tyro his own natural, inevitable mode of expression, even though he may have lifted prosodic devices, turns of speech, and whole phrases, straight from the works of his chosen model. A poetic tradition is healthy when young writers can easily gravitate to literature of the past which will foster in them the basic virtues of honest feeling, clear thinking, and respect for language. When such a tradition has grown enfeebled or corrupt, young poets will glut themselves on debased emotionalism, self-indulgent posturing, and bloated rhodomontade.

A revolution in poetic thought and sensibility is almost always precipitated, or at least accompanied, by a radical change in the language of poetry. One could even consider the history of English verse as a series of experiments with diction, metre, and rhythm, such innovators as Donne, Milton, Dryden, Wordsworth, Hopkins, and Eliot playing the leading roles in the story. This would, admittedly, be a lopsided view of the matter, one that lays a disproportionate emphasis on technical originality. We ought to remember that poets as fine as Smart, Blake, Keats, Tennyson, and Yeats, for all their technical prowess, are not primarily concerned with poetry as linguistic change or development; while admirable minor poets, such as Herrick, Crabbe, and de la Mare, are content to lavish all their skill and subtlety upon the accepted idiom of their day, without feeling the need to forge a totally new style for themselves. Poets of our time, bringing to the practice of their art a self-consciousness which is sometimes termed Alexandrian or Byzantine, have become increasingly preoccupied with problems of technique. W. B. Yeats, so proudly and defiantly a traditional poet, is nonetheless a typical figure of this century when he asks Ezra Pound to comb his verse and to show him which lines are flabby or otiose;

when he reads Donne in order to gain a seventeenth-century metaphysical strength and intensity; when he remoulds his poetry in order that he may remake himself. An age such as our own that has lost its belief in personal immortality will acknowledge the dominion of time and look to language in the hope that its power may save something from the wreckage:

> Time that is intolerant
> Of the brave and innocent,
> And indifferent in a week
> To a beautiful physique,
>
> Worships language and forgives
> Everyone by whom it lives;
> Pardons cowardice, conceit,
> Lays its honours at their feet.
>
> Time that with this strange excuse
> Pardoned Kipling and his views,
> And will pardon Paul Claudel,
> Pardons him for writing well.[1]

It is, therefore, not astonishing that, after the Second World War, the younger poets should have been searching for guides and models. They recognized Yeats, Eliot, and Pound as great poets who were, for a variety of reasons, inimitable. Muir and Graves, although generally admired and respected, had not at this time gained the popularity which they were to enjoy within the next ten years. A young poet seeking a master was likely to look either to Edith Sitwell and Dylan Thomas, or to William Empson, regarding with violent antipathy those of his contemporaries who had made the wrong choice. Every age overemphasizes the contrasts between artistic styles prevalent at a given moment, forgetting that future generations will fix upon all the work of a period an indelible date-stamp. The partisans of Wagner and of Brahms would have been furious and incredulous had they been told that, sixty years on, the music of both these idols would be calmly accepted as logical de-

[1] W. H. Auden, 'In Memory of W. B. Yeats'.

velopments of the same nineteenth-century Germanic tradition. So, in the year 2000, readers of English poetry, wondering why young poets in 1945 reacted in such violently differing ways to the verse of Dylan Thomas and of Empson, may recollect John Byrom's epigram on the conflict between the admirers of Handel and of Bononcini:

> Strange! all this difference should be
> 'Twixt Tweedle-DUM and Tweedle-DEE!

The fact remains that many young writers in the immediate post-war years felt an almost physical compulsion to choose between the ways of looking at the world, and the uses of language, exemplified in the following typical passages:

> Never until the mankind making
> Bird beast and flower
> Fathering and all humbling darkness
> Tells with silence the last light breaking
> And the still hour
> Is come of the sea tumbling in harness
>
> And I must enter again the round
> Zion of the water bead
> And the synagogue of the ear of corn
> Shall I let pray the shadow of a sound
> Or sow my salt seed
> In the least valley of sackcloth to mourn
>
> The majesty and burning of the child's death.[1]
>
> Feign then what's by a decent tact believed
> And act that state is only so conceived,
>   And build an edifice of form
>   For house where phantoms may keep warm.
>
> Imagine, then, by miracle, with me
> (Ambiguous gifts, as what gods give must be)
>   What could not possibly be there,
>   And learn a style from a despair.[2]

[1] Dylan Thomas, 'A Refusal to Mourn the Death, by Fire, of a Child in London'.
[2] William Empson, 'This Last Pain'.

We cannot justly relegate these poems to some neat, preconceived literary category (such as classical or romantic) and praise or condemn them for exhibiting the qualities supposedly to be found in the category. It would be a superficial reading of these poems that discovered in 'A Refusal to Mourn' nothing but a splurge of rhetoric, and in 'This Last Pain' only an ingenious manipulation of frigid concepts. The most remarkable feature of Thomas's poem is the intellectual control which he displays as he allows the logic of his argument to unfold itself in the progression of his imagery and the sequence of his cadences. Nor does the merit of Empson's poem reside in its intellectual power and coherence: despite the subtlety and apparent rigour of the poet's logic, despite the brilliance of his individual conceits, the continuity of his argument is difficult to perceive. His lines move us by their emotional intensity, for beneath the poem's flawless surface and elegant formality there lies concentrated a world of experience and of suffering.

Yet there is a marked difference between these two poems, and one which it is easier to recognize than to analyse: a difference of tone. There flourish in every age men whose peculiar distinction and charm, though generally apparent to their contemporaries, can never be communicated to posterity. In much the same way, one generation responds intuitively and keenly to variations of tone which a succeeding generation can barely distinguish and to which it remains totally indifferent. G. M. Young is making a similar point when he is discussing Swinburne's hold over the readers of his day:

In every work of art there is something which addresses the nerves, a thrill, beside those other things which reach the spirit. It is in virtue of this thrill, very often, that a writer makes his entry and secures his public ... and I believe the curious anger, or detestation, so much beyond any reasonable ground of distaste, with which each age for a time regards the literature of the last, has its cause in this: it perceives the appeal, but cannot answer it. Nothing is more exasperating to the nerves or the temper than a thrill which has begun to be a bore.[1]

[1] G. M. Young, *To-Day and Yesterday* (Hart-Davis, 1948), p. 49.

It was this 'something which addresses the nerves' that divided opinion so deeply among the poets of the early post-war years. In the extract from Thomas we are borne irresistibly on by a mounting wave of sound prolonged for thirteen lines, where the main verb delays its appearance until the tenth line; where it is hard to distinguish present participle from compound adjective or to determine which adjective qualifies which noun; and where no punctuation marks halt the resonant flow of the oratory until the lengthy sentence finally subsides and dies away. In the passage from Empson, we encounter a firm, well-articulated syntax, a trenchant diction and a sharp clarity of outline in the structure of the verse. The commas and the brackets, placed with precise care, retard the movement of the lines and qualify their meaning; while the transition from the easy conversational manner, stiffened by irony and sharpened by wit, into the grand style of the final stanza, is managed with consummate skill.

While it is clear that Thomas and Empson, like rival *virtuosi*, employ widely dissimilar devices to subdue and enchant their readers, it may be less clear why young poets felt obliged to take sides, to praise one mode of excellence and to damn the other. Why should we impoverish ourselves by passing a self-denying ordinance, and by adopting a crabbed narrowness of judgement, which remains stultifying even though we dignify it by the title of austere discrimination?

This easy-going, all-embracing tolerance ignores the distinction which practising poets constantly draw between the merits of a writer and the influence of his work at a given moment. Some poets, whatever one may think of their achievement, set an example which later and lesser men will imitate at their peril. It is difficult to believe that the influence of Swinburne can ever be anything but vicious, although his best poetry triumphs over even the most outrageous of its lapses and excesses. Conversely, some poets have left behind not only a considerable body of fine work, but a salutary example for all to follow. A young writer who studies Ben Jonson or Dryden will nurture and strengthen his imagination without running the risk of picking up deplorable poetic habits. Midway between the poles represented by Swinburne and by Jonson, there stand those writers whose value as exemplars fluctuates from age to age, and varies according to the intelligence which is brought to bear upon them. At certain periods the verse of Donne may serve as a reminder that intellectual passion and emotional daring are twin elements, and that poetry cannot afford to dispense with either of them; at other times an admiration for Donne may lead poets to over-value metaphysical subtlety and to attempt emotional acrobatics in order that they may not be judged insipid or deficient in originality. Hopkins may help a poet to revivify and to order the English language in such a way that his verse will express with the utmost fidelity and concentration the fierce, intricate motions of mind and spirit. He may also, if crudely imitated, appear to justify a licentious extravagance of feeling, a grotesque deformation of linguistic patterns, a monstrous jargon equally remote from the living speech of the day and from the normal mental processes of its author.

Poets are singularly ill-fitted to pass an impartial judgement on the work of their contemporaries, because they are, knowingly or unknowingly, engaged in framing an apology for their own verse just as they are perpetually ransacking other men's poetry to enrich their own. The acuteness, the urgency, of criticism written by poets spring from this personal concern, which sharpens, even though it may distort, their perceptions. T. S. Eliot admits that his best literary criticism 'is a by-product of my private poetry-workshop; or a prolongation of the thinking that went into the formation of my own verse'.[1] His strictures on Milton and his subsequent essay on the same theme become intelligible in the light of that admission. Keats had pronounced a similar verdict: writing to Reynolds on 24 August 1819, he remarks that day by day 'Paradise Lost becomes a greater wonder'; yet in the long letter to George and Georgiana Keats, dated 17–27 September of that same year, he speaks as a practitioner of verse: 'I have but lately stood on my guard against Milton. Life to him would be death to me.'

[1] T. S. Eliot, 'The Frontiers of Criticism'. *On Poetry and Poets* (Faber, 1957), p. 106.

It was, therefore, understandable that a young poet after the war should feel obliged to choose between the poetic worlds of Thomas and of Empson, to commit himself to one of them as an act of faith. We can even make a rough division of post-war poets into two groups: those who believe that the example of Thomas (which they distinguish from his achievement) has been entirely baneful, fostering the notion of poetry as a dithyrambic outpouring, and of a poet as a man exempt from customary social obligations and restraints; and those who hold that Thomas had grasped the central truth that poetry is a celebration of visionary reality. The first group commonly argue that although Empson is not a man to be slavishly imitated, he at least offers a salutary, astringent antidote to the legacy of the Welsh bard, 'the little spellbinder of Cader Idris', 'the canary of Swansea', 'the Baby of Taliessin'.[1] The second group take a diametrically opposed view and, while praising a dozen of Empson's best poems, maintain that his work points the way to a desolate blind alley. Moreover, the first group, unlike the second, attack Edith Sitwell as a vastly overrated poet who has debased the poetic currency and vulgarized every valuable innovation of the past forty years.

Thus we find Donald Davie writing a letter to the *London Magazine* in March 1954:

The death of Dylan Thomas was very sad, and it is clear that some of the poems he wrote are going to be remembered for a very long time. . . . But the saddest thing about it, to my mind, was the fulsome ballyhoo it evoked on both sides of the Atlantic.

Davie was among those who took part at this time in a number of critical skirmishes about the merits of Edith Sitwell, the literary pages and correspondence columns of *The Spectator* providing a convenient field for the battle, which was waged also in the *London*

[1] These phrases are taken from Kenneth Rexroth, 'Thou Shalt Not Kill: A Memorial for Dylan Thomas'. When Thomas used such phrases about himself it was in a mocking tone: '. . . good old 3-adjectives-a-penny belly-churning Thomas, The Rimbaud of Cwmdonkin Drive'. *Letters to Vernon Watkins*, ed. Vernon Watkins (Dent and Faber, 1957), p. 104.

Magazine and in the *Times Literary Supplement*. The opposing factions exchanged comparatively genial abuse, a typical example being John Lehmann's Foreword to the October 1954 issue of the *London Magazine*, where he awards 'the booby prize for the most inept remark of 1954 to Messrs. Davie and Cruttwell who have solemnly announced that they consider the author of *Façade*, *Gold Coast Customs* and *Street Songs* to be "no poet at all" '.

Many of those who gleefully mounted the assault on Edith Sitwell's reputation were young teachers of English literature, who either worked in or were graduates of the newer provincial universities. Some of them had been reared in the ethos of political radicalism and of protestant non-conformity; and although most of them had abandoned the religion of their childhood for a watchful agnosticism tinged with moral earnestness, the Puritan within them was eager to trample upon any frivolous, idolatrous cult inaugurated by the Cavaliers. The adulation of Edith Sitwell and of Dylan Thomas seemed to them just such a cult, organized by that sinister, nebulous Establishment whose agents gave smart cocktail-parties, controlled the influential periodicals, the B.B.C., the British Council and all those sources which, in the small, tightly-organized realm of English letters, can make or break a fashionable literary reputation. The conflict was not about poetic styles alone: it embraced a wide area of disagreement about ways of thought, modes of living, standards of value. It was epitomized frivolously by the setter of a *New Statesman* competition, who offered the usual prizes for a Byronic satire to be entitled 'Provincial Bards and Metropolitan Reviewers'. On a more serious level, it was a continuation of the campaign which F. R. Leavis and his colleagues had fought so unrelentingly in *Scrutiny* for over twenty years.

A belief that the influence of Edith Sitwell and of Dylan Thomas has been wholly malevolent does not, by itself, constitute an adequate poetic credo. To discover whether those poets who subscribed to this article of faith shared any more positive beliefs and aspirations is not an easy task. In this country poets seldom form themselves into schools, issue manifestoes or draw up a doctrinaire aesthetic programme, leaving such un-English activities to continental writers and to energetic Americans like Ezra Pound, who come over here to disturb our lazy empiricism, and who may even, once in half a century, goad a native poet to circulate a document, such as the so-called Imagist Manifesto of Richard Aldington. Enterprising journalists occasionally huddle a few assorted and mildly protesting writers into a little group, which they proceed to label; an alert critic may edit a small anthology designed to suggest that a new school of poets has emerged; there will be avowals and retractions, charges and counter-charges, assertions and indignant denials, until, after a few years, the individuals will go their own ways, quick to deny that they ever really belonged to any school and lamenting the misleading publicity (which may at the time have been useful in advancing their reputations).

A process of this kind caused readers of contemporary verse to become aware, early in 1954, of the fact that certain poets aged about thirty seemed to share a common way of looking at the world, to speak in the same tone of voice. The appearance of *Poets of the 1950's*, edited by D. J. Enright (1955), and of *New Lines*, edited by Robert Conquest (1956), confirmed these suspicions. All eight poets in Enright's team turned up again in Conquest's anthology, which contained a provocative introduction but lacked the brief notes on their own work contributed by the writers of Enright's choice. Since even these introductory comments are revealing snippets of autobiography rather than a coherent statement of poetic doctrine, critics found it difficult to invent a satisfactory name for the group whose existence they were determined to prove. In the end, despite some half-hearted attempts to christen them the Academics, or the University Wits, or neo-Empsonians, they were most widely known by the curious appellation of the Movement, a title derived from an anonymous article in *The Spectator*, 1 October 1954, headed 'In the Movement'.

Although the poets represented in these anthologies advance no systematic theory of poetry and offer no rigid set of dogmatic beliefs, it is possible to trace their immediate literary ancestry and to summarize the main characteristics of their work. Most of them had learned from George Orwell to mistrust what he called the smelly little orthodoxies to which politicians, public relations men, academics and tidy bureaucrats pay lip service. Orwell had taught them to develop a keen nose for cant and humbug, no matter how cunningly they might be disguised and packaged. He had warned them also that advertisers and confidence men, whether they were selling commercial wares or political slogans, would, by the nature of their trade, tend always to debase the currency of language, whose purity it is the poet's task to preserve. These poets owed an even more profound debt to F. R. Leavis who, whether or not they agreed with his judgements on individual writers, stood for a serious, uncompromising devotion to the idea of literature as a great moral and imaginative discipline and who had dedicated the labours of a lifetime to the defence of his principles. One or two of these poets had studied the writings of Wittgenstein and of the Logical Positivists; all of them had come to maturity in a climate of opinion where the assumptions of these philosophers had flourished and become an accepted part of the landscape.

The poets who appeared in *New Lines* found many of the qualities which they admired and sought to emulate in the early poems of T. S. Eliot and in the work of Empson. They borrowed from Robert Graves his dry, rueful, ironical wit, and from W. H. Auden the sudden twists of mood and diction which he perfected in the sonnet sequences *In Time of War* and *The Quest*. Just as it is possible to trace a 'line of wit' in seventeenth-century poetry, so one can discern a similar line descending from Eliot and Empson, taking in Graves and Auden, and branching out to include such varied poets as Norman Cameron, Demetrios Capetanakis, and Roy Fuller. The characteristic tone of voice which echoes through *New Lines* can be detected in Cameron's 'The Compassionate Fool', where a quizzical irony, self-scrutiny, and calm acceptance of life's absurdity govern the poem:

> My enemy had bidden me as guest.
> His table all set out with wine and cake,

His ordered chairs, he to beguile me dressed
So neatly, moved my pity for his sake.

I knew it was an ambush, but could not
Leave him to eat his cake up by himself
And put his unused glasses on the shelf.
I made pretence of falling in his plot,

And trembled when in his anxiety
He bared it too absurdly to my view.
And even as he stabbed me through and through
I pitied him for his small strategy.

One finds a similar blend of colloquial ease and dramatic intensity
in these stanzas from 'Abel' by Capetanakis:

My brother Cain, the wounded, liked to sit
Brushing my shoulder, by the staring water
Of life, or death, in cinemas half-lit
By scenes of peace that always turned to slaughter.

He liked to talk to me. His eager voice
Whispered the puzzle of his bleeding thirst,
Or prayed me not to make my final choice,
Unless we had a chat about it first.

Auden's contribution to the style of this new school is less easy to
define, but in the opening lines of the second sonnet from *The Quest*
he strikes a note which was to become increasingly familiar in the
mid-1950's, a note in which an insolent, yet melancholy, wit glances
obliquely at a hidden reserve of powerful emotion:

All had been ordered weeks before the start
From the best firms at such work; instruments
To take the measure of all queer events,
And drugs to move the bowels or the heart.

Roy Fuller, who began to publish his verse in periodicals before
1939, serves as a bridge between Auden and this group of post-war
poets, not only as a craftsman but also as a student of Freud.
English poets seldom incorporate in their verse an elaborate meta-

physical system or expound in detail a consistent philosophical theory. One finds in our poetry moments of sudden illumination, a sense of the mystery of the world, and it is in this total response to life's intricacy and wonder rather than in an adherence to any formal doctrinal scheme that the genius of English poetry resides. Yet from time to time our poets may find in the speculations of a philosopher something congenial to their temperament, something which, corresponding to their emotional needs, helps to define the vague intellectual promptings and perplexities by which they have been haunted. They may be excited by the work of a metaphysician whom they have studied very superficially and whom they understand imperfectly. There is even such a thing as fruitful misunderstanding, for a poet's first duty is to write poems, and as a bird will gather for its nest a variety of incongruous objects, so a poet will carry away from his raid upon a formidable edifice of metaphysical concepts only a few coloured fragments which have caught his fancy and which may be useful to him in the construction of his poetry. Auden, in his early work, employs in this way the teaching of Freud, Groddeck, and Homer Lane, peppering his verse with terms derived from their psychoanalytical theories, depicting the violence and febrile turmoil of our civilization as though they were neuroses, and vaguely hoping for the advent of a Healer who will cure men of their ills. When we recall the recurrence of Freudian motifs in *The Ascent of F6* and in *On The Frontier*, as well as his long elegy on Freud, we shall find further proof of Auden's indebtedness to him as a source of ideas, themes, and imagery.

Fuller stands alone among post-war poets in his persistent efforts to weave Freudian concepts into the texture of his verse. The poets of *New Lines* are, by temperament, more sympathetic towards the work of Freud, which offers a vast range of daring hypotheses that seem to be capable of verification by scientific experiments, than towards the theories of Jung, which apparently rest upon metaphysical presuppositions that do not lend themselves to empirical proof or disproof. It is therefore of some importance that they were able to find readily available in Fuller's verse an example of how a poet could assimilate Freudian doctrine into poetry without any sense of eccentricity or of strain. The first stanza of his poem, 'The Image', foreshadows several features of the style of verse which was to become predominant in the late nineteen-fifties:

> A spider in the bath. The image noted:
> Significant maybe but surely cryptic.
> A creature motionless and rather bloated,
> The barriers shining, vertical and white:
> Passing concern, and pity mixed with spite.

Here we have a quiet conversational opening, a casual tone, a reference to a trivial, domestic, everyday occurrence, with the under-lying suggestion that the object of our scrutiny may yield a disturb-ing symbolical meaning. The sinister implications of the third line are partially contradicted by the use of the qualifying word 'rather', designed to reassure us and yet to terrify us by its menacing hint. This deliberate ambiguity, like the wary refusal to commit oneself, and the protective use of irony, is typical of much post-war verse. Fuller continues to juxtapose the familiar, the whimsical, and the portentous, introducing in the second stanza a grotesque, horrify-ing image, bred by Auden out of Freud, which compares the spider with

> The filthy aunt forgotten in the attic.

Then in the fourth stanza he reverts to the faintly jocular style of the poem's two opening lines and describes how one lifts up the spider before throwing it out of the window:

> One jibs at murder, so a sheet of paper
> Is slipped beneath the accommodating legs . . .

In the final stanza Fuller at last speaks out unequivocally, his tone of voice growing firm and resonant as the poem reaches its climax:

> We certainly would like thus easily
> To cast out of the house all suffering things.
> But sadness and responsibility
> For our own kind lives in the image noted:
> A half-loved creature, motionless and bloated.

The poets represented in *New Lines* are, in order of their appearance in the anthology, Elizabeth Jennings, John Holloway, Philip Larkin, Thom Gunn, Kingsley Amis, D. J. Enright, Donald Davie, Robert Conquest, and John Wain. I shall consider some of these poets individually in later chapters: meanwhile I shall quote brief passages from four of them, and from a slightly younger poet not wholly in sympathy with them, in order to indicate the characteristic flavour of their work and to show its family likeness to the poetry of Empson, Auden, Cameron, Capetanakis, and Fuller which I have already cited:

> Proust who collected time within
> A child's cake would understand
> The ambiguity of this —
> Summer still raging while a thin
> Column of smoke stirs from the land
> Proving that autumn gropes for us.
>   ELIZABETH JENNINGS, 'Song at the Beginning of Autumn'

> When love as germ invades the purple stream
> It splashes round the veins and multiplies
> Till objects of desire are what they seem;
>   JOHN WAIN, 'Eighth Type of Ambiguity'

> No ripening curve can be allowed to sag
> On cubist's canvas or in sculptor's stone:
> Informal fruit, that burgeons from the swag,
> Would spoil the ripening that is art's alone.
>   DONALD DAVIE, 'Cherry Ripe: On a Painting by Juan Gris'

> For since you were so thankfully confused
> By law with someone else, you cannot be
> Semantically the same as that young beauty:
> It was of her that these two words were used.
>   PHILIP LARKIN, 'Maiden Name'

The sun's occasional print, the brisk brief
Worry of wheels along the street outside
Where bridal London bows the other way ...

PHILIP LARKIN, 'Deceptions'

You stand in the first dumbness of the snow
As finely, the gauze drop in pantomime,
All detail fades upon your startled face
And back to darkness line and colour flow.

A. ALVAREZ, 'The Vigil'

These five poets, it is plain, share certain assumptions and speak in a common tone of voice. Poetry, they seem to say, should observe the world coolly and intelligently, construct satisfying patterns, employ rational processes of thought, try to make sense of what it contemplates. They all display a cautious scepticism, favour an empirical attitude, speak in carefully measured accents, and examine a problem with an alert wariness. Believing that the virtues of good prose are not out of place in poetry, they leave room in their verse for coherent argument, subtlety, irony, and erudition, because rational men ought not to exclude from their poems those qualities of mind which have played so large a part in shaping our intellectual heritage. Verse in their hands may on occasion become an instrument of overt moralizing; nor will they hesitate to be didactic, since poetry should have enough weight and strength to bear the burden of instruction. They frown severely on loose emotional gestures, inflated rhetoric, the cult of the poet as rebel, inspired madman, or Bohemian, since these aberrations permit the fool and the charlatan to debauch their readers' sensibility and the English language.

They all habitually employ traditional verse patterns, with a special fondness for the quatrain, or for such exacting forms as the *sestina*, the *villanelle* or *terza rima*. Wain in his early verse is avowedly a disciple of Empson, who, together with Donne, is clearly a pervasive influence throughout the work of Alvarez. All these poets, mistrusting or ignoring the legacy of the Romantics and aiming at colloquial ease, decorum, shapeliness, elegance, are trying to bring back into the currency of the language the precision, the snap, the gravity, the decisive, clinching finality which have been lost since the late Augustan age.

Although the tone of voice which they favoured and the critical values for which they stood won general approbation during the nineteen-fifties, both their theory and their practice drew some hostile fire. Edith Sitwell announced her regal displeasure:

We know, now, that the proper study for Man is, in poetry, not Man, but troubles about bicycle clips, or the discovery of a spider in one's bath.[1]

We have already observed that Roy Fuller's poem is, pre-eminently, a study of Man in relation to his fellows; and the most casual glance at Philip Larkin's 'Church Going' reveals that it is a study of Man as a creature isolated in a universe from which God seems to have withdrawn. A gibe, to be effective, needs to contain a modicum of truth, just as the most telling satire is that which credits its victim with one or two attractive qualities. John Heath-Stubbs, in his 'Brief Letter to a Friend', dated 10 November 1953, is scarcely more convincing than Edith Sitwell although he displays more good-humour. His targets in these lines are academic poets and critics in general, Donald Davie, John Wain, and F. R. Leavis in particular, whom he accuses of maltreating English poetry, now become an under-nourished brat:

> While one in Dublin, kindly-cruel
> Feeds her with thin and neutral gruel;
> And one in Berkshire will not fail
> To prove that Reading has a gaol;
> By the whole gang she's soundly rated
> By one she's robbed, by one she's bated,
> And last, at Downing, suffocated.

A juster criticism would be that even the best of these poets display a self-awareness which all too frequently hardens into a crippling self-consciousness. In the very act of writing a poem they

[1] Letter to the *Times Literary Supplement*, 29 November 1957, p. 721.

seem to ask themselves whether it is critic-proof, whether it is vulnerable to rigorous analysis or to mockery, whether they have been guilty of unpardonable emotion or unregulated enthusiasm. Hence they feel constrained to adopt a nonchalant pose of self-deprecating irony, as if to make it clear that they see both sides of the question, and that it would be an error to take them too seriously or tragically. Their carefully cultivated tone of conversational ease, especially when combined with the employment of strict verse-forms, at times degenerates into affectation and mannerism. More-over, the practice of scattering here and there such empty phrases as 'of course', 'I'm afraid', 'it seems', in so far as it is not just metrical padding, appears to be a vaguely reassuring gesture intended to show that these highly intellectual poets want their readers to relax and to feel at home in a genial atmosphere. Kingsley Amis, with his customary frankness, admits as much:

The trouble with the newer poets, including myself, is that they often are lucid and nothing else — except arid and bald, and that, on the other hand, the strict forms seem to give some of them the idea that they can be as sentimental and trite as they please, provided they do it in *terza rima*.[1]

Some of these poets display a brittle ingenuity and a precocious cleverness which fail to conceal a radical uncertainty of purpose and of tone. John Wain, taking as an epigraph a passage from one of Keats's letters to Fanny Brawne — 'For God's sake save me, or tell me my passion is of too awful a nature for you' — composes a set of verses on the dying poet's cry. This poem, entitled 'Don't Let's Spoil It All, I Thought We Were Going To Be Such Good Friends', and written in *terza rima*, is meant to be a terse, poised commentary on a tragic situation. Wain, understandably, desires to avoid the perils of adopting an inflated neo-Romantic jargon and of exhibiting a gaseous emotionalism. To guard against these dangers he uses slang and understatement, hoping to persuade his readers that only his iron restraint and strict technical control can hold in check the emotional intensity which would otherwise shatter the poem's fine equilibrium. Yet, reading this poem, one

[1] *Poets of the 1950's*, ed. D. J. Enright, p. 17.

recalls R. P. Blackmur's quiet condemnation of 'deliberate flatness: which is only the contemporary form of Georgian deliquescence'.[1] One remembers also that irony is often an elegant form of evasion, a defensive gesture to conceal the absence of deep feeling, the flaking coat of paint which gives lath the appearance of iron. However serious Wain's intentions may have been, the result is an uneasy mixture of hard-boiled facetiousness, knowing cynicism, and facile melodrama. The poem opens with an elaborately casual remark, and speedily adopts a tone of affable, condescending superiority:

> It seems the poet made a bad mistake.
> How could she know how awful passion was?
> The lesson is that breaking hearts must break.
>
> Now sage biographers are sad because
> She did not play the game they like to see,
> The necessary did not come across. . . .

Then, after teasing us with a few more observations of this kind, the poet gives the verse a sudden theatrical twist, portraying Keats as 'choking in his fear', and pointing the moral of the tale in a resounding curtain-line:

> The lesson is that dying hearts must die.

A similar modish ingenuity and perverted intelligence can be found in the work of Gordon Wharton. His 'Poem for the Photograph of Miss Marilyn Monroe on a Calendar for 1956', written, one need hardly say, in *terza rima*, celebrates the charms of Marilyn Monroe with an erudite, pedantic wit, in the manner of one of Rowlandson's elderly lechers peering at a buxom nude:

> Not the geologist's but geographer's art
> Would do you justice. The bland surveyor sees
> Your landscape indolent upon his chart
>
> And notes, from hair to modelled Alpine knees,
> No easy reference to the deciduous year,
> Finds no Alaska where his glance might freeze.

[1] R. P. Blackmur, *Language as Gesture*, p. 429.

John Donne, it is true, resorts to a comparison of this kind in

O my America! my new-found land

but whereas in his poem we can sense an exuberant imagination seizing upon all kinds of imagery to convey the nature of his passion, we can detect in the verses quoted above only a laboured attempt to sustain a forced simile. In 'The Laws of Cooling' Wharton produces a series of metaphysical conceits which, lacking imaginative coherence and intensity, are no more than fanciful decorations:

> Quite still, like goldfish packed in ice,
> Our bodies, lazy, may append
> No action, tremor or surprise
> To realise a decent end. . . .

> We like Alaskan rivers tilt
> Out of our beds in parallels;
> Desire out of the ice may melt
> But leave our bodies somewhere else.

These lines yield the same kind of pleasure that we derive from the most outrageous conceits of John Cleveland or from Marvell's salmon fishers in *Appleton House*, who

> . . . like *Antipodes* in Shoes
> Have shod their *Heads* in their *Canoos*.
> How *Tortoise like*, but not so slow,
> These rational *Amphibii* go.

Wharton's stanzas compel from us a smile which is, in part, a tribute to his adroitness and, in part, a recognition of the fact that his lovers, 'like goldfish packed in ice', are figures of an endearing absurdity.

It is, after all, better to misuse than to abandon intelligence, and those who master a technique have acquired an instrument on which they may come to play good tunes. The *New Lines* poets and their followers, even at their most arid, deserve the tribute paid by Dr. Johnson to the Metaphysical poets:

To write on their plan it was at least necessary to read and think. No man could be born a metaphysical poet, nor assume the dignity of a writer by descriptions copied from descriptions, by imitations borrowed from imitations, by traditional imagery and hereditary similes, by readiness of rhyme, and volubility of syllables.[1]

The severest of their critics deny that they merit a more positive commendation. In a review of *New Lines*, Charles Tomlinson discerns in all these poets an imaginative poverty and dullness, a total failure to apprehend the splendour or the mystery of the world, a parochialism of the senses no less than of the intellect:

They show a singular want of vital awareness of the continuum outside themselves, of the mystery bodied over against them in the created universe, which they fail to experience with any degree of sharpness or to embody with any instress or sensuous depth.[2]

Kathleen Raine has condemned these poets, although she does not specifically name them, for their philosophical crudity and inadequacy. In two letters printed in the *Times Literary Supplement*, dated 25 May and 8 June 1956, she enlarges upon the view of poetry which she had expounded in the introduction to her *Collected Poems*:

Poetry, as I understand it, is of value insofar as it is imaginative — insofar, that is, as it is an expression of a timeless metaphysical order that has been variously named. . . . A philosophy so unfashionable as Platonism is unlikely to find favour with a generation raised on a diet of materialism, positivism, and the like (can these be called *love of wisdom?*). . . .

There seems to be a school of young poets who have never heard of Muse or daimon, and who write only from personal experience. Inspiration is one thing, personal Memory quite another; and as Blake never tired of pointing out, memory is not a Muse.

One could reply that a love of wisdom is not confined to Platonists (unless the word 'wisdom' be given an esoteric connotation); that the real question is not whether Platonism is unfashionable but whether it is true; that Blake's assertion about memory is a starting-point for an argument rather than an *ex cathedra* pronouncement by an infallible authority; and that in poetry, no less than in daily life,

[1] *Life of Cowley*.
[2] 'The Middlebrow Muse'. *Essays in Criticism*, VII, No. 2 (April 1957), p. 215.

it is desirable to cultivate good sense, empiricism, and the habit of scrupulously examining all the available evidence. Yet we must admit that some gifted post-war poets who do not share Kathleen Raine's metaphysical presuppositions agree with her in lamenting the emotional poverty and dryness of the authors whom she has attacked. Vernon Watkins, George Barker, David Gascoyne, Thomas Blackburn, W. S. Graham, and David Wright, dissimilar as they are in their religious convictions and in their view of the world, hold in common with Kathleen Raine and with one another certain beliefs about the nature of poetry which are reflected in their verse.

When considering the work of the *New Lines* poets, I suggested that one could map their descent from a line of wit going back to Eliot and to Empson. It is less easy to trace the literary and philosophical ancestry of this second group: they have learned something from the esoteric poems of Yeats, from Rilke and from Symbolism; they find the speculations of Jung more congenial than the ideas of Freud; they admire the poetry of Kathleen Raine and of Dylan Thomas; and while they may find it hard to swallow Robert Graves's notion of the White Goddess, they acknowledge the mystical nature of poetic inspiration. Our concern, however, is with achievement rather than with ancestry, and the following characteristic passages may serve to illustrate the kind of poetry which these poets habitually write:

> So the green Earth is first no colour and then green.
> Spirits who walk, who know
> All is untouchable, and, knowing this, touch so,
> Who know the music by which white is seen,
> See the world's colours in flashes come and go.
> The marguerite's petal is white, is wet with rain,
> Is white, then loses white, and then is white again
> Not from time's course, but from the living spring,
> Miraculous whiteness, a petal, a wing,
> Like light, like lightning, soft thunder, white as jet,
> Ageing on ageless breaths. The ages are not yet.
> VERNON WATKINS, 'Music of Colours: The Blossoms Scattered'

Let my body sweat
let snakes torment my breast
my eyes be blind, ears deaf, hands distraught
mouth parched, uterus cut out,
belly slashed, back lashed,
tongue slivered into thongs of leather
rain stones inserted in my breasts,
head severed

if only the lips may speak,
if only the god will come.

KATHLEEN RAINE, 'Invocation'

And I no longer boy still seek to find
    That sacred instrument —
The haunted chord struck by a dawn wind
    Which by presentiment
Of breath lifts the dead feathers of the mind
    Exalting a transcendent.
So, holy poem, I see the idea enshrined
    With all altared thought,
And bleeding eagles, as they strike to blind,
    Shall tear a vision out.

GEORGE BARKER, 'Consolatory Verses for the Middle Years'

In whatever condition, whole, blind, dumb,
One-legged or leprous, the human being is,
I affirm the human condition is the same,
The heart half broken in ashes and in lies,
But sustained by the immensity of the divine.

Thus I too must praise out of a quiet ear
The great creation to which I owe I am
My grief and my love. O hear me if I cry
Among the din of birds deaf to their acclaim
Involved like them in the not unhearing air.

DAVID WRIGHT, 'Monologue of a Deaf Man'

All these poets lay stress upon the forces in the universe and in
man's personality which lie beyond the control of human reason.

A poet must acknowledge these forces, submit to them, become an instrument devoted to the service of daimonic powers, a mouthpiece by which arcane spiritual truths and intimations are conveyed to mankind. Those who hold this belief normally adopt a lofty, solemn tone when speaking about the poet's vocation since, on this view, he is a guardian of sacred mysteries, a bard, a prophet, a priest of a hidden God or White Goddess. Their verse abounds in apostrophes and invocations; and, believing with Milton that a poet must soar 'into the high region of his fancies with his garland and singing robes about him',[1] they are untroubled by the suspicion that such a rig-out is all too easily obtainable from any theatrical costumier. The poets of *New Lines*, although taking their art no less seriously, mistrust extreme claims couched in quasi-religious terms, and believe that a pinch of salt is healthier than an unrelieved diet of incense.

The qualities which we find in this second group of poets are a lyrical purity and intensity, a Dionysian abandon, a reliance upon the evocative power of myth and symbol, a prophetic fervour, a deliberate raising of the emotional temperature, a willingness to make large claims and to indulge in sweeping gestures. Responding passionately and intuitively to human suffering and joy, desiring above all to record faithfully their vision of the world, they are far less concerned with the careful analysis of moral problems, the witty, penetrating observation of human manners and foibles, or the construction of intellectual patterns and of philosophical systems. Their poetry affirms and celebrates the splendours and miseries of creation, the spiritual glory and wretchedness of man. In contrast to the tone of austere stoicism and dignified agnosticism pervading the work of the *New Lines* poets, a note of religious ecstasy vibrates in their verse, which is essentially a poetry of revelation rather than of discourse, of incantation rather than of argument. The poem is for them a rune, a spell, a sacred hieroglyph.

Unlike those who regard a poem as primarily an artefact deliberately fashioned by human skill, these poets favour the meta-

[1] John Milton, *Reason of Church Government*.

E

phor of organic growth when speaking of the way in which a poem is written. They follow Romantic and Symbolist tradition both in their fondness for this metaphor, and in their high, almost sacramental view of the poetic image, which they endow with enormous potency. They would accept as valid Dylan Thomas's account of a poem's genesis and development, whereas poets whose turn of mind is more analytical and sceptical would shrug it aside as a piece of heady rhetoric which obscures a complex problem by emitting a smoke-screen of verbiage and of mystification:

... a poem by myself needs a host of images, because its centre is a host of images. ... Out of the inevitable conflict of images — inevitable, because of the creative, recreative, destructive and contradictory nature of the motivating centre, the womb of war — I try to make the momentary peace which is a poem.[1]

When we read a good poem by Fuller, Davie, or Larkin we feel that the poet must have planned it from start to finish with the same care, the same regard for proportion, that an architect employs in the design of a building. Or, to vary the simile, their verse resembles the speech of an advocate, who calculates the weight of every word, manipulates his epithets, varies his tone of voice and pace of delivery, as with a finely tempered skill and lucidity he moves from his exordium to his peroration. A good poem by Barker, Watkins, or Gascoyne achieves its effect by different means: it passes from image to image and from cadence to cadence as though it were obeying a law of its own nature, and the poet appears to be exploring the world of the poem in order to discover the secrets which it may yield. While we need not condemn either of these procedures in the name of the other, we must admit that these contrasting modes of composition reflect a radical divergence of beliefs about the nature and purpose of poetry.

Even the best poets of this second group reveal, from time to time, the characteristic vices of Dionysian poetry: a lack of earthiness, sinewy vigour, and plain good sense; a posturing in the role of

[1] Quoted by Henry Treece, *Dylan Thomas* (Lindsay Drummond, 1949), p. 47, n. 1.

the artist as seer, or defiant outcast, or Sybil uttering cryptic words of aetherial wisdom; a reliance upon a lofty Romantic argot; a tendency, when imaginative passion grows feeble, to relapse into grandiloquent rhetoric. Of the inferior writers in this genre it is difficult to speak with moderation. Poets who accept the standards recognized by the contributors to *New Lines* retain, even in their moments of perverted ingenuity, a framework of rational order, as we saw in those lines by John Wain and by Gordon Wharton on which I made some unfavourable remarks. Those who ignore such restraints flaunt, at their worst, a disrespect for language, a contempt for decorum and coherence, an addiction to proliferating nonsense, which degrade the art of poetry to the level of vulgar exhibitionism. To read them is painful: to quote them would be unnecessarily cruel. Alexander Pope has portrayed them with prophetic accuracy:

> The Dog-star rages! nay 'tis past a doubt,
> All *Bedlam*, or *Parnassus*, is let out:
> Fire in each eye, and Papers in each hand,
> They rave, recite, and madden round the land.[1]

And in the Preface to his *Poems* (1853), Matthew Arnold has given us a warning which is still relevant to-day:

Two kinds of *dilettanti*, says Goethe, there are in poetry: he who neglects the indispensable mechanical part, and thinks he has done enough if he shows spirituality and feeling; and he who seeks to arrive at poetry merely by mechanism, in which he can acquire an artisan's readiness, and is without soul and matter. And he adds, that the first does most harm to Art, and the last to himself. If we must be *dilettanti* . . . let us, at least, have so much respect for our Art as to prefer it to ourselves.[2]

It would be a mistake to believe that all good poets in recent years have belonged to one of two mutually hostile camps, movements, trends, or schools (those abstractions dear to the systematizing critic). For although it is true that the publication of *New Lines* and of a rival anthology, *Mavericks*, started an acrimonious debate,

---

[1] Alexander Pope, *An Epistle to Dr. Arbuthnot*, 3–6.
[2] Cf. Blake's dictum: 'Mechanical Excellence is the Only Vehicle of Genius'.

English poets are too sceptical, empirical, and wayward to group themselves into disciplined phalanxes for the propagation of clearly-formulated poetic doctrines.[1] Moreover, in the small literary world of England where most poets know and frequently meet one another, personal friendships, loyalties, and animosities continually modify, blur, and soften the lines of demarcation between rival literary theories. Even a cursory glance at my neat categories would reveal certain quirks and irregularities, which are the despair of the schematic philosopher and the very life of poetry. Thus, John Holloway and Kathleen Raine, whose views are often diametrically opposed, unite in venerating the work of Edwin Muir; Thom Gunn, whom G. S. Fraser and Iain Fletcher describe in their anthology, *Springtime*, as a neo-Empsonian, ends a severely critical review of Empson's *Collected Poems* by remarking that he is no less dangerous a model for young poets than Dylan Thomas,[2] a judgement which finds support in Robert Conquest's reference to 'that pole of darkness where . . . Dylan Thomas and William Empson meet'. Nor do the poets of *New Lines* present a united front to the world: Davie and Holloway share many basic principles which are anathema to Larkin and to Amis; Davie holds a number of aesthetic beliefs in common with Charles Tomlinson who, denied a place in their anthologies by Enright and by Conquest, has exposed what he considers to be the radical deficiencies of their chosen poets.

Yet the distinctions which I have drawn are not merely verbal

[1] See Charles Tomlinson, 'The Middlebrow Muse' in *Essays in Criticism*, VII, No. 2 (April 1957), pp. 208–17, and subsequent correspondence; the Introduction to *Mavericks*, ed. Howard Sergeant and Dannie Abse, pp. 9–14; various articles in *Delta*, No. 8 (Spring 1956), pp. 6–31, and a letter from Donald Davie in No. 9 (Summer 1956), pp. 27–28; a review entitled 'Too Late the Mavericks' in the *Times Literary Supplement*, 8 March 1957, pp. 137–8; John Wain, 'English Poetry: The Immediate Situation' in *Sewanee Review*, LXV, No. 3 (1957), pp. 353–74; Donald Davie, 'Remembering the Movement' in *Prospect* (Summer 1959), pp. 13–16. All these are partisan statements, and they are of unequal value, the *TLS* article being a classic example of how irresponsible malice can flourish beneath the cloak of anonymity. A general survey of the period is to be found in the symposium on 'English Poetry since 1945', *London Magazine*, vol. 6, No. 11 (November 1959), pp. 11–36.

[2] This review is printed in *London Magazine*, vol. 3, No. 2 (February 1956), pp. 70–75. For a reply see Kathleen Raine's letter in the March issue, pp. 66–67; and Gunn's rejoinder in the April issue, pp. 64–65.

quibbles: they mark genuine disagreements about poetic theory and divergencies in practice. Consider, for example, how three poets celebrate the figure of Orpheus:

> Orpheus, beloved famulus,
> Known to us in dark congeries
> Of intimations from the dead:
> Encamping among our verses —
> Harp-beats of a sea-bird's wings —
> Do you contend in us, though now
> A memory only, the smashed lyre
> Washed up entangled in your hair . . . ?
>
> LAWRENCE DURRELL, 'Orpheus'

> Now on a salt, unbridled stream,
> His sacred essence walks abroad,
> Through cold futurities of dream
> In hopeless and plutonian love.
> The clouded animals of sense
> Are touched by that grief stricken eye,
> And from their blind experience
> Follow a vagrant, orphic cry.
>
> THOMAS BLACKBURN, 'Orpheus'

> And now I'm tired of being the trade-name
> of boxes of assorted junk; tired of
> conscription as the mouthpiece of your brash
> theories, of jigging to your symbol-crash.
> Speak up for yourselves, or not at all; this game
> is up — your manikin has had enough.
>
> KINGSLEY AMIS, 'Sonnet from Orpheus'

Durrell and Blackburn, with appropriately deferential postures and tones of voice, pay a reverent tribute to an undying myth; Amis smiles tolerantly at a poor little marionette, a battered idol grown weary of his devotees' mumbo-jumbo and genuflexions.

Even more striking is the contrast between the 'Oedipus' of Anthony Thwaite and the 'Oedipus' of Thomas Blackburn. Thwaite's concern is with the agony of a man who comes to realize the truth about his love for Jocasta, a truth which he cannot bear to contemplate:

> If she who first embodied me
> From swollen foetus crouched beneath
> Hot sallow blood and milk, if she
> Speaks through your eyes, tastes of your breath,
> Then hide me where I cannot see.

The restraint of the language serves to emphasize the growing intensity of the horror, until the final line of the poem descends with the decisive flash of the guillotine:

> Held fast against your breast, I find
> A shapeless memory takes shape
> Upon the pillow. Heart and mind
> Blunt both my eyes in blind escape
> And when I waken, I am blind.

In Blackburn's poem, the protagonists are less human beings than mythical figures rehearsing the destiny of Man in declamatory operatic strains:

> Then up and blind him, hands, pull blackness down
> And let this woman on the strangling cord,
> Hang in the rich embroidery of her gown;
> Then up and blind him, pull the blackness down.

As Oedipus moves away in the final stanza, we feel that his exit demands the kind of gorgeous orchestral flourish which brings to an end the *Ariadne auf Naxos* of Richard Strauss:

> But as he stumbles to the desert sands,
> Bleeding and helpless as the newly born,
> His daughters leading him with childish hands,
> I see beyond all words his future shape,
> Its feet upon the carcass of the ape
> And round its mighty head, prophetic birds.

To simplify is to distort; and a brief survey of this nature inevitably blurs or ignores those subtle and minute variations of tone and feeling that endow poems with their individual significance. It may, however, help us to detect a coherent pattern in the babel of post-war verse and to distinguish there two dominant voices: the voice which argues, teaches, sets in order; and the voice which chants, affirms, prophesies. The dialogue between them has moulded and defined the history of poetry in England since the war.

III

THE FOURFOLD VISION

WE can divide poets into those for whom the visible world
not only exists but is sufficient, and those who value it
only in so far as it nourishes the visionary imagination and
embodies those unchanging spiritual forms which are the source of
all energy and beauty. Poets of the first kind take as their theme the
intellectual achievements and the sensual desires of men and women,
the actions of man as a political animal, the psychological complexities of individual human beings. Whatever may be their moral,
metaphysical, and religious beliefs, they are more concerned with
portraying life as it is lived day by day in the busy world of men
than with exploring the depths of the psyche or the regions of the
unconscious. Chaucer, Jonson, Shakespeare, Dryden, and Pope,
for all their range and intensity, seldom forget that they are terres-
trial creatures: their hopes may be in heaven, but their conversation is of the earth. In this they differ from such poets as Spenser,
Milton, Blake, Coleridge, and Shelley who, despite their rich
sensual endowment, constantly have recourse to a symbolic vocabulary, since it alone can formulate their apprehension of spiritual
reality.

In Blake, more than in any other poet, we find an absolute conviction that the created world is of no value until it is transmuted by
the Divine Imagination in Man. Rejecting the mechanistic universe
of that unholy Trinity, Bacon, Newton, and Locke, he affirms that
Imaginative Art is 'a Representation of what Eternally Exists,
Really and Unchangeably'.[1]

Blake repeatedly emphasizes the primacy of Imagination and of
Vision:

[1] *A Vision of the Last Judgment.*

And I know that This World Is a World of Imagination & Vision . . . to the Eyes of the Man of Imagination, Nature is Imagination itself. As a man is, so he sees. As the Eye is formed, such are its Powers. You certainly Mistake, when you say that the Visions of Fancy are not to be found in This World. To Me This World is all One continued Vision of Fancy or Imagination, & I feel Flatter'd when I am told so.[1]

I assert for My Self that I do not behold the outward Creation & that to me it is hindrance & not Action; it is as the dirt upon my feet, No part of me. 'What', it will be Question'd, 'When the Sun rises, do you not see a round disk of fire somewhat like a Guinea?' O no, no, I see an Innumerable company of the Heavenly host crying, 'Holy, Holy, Holy is the Lord God Almighty'. I question not my Corporeal or Vegetative Eye any more than I would Question a Window concerning a Sight. I look thro' it & not with it.[2]

A Spirit and a Vision are not, as the modern philosophy supposes, a cloudy vapour, or a nothing: they are organized and minutely articulated beyond all that the mortal and perishing nature can produce. He who does not imagine in stronger and better lineaments, and in stronger and better light than his perishing and mortal eye can see, does not imagine at all.[3]

Blake prays to be delivered from the tyranny of the eye which sees only the corporeal world:

> Now I a fourfold vision see,
> And a fourfold vision is given to me;
> 'Tis fourfold in my supreme delight
> And threefold in soft Beulah's night
> And twofold Always. May God us keep
> From Single vision & Newton's sleep![4]

Bernard Blackstone has explained that, in Blake's view, the task of the prophet and poet

is to overthrow the weight of custom and restore the power of double vision which will enable us to see the eternal form under the disguise of the temporal, of threefold vision which will enable us to reach unity

---

[1] Letter to Dr. Trusler, 23 August 1799.   [2] *A Vision of the Last Judgment.*
[3] *A Descriptive Catalogue.*   [4] Letter to Thomas Butts, 22 November 1802.

through love, and of fourfold vision which destroys completely the doubting selfhood.[1]

A study of Blake is the best introduction to the work of the three poets whom we are about to consider — Vernon Watkins, George Barker, and David Gascoyne. To say this is not to argue that they are disciples of Blake or that they share his beliefs: what all have in common with him and with one another is a desire to interpret the visible world symbolically, to see all things transformed in the visionary light of imagination which reveals 'what Eternally Exists, Really and Unchangeably'.

Although Vernon Watkins (b. 1906) is a little older than Auden, Spender, and MacNeice, it was not until 1941 that he brought out his first collection of poems, *Ballad of the Mari Lwyd*. The title of the opening poem, 'The Collier', might suggest that Watkins is going to describe the life of a Welsh mining village during the depression of the nineteen-thirties, but it soon becomes clear that his purpose is to portray the inner life of a man, the griefs of a soul:

> They dipped my coat in the blood of a kid
> And they cast me down a pit,
> And although I crossed with strangers
> There was no way out of it. . . .
>
> And one said, 'Jack was not raised up
> When the wind blew out the light
> Though he interpreted their dreams
> And guessed their fears by night.'

The story of Joseph is thus re-enacted in the valleys of Wales.

We seldom find in Watkins a description of people or of objects for their own sake, nor does he try to analyse the subtleties of human relationships. The poem 'Before a Birth' characteristically ignores the natural hopes and fears of the parents, the facts of parturition, the circumstances of the event, in order to emphasize the mystery and ecstasy of Birth, the sacredness of Woman as the vessel of God-given life:

[1] Bernard Blackstone, *English Blake* (Cambridge, 1949), pp. 233–4.

Touch, finger of Wine, this well of Crystalline water
And this earthenware jug, that knows the language of silence;
Touch, for darkness is near, that brings your glory to bed.

A much earlier poem, 'The Mother and Child', also depicts an archetypal pattern of mother and child, rather than two creatures of flesh and blood living in a particular time and place:

Let hands be about him white, O his mother's first,
Who caught him, fallen from light through nine months' haste
Of darkness, hid in the worshipping womb, the chaste
Thought of the creature with its certain thirst.

It is a far cry from these icons of Motherhood to the warm humanity of Shakespeare as he shows us what childbirth can mean, in terms of physical suffering, to a woman, and of mental pain, to a man:

A terrible Child-bed hast thou had, my deare,
No light, no fire, th' unfriendly elements
Forgot thee utterly. . . .[1]

Again and again we encounter in the poetry of Vernon Watkins this preoccupation with symbols of Reality, this indifference to the temporal and the local, this desire to reduce the multifarious activities of men into the unity of Myth. It is instructive to compare his sonnet 'Westminster Bridge' with the sonnet by Wordsworth on the same theme. Both poets are communicating a visionary experience; but Wordsworth's poem depicts a recognizable London, with literal accuracy, whereas the bridge in Watkins's sonnet might be a bridge seen in the underworld by Dante:

These figures around an urn
Cross the bought flood; they fix you with bartered eyes.
The bridge is a treadmill; alone the bathers, naked, are born.

This ability to ignore the transitory and the accidental, so as better to celebrate what is essential and unchanging, enables Watkins to attempt themes which would defeat most of his contemporaries. In his stanzas on the coronation of Elizabeth II, he can evoke, without

[1] *Pericles*, III, i.

any trace of embarrassment, the solemnity of the moment, the sacred
character of the ceremony:

> God's true fear, the rebuke of power, attended
> Her the trumpets proclaimed and the moment crowned
> Throned by the Thames, just past this
> Century's noon, in the midst of summer.
>
> Then, as the mantle fell and the crown was lowered,
> Set with emeralds, rubies and precious stones,
> Minstrels bade the anointed
> Keep, like the morning star, her stillness.

Even if we find the hieratic style of this 'Ode' not wholly to our
liking, we must admit that the poet has employed it with unfaltering
dignity and eloquence.

Watkins, like Blake, continually turns to the natural world in
order to renew his vision, and finds, in the landscapes and seascapes
of the Welsh coast where he has spent all his life, the symbols that
are the elements of his mythical world. His poetry abounds in
images drawn from nature and from the cosmos: birds, flowers,
trees, sand, water, sea, frost, light, darkness, sun, stars, thunder,
lightning. He is fascinated by the play of light upon the surfaces of
things, verbs such as *glint*, *flicker*, *ripple*, *shine*, *dazzle*, *sparkle*
recurring in his poetry as he seeks to convey the quality of the
divine energy which animates the universe. The appearance of
blossom on the trees inspires two poems, 'Music of Colours —
White Blossom' and 'Music of Colours: The Blossom Scattered',
in which he sustains a long, elaborate meditation on the mystical
significance of whiteness. The following stanza may conceivably
owe something to Gautier, although even in describing the hard,
pagan, classical world, Watkins invests it with a radiant tenderness,
a warm softness, a mystical ecstasy, alien both to ancient Greece and
to the poet of 'Symphonie en Blanc Majeur':

> Lovers speak of Venus, and the white doves,
> Jubilant, the white girl, myth's whiteness, Jove's
> Of Leda, the swan, whitest of his loves.

> Lust imagines him, web-footed Jupiter, great down
> Of thundering light; love's yearning pulls him down
> On the white swan-breast, the magical lawn,
> Involved in plumage, mastered by the veins of dawn.

But for Watkins the sensuous properties of whiteness are of minor import; he is seeking to discover its spiritual origin, to fathom its metaphysical depths. The white objects visible on earth are merely reflections of spiritual glory, of the whiteness created or revealed by Christ:

> If there is white, or has been white, it must have been
> When His eyes looked down and made the leper clean.

It is not easy to give a coherent account of the themes which dominate the six volumes so far produced by Vernon Watkins.[1] A clue may be found in an early poem, 'Discoveries', where in a series of gnomic couplets he epitomizes the life-work of enigmatic figures who explored the earth, the heavens, the realms of metaphysical speculation and the world of art. The list includes Heraclitus, Ptolemy, Columbus, Copernicus, Michelangelo, Galileo, Milton, Voltaire, Blake, Kierkegaard, Rilke, and Yeats. It would be possible, though unrewarding, to trace in the poems of Watkins references to these spiritual ancestors, to note the sonnet on Blake, the allusions to him in a long poem, 'The Broken Sea', the influence of Dante upon 'The Lady with the Unicorn'. The best way to approach his work is to regard it as a huge symphonic poem in which he composes variation after variation on the themes of birth, death, resurrection, love, the cycle of the seasons, the ever-changing forms of nature, the artist's imagination, and the divine spirit which sustains all created things. Two passages, the first from the poet's own Note on 'The Mari Lwyd', the second from his Note on 'The Death Bell', are valuable for the light they throw upon his cast of mind and upon the faculty which permits him to discover, in pagan myth no less than in the natural world, hints of the Christian revelation and foreshadowings of the Beatific Vision:

---

[1] I exclude from this reckoning his translation from Heine, *The North Sea.*

I have attempted to bring together those who are separated. The last breath of the year is their threshold, the moment of supreme forgiveness, confusion and understanding, the profane and sacred moment impossible to realize while the clock-hands divide the Living from the Dead.

The pathos of pre-Christian love lies in its incompleteness, the prophetic nature of pre-Christian death in its reticence. Thus, Laocoön represents the bull's thirst for resurrection, and Abel, the nightingale's. Their deaths, and all future deaths, are simultaneous in the bell's tolling.... The harmony within the bell, and within the dead body, is musically controlled, and depends upon the mercy and judgment of heavenly scales for its peace. These scales are discernible everywhere in nature, but they may be discerned only by the intuition, not by the reason.

Although his poetry is continually irradiated by Christian mysticism, Watkins seldom expounds Christian dogma, and when he does so, in such poems as 'For a Christening' and 'Good Friday', the verse betrays a certain stiffness, as if it were constricted by its sacerdotal garments. He moves with much greater freedom in the realm of myth: the tranquil sonnet, 'Christ and Charon', owes nothing to religious orthodoxy and everything to the imagination of the poet who mounts from the underworld to paradise:

> I left that nightmare shore, and woke to naves
> Of daybreak.[1]

In 'The Return of Spring' Watkins makes it clear that he is not recording a pantheistic identification of the self with the universe, but portraying a sacramental world:

> What first I feared as a rite I love as a sacrament.

Yet the poem is far from being an exposition of Christian doctrine: it is, above all, a hymn to the renewal of life, a celebration of that blessed mood in which man is at one with the divine presence, and exquisitely wedded to the earth:

> Taut branches exude gold wax of the breaking buds.
> Sweet finches sing. The stream has a hundred voices

[1] Edwin Muir's sonnet, 'Milton', has something of the same calm and gentleness.

Unheard before. One leans on the grass like a bridegroom,
And death slips under the bride-sleep.

He is most successful in evoking the supernatural import of the
visible world when, laying aside his doctrinal beliefs about the
immortal in nature, he concentrates wholly upon recording the
minute particulars of the scene. In 'The Dead Shag' and 'The Heron'
he depicts, with an exulting lyrical freedom and precision, the clouds,
the rocks, the sea-birds, and the tumult of the bay as they appear to
the eye of flesh. There is no attempt to make them symbolical
counters in an elaborate metaphysical system, or to interpret them
in the light of theological dogma to which we may be indifferent or
hostile. It is the brilliance and the energy of these poems which
persuade us, while we are under their spell, that the forms of nature
are indeed the epiphany of a divine creator. The axioms of religion
are proved upon our pulses:

> Shag: a mummified bird.
> The sea-flash never is still.
> I have watched long, long,
> The craning neck that stirred
> To the fisherman's lightest sound.
> Jet-winged skimmer of sea
> Sped from the leaning hill;
> Under my net I found
> A blackened piece of a tree,
> Touched through the brilliant curd
> Of spray, a cold black thing;
> Then at once I caught the thrill
> Of a wing in the fire-wake charred.
> Shag: a mummified bird.
> The sea-flash never is still.[1]
>
> Yet no distraction breaks the watch
> Of that time-killing bird.
> He stands unmoving on the stone;
> Since dawn he has not stirred.

[1] 'The Dead Shag'.

Calamity about him cries,
But he has fixed his golden eyes
On water's crooked tablet,
On light's reflected word.[1]

Watkins was a generous friend to Dylan Thomas, with whom he felt a deep affinity, based less upon their common Welsh background than upon a profound agreement about the nature of poetry:

He disliked the sociological poetry of the thirties. My own themes were really closer to his; we were both religious poets, and neither of us had any aptitude for political reform . . . natural observation in poetry meant nothing to us without the support of metaphysical truth.[2]

Nevertheless their approach to technical problems and their method of shaping a poem were markedly dissimilar:

Dylan worked upon a symmetrical abstract with tactile delicacy; out of a lump of texture or nest of phrases he created music, testing everything by physical feeling, working from the concrete image outwards. I worked from music and cadence towards the density of physical shape.[3]

An anecdote recorded by George MacBeth yields another clue to the nature of Watkins's poetry:

I remember Vernon Watkins once saying to the Oxford University Poetry Society that he'd begun to write poetry with a large exercise book. On the first page of this he'd written in a bold, round hand the one word: ROMANTIC.[4]

But to what kind of Romantic poetry does Watkins owe allegiance? Closer in spirit to Coleridge and to Shelley than to Byron or to Keats, he can best be described as a poet of the high dream, a self-disciplined visionary, in whose verse there is nothing trivial, mean, or vulgar, nothing carelessly or shoddily made. For a quarter of a

[1] 'The Heron'.
[2] Vernon Watkins, Introduction to Dylan Thomas, *Letters to Vernon Watkins*, pp. 17–18.
[3] Ibid., p. 13.
[4] George MacBeth, 'Ancestors and Allegiances', *London Magazine*, vol. 6, No. 11 (November 1959), p. 21.

century, with a total lack of play-acting or of self-seeking publicity, he has dedicated himself to his sacred calling — he has, indeed, done much to redeem the dignity of this phrase, which has been degraded and bandied about by so many professional bohemians and wastrels.

The qualities and themes that one misses in his poetry are those whose presence would shatter the rapturous perfection of the high dream: humour, wit, irony, the harsh realities of politics, sexual desire, physical suffering, the monotonies of the daily round in a modern industrial society, the pleasures of food and drink and bodily activity, the bustle, the fun, the boredom of the workaday world. His poetic universe often appears insubstantial and aetherial, a refuge where trailing clouds of glory obscure the outer world of flesh and blood and machines in which we must all spend our waking lives. Yet, working devotedly within his deliberately chosen limitations, Vernon Watkins has produced a body of impressive verse, rooted in the landscape of Wales but always envisaging the heavenly city:

> So, in these Welsh hills,
> I marvel, waking from a dream of stone,
> That such a peace surrounds me, while the city
> For which all long has never yet been built.[1]

George Barker (b. 1913), although seven years younger than Vernon Watkins, began to win a fashionable reputation in the mid-nineteen-thirties. He was the youngest poet included by Yeats in his *Oxford Book of Modern Verse* (1936), and in a letter dated 29 December 1938 Dylan Thomas comments on the policy of a new periodical, *Poetry* (London), to be edited by Tambimuttu: '. . . it shouldn't want to pack its pages with the known stuff of the known boys; a new paper should give — (say) — Barker a rest: he must be very tired'.[2] After the publication of an early volume by the Parton Press, Barker became a Faber poet, five books of verse and the *Collected Poems 1930–1955* appearing under their imprint.[3] This collection bears the following Note:

[1] 'Peace in the Welsh Hills'.   [2] *Letters to Vernon Watkins*, p. 51.
[3] Barker's latest volume, *The View from a Blind I* (1962), appeared after this chapter was written.

F

One long poem, *The True Confession of George Barker*, which Mr. Barker wished to include in this volume, has been omitted at the publishers' request.

The True Confession has had a rough passage. After it had been broadcast in the Home Service of the B.B.C., the Director-General apologized for this lapse of taste — and very properly so: those with ears attuned to the delicacy of music-hall comedians and minds purified by the ritual of parlour-games on television cannot be expected to stomach a poem whose pages exude so rank a smell of the Old Adam. *The True Confession* bristles with coarse words and lewd thoughts, for Barker describes in brutal and gross detail aspects of sexuality which almost all poets have shunned or tried to transcend. He depicts himself as a dirty small boy and as a grubby adolescent, tormented and fascinated by the power of sex, and it is a mark of his rare honesty that he has omitted none of the warts on this unprepossessing self-portrait. Scatological and distasteful as the poem is in places, it remains essential to any understanding of Barker's work; a few vigorous Rabelaisian passages and some finely-sustained lyrical stanzas are among the best things that he has written; and nowhere does it sink to the incoherent ranting of the *Collected Poems* at their most delirious.[1]

Critical opinion is sharply divided about the merits of his verse. One reviewer of the *Collected Poems* describes *The True Confession* as 'the masterpiece of one of our few major contemporary poets',[2] a eulogy which many good judges would wave aside as ludicrously extravagant. Some critics salute him as a splendid visionary poet; others hold him to be no more than a concoctor of inflated nonsensical rhetoric. To survey calmly but sympathetically the work of a poet who arouses such angry dissension is no easy task.

A brief essay by Barker which came out in 1949 provides a useful introduction to his beliefs about the nature and function of poetry.[3] The title, the hieratic tone, and the exalted doctrine of the poetic

---

[1] *The True Confession*, which first appeared in 1950, was republished by the Parton Press in 1957.
[2] *Times Literary Supplement*, 16 August 1957, p. 494.
[3] 'The Miracle of Images', *Orpheus*, vol. 2 (1949), pp. 133–6.

image point towards the kind of effect at which Barker is aiming in
his poems:

The image is what the imagination ascertains about the hitherto un-
imaginable. The image is what Michaelangelo saw lying hidden in a piece
of dirt. . . . The image is made up of words, words are made up of the alphabet, and the alphabet is the twenty-six stations of the cross to the Logos.

The unknown can very seldom be embodied properly or best in images
taken without distortion from existence as we normally know it, because
into such known images the unknown could not, by definition, easily or
properly fit.

The question is whether and to what extent images can be systematically distorted without their becoming grotesque, and the
danger is that a poet who resorts to this practice will be driven to
use ever more and more extravagant imagery. Barker reinforces this
violent, mystical doctrine of the image by making immoderate,
portentous claims for the transcendental power of poetry:

> There is that whispering gallery where
> A dark population of the air
> Gives back to us those vocables
> We dare not robe in syllables:
>
> I speak of the whispering gallery
> Of all Dionysian poetry
> Within whose precincts I have heard
> An apotheosis of the word
>
> As down those echoing corridors
> The Logos rode on a white horse;
> Till every No that sense could express
> Turned to a transcendental Yes.

Then, after speculating on the turbulence of the world and of man's
heart, Barker affirms the reconciling power of poetry:

> But over the known world of things
> The great poem folds its wings
> And from a bloody breast will give
> Even to those who disbelieve.

Finally, in an image which refers us back to the first stanza, he postulates a mystery at the heart of things to which Dionysian poetry may lead us and at whose nature it may hint:

> That dark population of the air
> Leans downward, singing, to declare
> The mystery of the world is this:
> That we do not know what is.[1]

A similar vision inspires the 'Verses for the 60th Birthday of Thomas Stearns Eliot', in which Barker portrays 'this gentle and gothic man' less as a poet of profound, subtle intelligence or as a great master of language than as a demiurge wrestling with negative powers of darkness:

> But as the huge negations ride
> And depredate all things outside
> His window, he puts out his hand
> And writes with whirlwinds on the ground
> Asseverations that tame
> The great negations with his name.

Barker is unequivocally committed to the belief that poetry is a Dionysian activity and that 'the function of the poem as a poem is to glorify'.[2] Although he is a prolific writer, he constantly recurs to a few obsessive themes and he tends to compose in sequences or groups or cycles of poems: 'Pacific Sonnets', 'Personal Sonnets', 'Sacred Elegies', 'Secular Elegies', 'Four Cycles of Love Poems', 'Cycle of Six Lyrics', and 'Nine Beatitudes to Denver' are characteristic titles. One leading motif in his work is poverty, not the ideal of Christian poverty as a vocation, but the sour fact of being poor in the chilly, drab English slums of the years between the wars. It is not fanciful to attribute much of the wildness, the resentment, the savage incoherence of Barker's verse to his understandable hatred of the world which bred him, or to see in the fantastic opulence of his imagery an attempt to find compensation for the dinginess of his early years:

---

[1] 'Letter to a Young Poet'.   [2] 'The Miracle of Images'.

It was hard cash I needed at my root.
I now know that how I grew was due
To echoing guts and the empty bag —
My song was out of tune for a few notes.[1]

For half a dozen simple years
    We lived happily, so to speak,
On twenty-seven shillings a week;
    And, when worried and in tears,
My mercenary wife complained
    That we could not afford our marriage,
'It's twice as much', I explained,
    'As MacNeice pays for his garage'.[2]

This personal discontent spills over into a more general hatred of the English social order as it was before the war. In the long, dull 'Vision of England '38', the poet talks with such worthies as St. George and William Blake, who denounce capitalist oppression, and the poem ends with an unconvincing invocation to a Political Prince who shall liberate England.

In his later verse, Barker occasionally reverts to this theme of English society, but the note of personal grievance and deprivation is no longer dominant. We find instead an impersonal survey of England's plight in the post-war world, an utterance tinged with a prophetic grandeur:

I thought of Britain in its cloud
Chained to the economic rocks
Dying behind me. I saw the flocks
Of great and grieving omens crowd
About the lion on the stone.
And I heard Milton's eagle mewing
Her desolation in the ruin
Of a great nation alone.[3]

'Stanzas on a Visit to Longleat House in Wiltshire, October 1953' expresses a Yeatsian contempt for 'the hog of multitude' tramping through a noble house now reduced to a 'fouled public nest'. Yeats,

[1] 'Epistle I'.   [2] *The True Confession*, Book IV.   [3] 'Channel Crossing'.

it was said, became so aristocratic that he started to evict imaginary tenants, and Barker assumes here the role of the Victorian squire, as he watches

> The ragged-arsed mechanics squat
> Owning what they haven't got . . .
>
> In car-park, garden and urinal
> The free and ignorant, almost
> As easy as at a Cup Final
> Gawk through the stone-transparent ghost
> Of this once noble house, now lost
> In the gross error of survival.

Yeats, who once declared: 'I am still of the opinion that only two topics can be of the slightest interest to a serious and studious mind — sex and the dead',[1] might have welcomed Barker's preoccupation with sexual experience, although he would probably have condemned the discordant brutality and vulgarity of certain passages in his work. The main weakness in his love poetry is the obsessive narrowness of its emotional range: we find there no concentrated intellectual passion as in Donne, nothing of Marvell's subtle intensity, small trace of gaiety or of human tenderness, no sense that there can exist a marriage of true minds, and very little of the dignity, majesty, and ardour which burn in Yeats's finest love-poems. The emphasis is on the violence, the horror, the enormity of the sexual act, the compulsive thrill of lust; or the pendulum swings to the other extreme, and we are transported into a world of ecstasy where all is fantasy and rapture. There is no attempt to explore the middle range of experience, the complicated world of sexual relationships which change their character as lovers themselves alter, mature, and come to terms with the world and with their own natures.

He conveys his sense of sexual passion's irresistible, monstrous power by piling one extravagant image upon another in surrealistic profusion:

[1] Letter to Olivia Shakespear, 2 October 1927.

The bride who rides the hymenaeal waterfall
Spawning all possibles in her pools of surplus,
Whom the train rapes going into a tunnel. . . .[1]

O long-haired virgin by my tree
    Among whose forks hung enraged
A sexual passion not assuaged
    By you, its victim. . . .[2]

His disgust at the whole process of generation reaches its climax in
the last three stanzas of *The True Confession*, Book I, in which
nausea almost overpowers him as he contemplates the sheer nastiness
of sexual reproduction (the nearest parallel is not with Dryden's
translation of Juvenal's Sixth Satire, where all is redeemed by gusto,
but with Swift's loathing of our bodily functions). Few lines in
English poetry are more direct and more tainted with hatred of the
flesh than the passage which begins:

    The act of human procreation
    — The rutting tongue, the grunt and shudder. . . .

He evokes the enchantment and the strangeness of sexual passion
by indirect suggestion rather than by analysis of the lovers' feelings
or by plain description. An example of this technique occurs in the
poem 'Turn on your side and bear the day to me':

    Turn on your side and bear the day to me
    Beloved, spectre-struck, immured
    In the glass wall of sleep. Slowly
    Uncloud the borealis of your eye
    And show your iceberg secrets, your midnight prizes
    To the green-eyed world and to me. Sin
    Coils upward into thin air when you awaken
    And again morning announces amnesty over
    The serpent-kingdomed bed.

Apart from the hint of sexual guilt and torment conveyed by the
fiercely compressed metaphysical conceit of the last line and a half,

[1] 'Secular Elegies' V.   [2] *The True Confession*, Book III.

the universe conjured up in this poem resembles the transformation-scene in a pantomime or ballet, wherein the lovers have cast off their humanity in order to taste more keenly the essence of carnal passion. Barker's ability to suggest the numinous quality of the sexual act is nowhere better shown than in the following stanza where, for a change, a note of tenderness is heard:

> Sleep at my side again, my bride,
> As on our marriage bed you turned
> Into a flowering bush that burned
> All the proud flesh away. Beside
> Me now, you, shade of my departed
> Broken, abandoned bride, lie still,
> And I shall hold you close until
> Even our ghosts are broken-hearted.[1]

The *Times Literary Supplement* reviewer discerns in Barker's poetry

a vision of perspicuous sanity never dodging any human pettiness yet never for a moment losing sight of the equally human nobility ... a clarity of statement derived from his clear and subtle understanding of man's position in the metaphysical and moral universe, a clarity that illuminates the darkest places of the mind, that is adept at 'telling Truth she's telling lies', and that is yet able to reveal with sympathy and acknowledge with grace the most diabolical and the most tender extremes of feeling.

The extremes of feeling certainly make their presence felt, but usually in such hysterical and melodramatic form that no central vision of the world survives unshaken. Although he employs Christian symbols in 'Holy Poems', 'Sacred Elegies', and 'Goodman Jacksin and the Angel', he dwells almost exclusively on the violence, the mystical terror, the paradoxical absurdity of religious experience. Just as in his celebration of sexuality he swings from disgust to ecstasy, so, in his religious poems, the mood is always corybantic, reminding us of Hopkins at his most grotesque, of Crashaw at his most luscious and palpitating, even of the Donne who

[1] *The True Confession*, Book III.

'Committed holy Rapes upon our Will'.[1] There is scarcely a trace
of the calmer elements in Christian devotion: confident trust in the
loving-kindness of God, obedience to the teaching of Jesus,
recognition of the divine order in the world. The whirlwind blusters,
the earthquake rumbles, the fire crackles, but the still, small voice
which speaks to George Herbert or to Andrew Marvell is never
heard. Barker affirms

> that a mystery crowns our lives
> With the smile of God's blood-flecked jaws[2]

and

> that when I shall the last time close my eye
> O God will smother me like a father
> Mothering the son still hanging in his thigh.[3]

The fifth of the 'Sacred Elegies' concludes with a nightmarish vision
of God as a torturer who hounds men to their salvation, the savagely
rhetorical language serving to emphasize Barker's deliberate viola-
tion of sense and decorum:

> Fiend behind the fiend behind the fiend behind the
> Friend. Mastodon with mastery, monster with an ache
> At the tooth of the ego, the dead drunk judge:
> Wheresoever Thou art our agony will find Thee
> Enthroned on the darkest altar of our heartbreak
> Perfect, Beast, brute, bastard. O dog my God!

The True Confession ends by plunging into a chaos of paradox,
uttering, as it falls, a cry of anguish:

> Snuff the game and the candle, for our state
> — Insufferable among mysteries —
> Makes the worms weep. Abate, abate
> Your justice. Execute us with mercies!

We find in Barker's avowal of his metaphysical beliefs the same
lack of steadiness and of wholeness which is so disturbing in his

[1] Thomas Carew, 'An Elegie upon the death of the Deane of Pauls, Dr. John
Donne'.
[2] 'Holy Poems' II.   [3] 'Holy Poems' III.

religious poetry. Again, we are in a world of tension and of frenzied ambivalence, where everything threatens to spin out of control and to involve the poet in the general ruin. The nearest approach to an explicit statement of his philosophy occurs towards the end of 'Goodman Jacksin and the Angel', where he envisages the cosmic process as dialectical:

> The law of dialectics is
> How Love evolves. There are no
> Two ones of any kind but must
> Bring forth a firstborn third to prove
> That the arithmetic of love
> Transcends our lonely dust.
>
> Thus Love and Death together got
> Under a dark constellation . . .
> Then from their open-eyed embrace
> Rose the first god that ever was,
> With doom in his face.

The nature and the significance of this primeval god remain an enigma, nor is Barker's concept of morality free of the mystery-mongering, the flirtation with chaos, which seem to be the main-springs of his poetry:

> Underneath
> The human heart, I believe,
> Lives a god who cannot grieve
> No matter how disastrous
> The crimes our passion brings on us
> Because this ungrieving god
> Knows that either bad or good
> Might look, from a better angle,
> Like a double-headed angel.[1]

A poet obsessed by this kind of paradox, which hovers above an abyss of nihilism, will find it hard to formulate any coherent imaginative vision of the world, and may be tempted to strike a variety of effective theatrical attitudes, to sound a note of grandilo-

[1] 'To my Son', Part II.

quent despair or of hollow triumph. Barker has not escaped these perils. The worst vices of his poetry — a fondness for such excruciating puns as 'I see phallic: you, cephalic';[1] an addiction to spattering his pages with rhodomontade and verbiage; a lack of self-criticism that permits him to reprint in his *Collected Poems* a poem as gristly as 'Calamiterror', in which for over thirty pages he works himself into an epileptic lather about blood, loins, and bowels — are symptoms of this radical uncertainty and instability rather than a product of technical clumsiness. He is capable of lapsing at any time into near-doggerel, an example of this being the quatrain which disfigures an otherwise serious, reflective love-poem:

> Down in the deep ground
> Bisexuals squirm
> O if only we found it
> As easy as worms.[2]

At his best he is a master of the piercing, unexpected image and of daring word-play:

> The seagull, spreadeagled, splayed on the wind,
> Span backwards shrieking, belly facing upward,
> Fled backward with a gimlet in its heart
> To see the two youths swimming hand in hand
> Through green eternity.[3]

> No peeping constellations may
> Eavesdrop upon you as you clip
> Each other in old Adam's nest,
> And in an evening silvered cup
> Love's upspringing sunrise catch
> Till the winged bloodhorses of sex
> Dead heat, and meet their match.[4]

> As he cried out
> A pawing gag of the sea
> Smothered his cry and he sank in his own shout
> Like a dying airman. Then she

---

[1] *The True Confession*, Book II.   [2] 'A Song of the Sea'.
[3] 'Pacific Sonnets', V.   [4] 'Epithalamium for Two Friends'.

> Deep near her son asleep on the hourglass sand
> Was awakened. . . .[1]

He can also, at least for a short while, sustain a note of singularly pure lyricism, as in 'Summer Song' II and in the last three stanzas of 'Summer Song' I, where tenderness, longing, and regret are subtly commingled in a melodic pattern which, trembling on the verge of dissolving into sheer fantasy, retains a crystalline delicacy and strength:

> Great summer sun, great summer sun,
>   Turn back to the designer:
> I would not be the one to start
> The breaking day and the breaking heart
>   For all the grief in China.
>
> My one, my one, my only love,
>   Hide, hide your face in a leaf,
> And let the hot tear falling burn
> The stupid heart that will not learn
>   The everywhere of grief.
>
> Great summer sun, great summer sun,
>   Turn back to the never-never
> Cloud-cuckoo, happy, far-off land
> Where all the love is true love, and
>   True love goes on for ever.[2]

What is missing all too often in his work is the power to shape his brilliant but erratic perceptions into a coherent design, to staunch the verbal haemorrhage that gushes over his poems, to subdue the frenetic waywardness of his temperament, and to bring poetic order into a universe which, for him as for his triple-headed Manichee,[3] appears to be incurably dualistic and anarchical. His nearest approach to a wholly satisfying poem is 'Channel Crossing', where he is in full command of his talents and where the rich profusion of imagery

[1] 'On a Friend's Escape from Drowning off the Norfolk Coast'.
[2] This lyrical purity is all the more welcome after the distortions of the first three stanzas, where we encounter a sequence of grotesque images: 'the hyena despair'; 'fishlipped lovers' who 'lie kissing catastrophes'; and a 'breasted tree'.
[3] See 'Sonnets of the Triple-headed Manichee'.

develops, instead of blurring, the intricate poetic argument. Barker meditates on the destiny of Europe, scarred by war, and on the fate of England, protected by the bulwark of the Channel against the worst ravages of continental fanaticism, yet facing an imminent decline. He hears 'the old lip of the sea' ask the question 'What can a dead nation say?' and gives us a melancholy answer. The lines about the fishes evoke a precise image of the deep-sea creatures' aimless dartings here and there, but they do more than convey an accurate picture of the swift movement. They remind us that we live in a world of displaced persons and that the freedom of the amoral natural world differs from that liberty which is the proper element of man. By drawing on the imagery of sun and sea in these two stanzas, Barker has transformed what might have been a common-place analysis of a political situation into an illuminating discourse on the state of Europe, into a vision of Albion:

> As these words wailed in the air
> I looked at Europe and I saw
> The glittering instruments of war
> Grow paler but not go from where
> Like a Caesarian sunset on
> The cold slab of the horizon
> They lay foretelling for tomorrow.
> Another day of human sorrow
>
> But when I turned and looked into
> The silent chambers of the sea
> I saw the displaced fishes flee
> From nowhere into nowhere through
> Their continent of liberty.
> O skipping porpoise of the tide
> No longer shall the sailors ride
> You cheering out to sea.

Johnson's strictures on Gray come to mind as one studies the bulk of Barker's poetry:

These odes are marked by glittering accumulations of ungraceful ornaments; they strike rather than please; the images are magnified by affectation; the language is laboured into harshness. The mind of the writer seems to work with unnatural violence.[1]

But the poet who has written 'Channel Crossing', parts of *The True Confession*, and a handful of other poems in which he has disciplined his turbulent, wayward talents, is not far from deserving the tribute paid by Johnson to the author of Gray's *Elegy*: 'Had [he] written often thus, it had been vain to blame and useless to praise him.'[1]

By the age of twenty-two, David Gascoyne (b. 1916) had published a volume of poems, which appeared in 1933, a novel, a prose work entitled *A Short Survey of Surrealism* (1935), a collection of surrealistic poems, *Man's Life is this Meat* (1936), and versions of Hölderlin's poems, entitled *Hölderlin's Madness* (1938). A five-years' silence was broken in 1943 by the publication of *Poems 1937–1942*, with drawings and decorations specially designed for the book by Graham Sutherland. Since 1943 Gascoyne has produced only one collection of poems, *A Vagrant* (1950), and one long poem, *Night Thoughts* (1956), which was commissioned by the B.B.C. and broadcast on the Third Programme in December 1955.

Gascoyne seems to have been drawn towards surrealism by its uncompromising hostility to all forms of bourgeois sham, and by the energy which it appeared to liberate. His own surrealistic poems, the only English poems of any merit inspired by the movement, have a certain rhythmical power, and manipulate a limited range of obsessive imagery with considerable effectiveness:

> The face of the precipice is black with lovers;
> The sun above them is a bag of nails; the spring's
> First rivers hide among their hair.[2]

> Supposing the breasts
> like shells on the oceanless shore
> at the end of the world
> like furious thrusts of a single knife
> like bread to be broken by hands
> supposing the breasts still untouched by desires

---

[1] *Lives of the English Poets.*   [2] 'In Defence of Humanism: To M. Salvador Dali'.

    still unsuckled by thirsts
    and motionless still
    breasts violently still and enisled in the
    night and afraid both of love and of death.[1]

Although Gascoyne rapidly broke away from any formal allegiance to the surrealist movement, his verse has continued to display the richness, the hallucinatory strangeness, the dream-like intensity, which are characteristic of much surrealistic art. Moreover, his prime concern has always been to explore the deepest and most mysterious elements of human experience, to seek the visionary truth which lies behind the screen of daily life and beneath the surface of the visible world. In his view, the construction of philosophical systems and the exercise of our rational faculties are often no more than means of evading the questions and the enigmas which are too horrifying for us to face. He has developed this theme in an essay on Leon Chestov, which, apart from its merits as an introduction to Chestov, serves as an admirable gloss upon the work of Gascoyne himself.[2] The following passage, in particular, helps us to understand why, in *Poems 1937–1942*, the emphasis is on the terror, the agony, the shattering fury of human life:

For most of us, this moment of dislocation, of panic, of abrupt unfamiliarity and questionableness of everything hitherto regarded as certain, is throughout our whole lives postponed, evaded, and its possibilities and implications absolutely denied and ignored. But as Chestov took pains to make vivid to his interlocutor, with the approach of death, this moment may become increasingly difficult to postpone. For it is in part the moment of fully recognizing the truth of the fact of Death itself, and of its immense enigmatic significance for the whole of the human life that leads to it.[3]

Gascoyne's 'Inferno' portrays such a moment when he

                    . . . wandering
        Through unnamed streets of a great nameless town,

    [1] 'The Supposed Being'.
    [2] David Gascoyne, 'Leon Chestov'. *Horizon*, vol. xx, No. 118 (October 1949), pp. 213–29.
    [3] Cf. 'I think profound philosophy must come from terror.' W. B. Yeats, *Essays 1931–36* (Cuala Press, Dublin, 1937), p. 21.

As in a syncope, sudden, absolute,
Was shown the Void that undermines the world:
For all that eye can claim is impotent —
Sky, solid brick of buildings, masks of flesh —
Against the splintering of that screen which shields
Man's puny consciousness from hell: over the edge
Of a thin inch's fraction lie in wait for him

   Bottomless depths of roaring emptiness.

In moments such as these Wordsworth tried to reassure himself of
the visible world's reality by clutching some material object. Other
poets have tried to find oblivion or comfort in sexual love or in
metaphysical speculation. Gascoyne has surveyed these anodynes
and found them wanting. In 'Amor Fati' the lovers inflict a mortal
wound upon each other:

     Do not break
That vacuum out of which our silence speaks
Of its sad speechless fury to the star
Whose glitter scars
The heavy heaven under which we lie
And injure one another O incurably!

Not only the sexual act but life in the body itself is a source of
contamination:

  But who has lived an hour
In the condemned condition of our blood
And not known how a wound like a black flower,
Exquisite and irreparable, can break
Apart in the immortal in us, or not felt
An intimation of the fault: to be alive![1]

Gascoyne's universe is one of guilt, pain, and terror, a universe
haunted by

  Turbulence, uproar, echo of a War
Beyond our frontier: burning, blood and black
Impenetrable smoke which only blast
Of Archangelic trumpet could transpierce!

    [1] 'The Fault'.

The fault of being alive, which is irreparable, is punished by

> Infernal armies sent us to avenge
> The too-long-suffered tyranny and
> Celebrated scandal of man's life![1]

Gascoyne peoples this world with mysterious figures, an Angel, a harlot queen, Venus Androgyne, and Eve,

> Insurgent, wounded and avenging one,
> In whose black sex
> Our ancient culpability like a pearl is set.[2]

These figures seem to be projections of Gascoyne's anguish and guilt, rather than symbols of any philosophical or religious belief. They emphasize the horror and the fascination of human existence, without helping us to escape from the nightmare in which we are trapped. Nor is there any salvation to be found in thought, however subtle it may be, and however tantalizingly it may offer us a

> Remote presentiment of some intensely bright
> Impending spiritual dawn, of which the pure
> Immense illumination seems about to pour
> In upon our existence from beyond
> The edge of Knowing!

For the excitement aroused by thought's pale odour will be obliterated

> ... when fear-benumbed and frail
> Our dying thought within the closely-sealed
> Bone casket of the skull has flickered out,
> And we've gone down into the odourless black soil.[3]

In three poems, 'Lines', 'Apologia', and 'The Writer's Hand', Gascoyne acknowledges that poetry is both a miracle and a helpless gesture in a hostile universe. The artist is driven by some irresistible need to pursue truth and to practise his art, even though he is doomed to failure. Elsewhere, he summons Dionysian desire to help us:

[1] 'Insurrection'.   [2] 'Eve'.   [3] 'Odeur de Pensée'.

> . . . out of our lowland rear
> A lofty, savage and enduring monument![1]

He looks towards the mountains, seeing them as symbols of ascent, thrusting their peaks upward out of mines of energy:

> And starbound snowfields, fortify
> With the stern silence of your white
> Our weak hearts dulled by the intolerably loud
> Commotion of this tragic century.[2]

And when he finds that his narrow road leads him to the Wall of Interdiction, he builds his faith upon the courage that is born of despair:

> But if my despair
> Is strong enough, my spirit truly hard,
> No wall shall break my will: To persevere.[3]

In the sequence of poems entitled *Miserere*, this determination to endure ceases to be a merely negative, Stoical resistance to adversity, and takes on a Christian significance. The cruellest wounds of man become the stigmata of Christ; we may descend into hell with Christ; and it is a divine hand that guides us, even when it seems to cast us down:

> Hand that I love! Lord Light
> How dark is thy arm's will and ironlike
> Thy ruler's finger that has sent me here!
> Far from Thy face I nothing understand,
> But Kiss the Hand that has consigned
>
> Me to these latter years where I must learn
> The revelation of despair, and find
> Among the debris of all certainties
> The hardest stone on which to found
> Altar and shelter for Eternity.

Gascoyne's Christ is Man's Son, not the Christ of the churches, as the final stanza of 'Ecce Homo', the last poem in the sequence, explicitly declares:

---

[1] 'Lowland'.   [2] 'Mountain's.   [3] 'The Wall'.

> Not from a monstrance silver-wrought
> But from the tree of human pain
> Redeem our sterile misery,
> Christ of Revolution and of Poetry,
> That man's long journey through the night
> May not have been in vain.

Much as one may admire the seriousness of Gascoyne's aims and the tragic splendour of his vision, it is questionable whether his language matches the range and the intensity of his themes. There is, as Goethe observed, a kind of poetry which does the poet's thinking and writing for him; and although the best verse in *Poems 1937–1942* is exempt from this fault, much of his work is vitiated by too great a reliance upon resonant poeticisms, and by too ready an indulgence in large rhetorical generalizations. This is particularly true of *Night Thoughts*, even if we grant that the demands of the medium for which it was composed may be responsible for the looseness and the emotional crudity of the passages about the emptiness and the terror of Megalometropolis. Since some critics, fastening on this weakness in Gascoyne's verse, believe that it invalidates his claim to be regarded as a serious poet, it is worth looking at three poems in order to discover to what extent the language is unworthy of the vision.[1]

In 'Winter Garden' Gascoyne has found words and images that evoke with fine precision the mood of spiritual desolation, the atmosphere of metaphysical unease, by which he is haunted. The contrast between the deadness of the landscape and the ability of the stranger to suffer pain because he is alive is conveyed with an impressive economy and verbal assurance:

> Pure music is the cry that tears
> The birdless branches in the wind.
> No blossom is reborn. The blue
> Stare of the pond is blind.

[1] 'Winter Garden' is from *Poems 1937–1942*, and the other two poems are from *A Vagrant*.

> And no-one sees
> A restless stranger through the morning stray
> Across the sodden lawn, whose eyes
> Are tired of weeping, in whose breast
> A savage sun consumes its hidden day.

'September Sun: 1947' begins with an invocation to the sun and with a lament for man's deliberate choice of spiritual darkness:

> Magnificent strong sun! in these last days
> So prodigally generous of pristine light
> That's wasted only by men's sight who will not see
> And by self-darkened spirits from whose night
> Can rise no longer orison or praise.

The poem ends with a foreboding of the world's annihilation at the hands of God:

> ... These days and years

> May bring the sudden call to harvesting,
> When if the fields Man labours only yield
> Glitter and husks, then with an angrier sun may He
> Who first with His gold seed the sightless field
> Of Chaos planted, all our trash to cinders bring.

A severe critic might argue that the poet is relying on the elaborate diction to do the work for him; that such grandiloquent adjectives as *magnificent, pristine, self-darkened* are being exploited too easily and superficially; that the reference to Chaos is Miltonic pastiche. In Gascoyne's defence one could plead that the semi-archaic, liturgical style gives the necessary effect of remoteness and solemnity; that the echoes from the past blend harmoniously with the poem's melodic line; and that he has unfolded a difficult poetic argument with remarkable cogency.

'The Sacred Hearth' exhibits a similar tendency to pull out the Romantic organ stops:

> I wandered out across the briar-bound garden, spellbound. Most
> Mysterious and unrecapturable moment, when I stood
> There staring back at the dark white nocturnal house,

And saw gleam through the lattices a light more pure than gold
Made sanguine with crushed roses. . . .

This lavish use of such conventionally evocative words as *spell-bound*, *mysterious*, *nocturnal*, *gleam*, *sanguine with crushed roses*, lends substance to the charge that Gascoyne is manipulating verbal counters which have lost their original value and brightness, that he is a neo-Romantic poet dressing up second-hand literary concepts in a worn-out, derivative language. Yet it is possible for a poem to triumph over such defects, and to survive critical thrusts which threaten to inflict on it mortal wounds. One recalls Yeats's verdict on a poem by Robert Bridges: 'Every metaphor, every thought a commonplace, emptiness everywhere, the whole magnificent.'[1]

Moreover, Gascoyne himself would be indifferent to the minute analysis of texture and of tone which is the chief stock-in-trade of most contemporary critics. In his essay on Carlyle[2] he quotes with approval half-a-dozen passages in which Carlyle insists on the sacred, prophetic character of literature:

Genius, Poet: do we know what these words mean? An inspired Soul once more vouchsafed us, direct from Nature's own great fire-heart. . . . Hear once more, ye bewildered mortals; listen once again to a voice from the inner Light-sea and Flame sea, Nature's and Truth's own heart.[3]

Innumerable 'Philosophies of Man', contending in boundless hubbub, must annihilate each other before an inspired Poesy and Faith for Man can fashion itself together.[4]

Gascoyne has struggled to be a mouthpiece for what Carlyle calls 'Nature's own sacred voice', and to create 'an inspired Poesy and Faith for Man'. His entire work merits the title which he has given to one of his poems, 'Fragments towards a *Religio Poetae*'; although few of these fragments are without serious flaws he deserves our respect in that, like William Blake, he has preserved his poetic integrity and kept the Divine Vision in time of trouble.

[1] *The Oxford Book of Modern Verse*, p. xviii.
[2] David Gascoyne, *Thomas Carlyle* (Longmans, 1952), pp. 22–25.
[3] Thomas Carlyle, *Past and Present*, Bk. II, Chap. 9.
[4] Thomas Carlyle, *Characteristics*.

IV

PROVINCIALISM AND TRADITION

WHEN we say that Norwich is a provincial English city, or that Queen Elizabeth II was crowned in Westminster Abbey with traditional ceremony, we are describing matters of fact in a dispassionate, scientific tone. On the other hand, an elegant woman who remarks that Mrs. Y's clothes are expensive but provincial neither knows nor cares where the garments were bought: the word *provincial* is unmistakably insulting. Such terms as *traditional* and *provincial*, when used in the sphere of literary criticism, almost always carry with them strong overtones of praise or of blame. We speak approvingly of a poet as being in the main tradition of English poetry; or we may subtly belittle the achievement of a contemporary writer by calling him a good poet who has been satisfied to employ traditional metre and diction. The adjective *provincial* frequently bears a derogatory sense, and to observe of a writer that he is provincial is to suggest that he is limited, narrow, imperfectly civilized, mentally restricted, and emotionally underdeveloped. F. R. Leavis, in stigmatizing Thomas Hardy as 'a provincial manufacturer of gauche and heavy fictions that sometimes have the corresponding virtues',[1] has selected the epithet as a means of rubbing salt into the wound.

In the course of this chapter I shall try to employ the concepts of provincialism and of tradition without bias, and not as terms of abuse or of praise. When I argue that Kingsley Amis and Philip Larkin are provincial poets, while Charles Tomlinson and Donald Davie are traditional poets, I am not passing judgement on their respective merits, but attempting to indicate the distinctive cast of their minds and the nature of their aesthetic principles.

[1] F. R. Leavis, *The Great Tradition* (Chatto, 1948), p. 124.

The provincial poet, in my sense of the term, is one who is primarily concerned with the values of his own cultural society, and who is largely indifferent to what lies beyond the world that he knows at first-hand. Thus he cares very little for the poetry and the civilization of other ages and other countries, nor does he feel the need to justify his own practice by reference to the past. He values above all else sincerity of feeling, fidelity to the truth as he conceives it, and he chiefly admires in poetry that individual flavour and uniqueness which he takes to be the surest token of an author's originality and personal integrity. He has a keen nose for anything that smacks of cultural snobbery, pedantic erudition, literary humbug, and sterile academicism.

The traditional poet is, like T. S. Eliot, acutely conscious that

no poet, no artist of any art, has his complete meaning alone. His significance, his appreciation is the appreciation of his relation to the dead poets and artists. . . . And the poet who is aware of this will be aware of great difficulties and responsibilities.[1]

Such an awareness will usually entail a corresponding turning away from the cultivation of one's own idiosyncrasies, and will lead to a belief in the impersonality of art:

What happens is a continual surrender of himself as he is at the moment to something which is more valuable. The progress of an artist is a continual self-sacrifice, a continual extinction of personality.[2]

Since the traditional poet regards the literature of his own age and country as part of a larger whole, he will constantly try to compare one civilization with another; and will seek to enrich his art by studying the achievements of artists in other times and places — of painters, musicians, novelists, and dramatists, and not of poets alone. And whereas the provincial poet fears that his sincerity may be corrupted by the artificiality of art, the traditional poet mistrusts any crude distinction that would relegate our experience of art to the category of the unreal and the second-hand.

[1] T. S. Eliot, 'Tradition and the Individual Talent'. *Selected Essays*, p. 15.
[2] Ibid., p. 17.

Although Kingsley Amis (b. 1922) is most widely known as the author of *Lucky Jim* and of subsequent novels, his first two published books were volumes of poems, *Bright November* (1947) and *A Frame of Mind*, privately printed by the School of Art, Reading University, in 1953. In 1956 he brought out *A Case of Samples*, a selection of verse written during the previous ten years. One of his pronouncements about poetry has gained a certain measure of notoriety:

... nobody wants any more poems on the grander themes for a few years, but at the same time nobody wants any more poems about philosophers or paintings or novelists or art galleries or mythology or foreign cities or other poems.[1]

It is strange that, holding these views, Amis should write a neat quatrain on 'The English Novel 1740–1820', poems such as 'Beowulf' and 'A Note on Wyatt', and poems whose starting-point is a knowledge of the literary models and conventions that are being mocked or parodied. The very titles — 'A Dream of Fair Women', 'The Triumph of Life', 'The Triumph of Time' — are enough to show how heavily Amis leans on the tradition which he is deriding. He is, in fact, a highly literary poet, whose carefully cultivated insular philistinism is only one element in the aesthetic doctrines to which he subscribes. He wants to obliterate from poetry all that is loose, careless, and sloppily made:

> Half shut, our eye dawdles down the page
> Seeing the word love, the word death, the word life,
> Rhyme-words of poets in a silver age:
> Silver of the bauble, not of the knife.[2]

In 'Against Romanticism' he delivers some shrewd blows, but makes no attempt to discriminate between the valid principles of Romanticism and the quagmire into which it may lead the less talented of its adherents:

> A traveller who walks a temperate zone
> — Woods devoid of beasts, roads that please the foot —

---

[1] *Poets of the 1950's*, ed. D. J. Enright, p. 17.   [2] 'Wrong Words'.

> Finds that its decent surface grows too thin:
>> Something unperceived fumbles at his nerves.
> To please an ingrown taste for anarchy
>> Torrid images circle in the wood,
> And sweat for recognition up the road.

This is merely a more sophisticated restatement of the objections levelled at the first Romantics by the partisans of neo-classicism determined to stand no nonsense from unhealthy young men.

Amis's contempt for all forms of humbug and pretentiousness, his cool, astringent observation of human behaviour, and his technical adroitness equip him to be a formidable writer of light verse. 'A Bookshop Idyll', originally entitled 'Something Nasty in the Bookshop', reviews with malicious accuracy the contents of the typical thin anthology of modern verse:

> Like all strangers, they divide by sex:
>> *Landscape near Parma*
> Interests a man, so does *The Double Vortex*,
>> So does *Rilke and Buddha.*
>
> 'I travel, you see', 'I think' and 'I can read'
>> These titles seem to say;
> But *I Remember You, Love is my Creed*,
>> *Poem for J.*,
>
> The ladies' choice, discountenance my patter
>> For several seconds:
> From somewhere in this (as in any) matter
>> A moral beckons.
>
> Should poets bicycle-pump the human heart
>> Or squash it flat?
> Man's love is of man's life a thing apart;
>> Girls aren't like that.

It is characteristic of Amis that he should make a serious critical point about the nature of poetry by employing a facetious image, and that the poem, which begins as an ironical survey of the differences between the verse written by men and by women, should develop into a deadly attack on masculine arrogance and self-satisfaction.

Having rejected all flabbiness and lushness, Amis offers instead a spry intellectual vigour and a ruthless honesty designed to sweep away every kind of sham. Like the more intelligent roaring boys of the Restoration, he is a serious writer who enjoys assuming the mask of a rake:

> Install me dozing in the car,
> Wined, dined, but still unconcubined,
> And take me where the good times are.[1]

Why is it that so many of his poems, for all their adroitness, are so bleak and depressing? It is not solely that he dwells upon the seamy side of life, as in 'Nocturne', where two lovers, fondling each other in a shop-doorway, seem in 'this wasteful/Voiding of sweat and breath' nastier and clumsier than animals:

> These keep the image of another creature
> In crippled versions, cocky, drab and stewed.

Nor is it that he finds no consolation in nature or healing wisdom in religious faith, for one must admire his refusal to wax sentimental over vegetables and to celebrate myths which his intelligence rejects. The valid criticism of his work is that his clever poems are often trivial and that, in his determination to liquidate conventional poetic words and to replace them with tough, gristly phrases, he has coarsened his sensibility as well as his language:

> When Party-Member Lech lifts up his knout,
> We know that's funny and unfunny;
> When he gives you a clout . . .[2]

> Fustily grinning at a leg-show.[2]

> To nab some hodge with bum and scruff like yours . . .[3]

These lines are, in their context, defensible, but it is hard to excuse 'A Poet's Epitaph' which, in its dreary vulgarity, ranks with the dullest and silliest epigrams of Herrick.

[1] 'They Only Move'.   [2] 'The Triumph of Time'.   [3] 'To Eros'.

'A Song of Experience' illustrates the merits and the inadequacies of Amis's poetry. It portrays, with a lewd, ingenious, faintly blasphemous wit, the exploits of a smooth, womanizing commercial traveller:

> He tried all colours, white and black and coffee;
>> Though quite a few were chary, more were bold;
> Some took it like the host, some like a toffee;
>> The two or three who wept were soon consoled.

Amis then ridicules the gospel of passion as expounded by three major prophets and mocks at the limitations of literary sex:

> The inaccessible he laid a hand on,
>> The heated he refreshed, the cold he warmed.
> What Blake presaged, what Lawrence took a stand on,
>> What Yeats locked up in fable, he performed.
>
> And so he knew, where we can only fumble,
>> Wildly in daydreams, vulgarly in art;
> Miles past the point where all delusions crumble
>> He found the female and the human heart. . . .
>
> I saw him, brisk in May, in Juliet's weather,
>> Hitch up the trousers of his long-tailed suit,
> Polish his windscreen with a chamois-leather,
>> And stow his case of samples in the boot.

Even if we allow for the poem's satirical extravagance and for Amis's obvious pleasure in showing his technical virtuosity, we are being asked to accept certain shallow, disreputable propositions: that the commercial traveller, with his rat-like sexuality, is a surer guide to sexual relationships and to the nature of women than Blake, Lawrence, and Yeats; and that life, as represented by the traveller, is somehow more real than the fantasies of art or the romantic day-dreams of Juliet. Amis's pose as a bluff, straight-forward chap who has cleared his mind of cant is revealed here as a shoddy masquerade unworthy of his intelligence and of his sensi-bility. When he allows his genuine moral perceptiveness and delicacy of feeling to assert themselves he can write a poem which is both highly accomplished and deeply felt. 'Masters', for example, opens by depicting, in lines that move with something of Auden's curt authority and laconic ease, those who are bred to command their fellows:

> Those whom heredity or guns have made
> Masters, must show it by a common speech;
> Expected words in the same tone from each
> Will always be obeyed . . .
>
> In triumph as in mutiny unmoved,
> These make their public act their private good,
> Their words in lounge or courtroom understood,
> But themselves never loved.

Then the poet suddenly turns from the contemplation of human strength and self-sufficiency to a compassionate portrayal of human weakness, in which alone lies the possibility of understanding and of love:

> By yielding mastery the will is freed,
> For it is by surrender that we live,
> And we are taken if we wish to give,
> Are needed if we need.

Amis appears to be a dual personality: the cool, sardonic mocker of academic stuffiness, who cocks a snook at his highbrow colleagues by reviewing science fiction and jazz records, cohabits uneasily with the serious teacher of literature struggling against all that debases learning and flatters ignorance. The best of his recent poems, 'After Goliath', suggests that he is aware of his own divided nature and of his inner uncertainty. To the nineteenth-century Romantics, David was the artist-hero who routed the stupid bourgeois Philistines. Much as Amis may detest the supporters of Goliath, he is equally scornful of the hangers-on who have made culture, aesthetic taste, progressive views and sensitivity dirty, threadbare words:

> Academics, actors who lecture,
> Apostles of architecture,

> Ancient-gods-of-the abdomen men,
> Angst-pushers, adherents of Zen,
> Alastors, Austenites, A-test
> Abolishers — even the straightest
> Of issues looks pretty oblique
> When a movement turns into a clique.

Looking at his fallen opponent's sword, David wonders whether to keep it as a

> Trophy, or means of attack
> On the rapturous crowd at his back?
> He shrugged and left it, resigned
> To a new battle, fought in the mind,
> For faith that his quarrel was just,
> That the right man lay in the dust.

In these last four lines there may lurk a recognition that a mistrust of artistic snobbery and humbug, an impatience with woolly-minded sentimentalists, and a cynical resolve to be a clear-eyed, plain-speaking realist are limited virtues for an artist to cultivate; that the effort to preserve civilized values in every branch of life is painful and unending; that provincialism, like patriotism, is not enough.

Philip Larkin (b. 1922), a contemporary and friend of Amis at Oxford, has been widely and justly acclaimed as one of the finest poets of his generation. Like Amis, he reviews jazz records for a 'posh' newspaper, has an alarmingly keen nose for the phoney, and is plagued by a suspicion that modern poetry and literary criticism are top-heavy with Alexandrian expertise and pedantry. In his long, enthusiastic review of John Betjeman's *Collected Poems*,[1] he observes with a wistful envy that for Betjeman

there has been no symbolism, no objective correlative, no T. S. Eliot or Ezra Pound, no rediscovery of myth or language as gesture, no *Seven Types* or *Some Versions*, no works of criticism with titles like *Communication as Discipline* or *Implicit and Explicit Image-Obliquity in Sir Lewis Morris*.

[1] Philip Larkin, 'Betjeman en Bloc'. *Listen*, vol. 3, No. 2 (Spring 1959), pp. 14–22.

Elsewhere[1] he reveals his mistrust of the new and largely student audience for contemporary verse:

But at bottom poetry, like all art, is inextricably bound up with giving pleasure, and if a poet loses his pleasure-seeking audience he has lost the only audience worth having, for which the dutiful mob that signs on every September is no substitute.

His distaste for elaborate speculation about the nature of poetry, his warm approval of Betjeman's passionate, exclusive love for 'Dear old, bloody old England', his longing, backward look at the prelapsarian innocence of English poetry in the days before the cosmopolitan heirs of Symbolism brought obscurity into the world, all point to one conclusion: that Larkin is a classic example of the provincial poet. He has expressed no less scathingly than Amis a strong antipathy to poems which spring from a contemplation of art rather than from an experience of life:

As a guiding principle I believe that every poem must be its own sole freshly-created universe, and therefore have no belief in 'tradition' or a common myth-kitty or casual allusions in poems to other poems or poets, which last I find unpleasantly like the talk of literary understrappers letting you see they know the right people.[2]

In practice Larkin breaks his own self-denying ordinance whenever he finds it convenient to do so. He assumes in 'I Remember, I Remember' that the reader will be familiar with Hood's poem about his childhood, and with those terribly sensitive evocations of early life which Larkin is satirizing. Worse still, 'If, My Darling' makes a reprehensible casual allusion to *Through the Looking-Glass*; and he has ironically smuggled into 'Lines on a Young Lady's Photograph Album' a hidden quotation from Tennyson. Larkin is as ready as any follower of Eliot to exploit literary echoes, the truth being that every poet draws on 'tradition' and a common myth-kitty, and alludes to other poets. The only question is how sys-

---

[1] Philip Larkin, 'The Pleasure Principle'. *Listen*, vol. 2, No. 3 (Summer–Autumn 1957), pp. 28–32.
[2] *Poets of the 1950's*, ed. D. J. Enright, pp. 77–78.

tematically and intelligently he does so, to what extent he uses or misuses this device, how widely he ranges in his allusions, and what degree of knowledge he demands from his audience. Why are references to Hood, Carroll, and Tennyson more legitimate than references to Virgil, Baudelaire, and Dante? No poet can, without imposing on himself a crippling and unnecessary handicap, disregard the inheritance or escape from the responsibilities of art, as Larkin admits, however grudgingly:

> What calls me is that lifted, rough-tongued bell
> (Art, if you like) whose individual sound
> Insists I too am individual.[1]

Larkin has said of his verse:

I write poems to preserve things I have seen/thought/felt ... both for myself and for others, though I feel that my prime responsibility is to the experience itself, which I am trying to keep from oblivion for its own sake. Why I should do this I have no idea, but I think the impulse to preserve lies at the bottom of all art.[2]

In some of his most successful poems he appears to be cherishing the past because it is inviolable, because it is, paradoxically, the only thing which time cannot deface. The old racehorses in 'At Grass' hold a secure place in fable because of

> faint afternoons
> Of Cups and Stakes and Handicaps,
> Whereby their names were artificed
> To inlay faded, classic Junes.

The poet, in 'Lines on a Young Lady's Photograph Album', rummages through the album in order

> to condense

> In short, a past that no one now can share,
> No matter whose your future; calm and dry,
> It holds you like a heaven, and you lie

[1] 'Reasons for Attendance'.
[2] *Poets of the 1950's*, ed. D. J. Enright, p. 77.

> Unvariably lovely there,
> Smaller and clearer as the years go by.

In 'Maiden Name' the girl, become a married woman, is past and gone, but her maiden name preserves something that is more than a memory:

> It means what we feel now about you then:
> How beautiful you were, and near, and young,
> So vivid, you might still be there among
> Those first few days, unfingermarked again.
> So your old name shelters our faithfulness,
> Instead of losing shape and meaning less
> With your depreciating luggage laden.

Since Larkin's verse has, by some critics, been called dry, cerebral, prim, and devoid of genuine feeling, it is worth stressing the obvious fact that his poetry is suffused with a plangent melancholy, a hopeless, tender compassion for all who suffer. In 'Myxomatosis' the victim is a rabbit; in 'Deceptions' a young girl from the pages of Mayhew's *London Labour and the London Poor*, who was drugged and raped: their pain and grief seem to Larkin equally meaningless and inconsolable. He observes defeat everywhere, and in 'Wants' he quietly acknowledges what he takes to be the truth about human destiny and passions:

> Beyond all this, the wish to be alone:
> However the sky grows dark with invitation cards
> However we follow the printed directions of sex
> However the family is photographed under the flagstaff —
> Beyond all this, the wish to be alone.
>
> Beneath it all, desire of oblivion runs:
> Despite the artful tensions of the calendar,
> The life insurance, the tabled fertility rites,
> The costly aversion of the eyes from death —
> Beneath it all, desire of oblivion runs.

The absence of complaint or of self-pity, like the alertness and muted wit of the writing, cannot hide the fact that this is a poem of utter sadness and exhaustion, the testament of a man who has grown resigned to the dull ache of existence.

What one admires in Larkin's verse is the unfailing precision and the sharp flavour of his observation and of his language, the restrained tenderness, the finely-managed irony which is never cruel and which is often turned against himself. He has the gift of concentrating into a line or two a world of experience, the visual aspects of his images fusing perfectly with their emotional and intellectual resonance. Examples of this are the last line of 'Maiden Name' and two lines from 'Dry-Point':

> And how remote that bare and sunscrubbed room,
> Intensely far, that padlocked cube of light.

Such images, which even in isolation have the ring of authenticity, take on a still greater authority in their proper context. When in 'Deceptions' Larkin sketches for us

> The sun's occasional print, the brisk brief
> Worry of wheels along the street outside
> Where bridal London bows the other way

we recognize not only the beautiful felicity of the description but also the overwhelming rightness of the epithet *bridal*, which contrasts so poignantly with the sexual degradation inflicted on the girl lying at the mercy of greed and lust. The poem's ending is a triumph of artistry, sustained by the image of the desolate attic, scene of the rape and symbol of the pitiable debauchee's furtive, desperate lechery:

> For you would hardly care
> That you were less deceived, out on that bed,
> Than he was, stumbling up the breathless stair
> To burst into fulfilment's desolate attic.

A poet can achieve this kind of unemphatic mastery only when a rich technical resourcefulness is allied with a generous measure of imaginative understanding.

His most ambitious and best-known poem, 'Church Going', has

H

been criticized by the American poet Donald Hall for being too long and diffuse: an American writer, Hall argues, would have produced a more elegant result with a greater economy of means. Much the same criticism could be made of *Tintern Abbey*: Larkin's poem is Wordsworthian in its brooding meditation, its slow amplitude, its tentative honesty as it explores a puzzling theme and gropes towards its weighty conclusion. 'Church Going', though admittedly not a flawless poem, exhibits Larkin's virtues at their richest and strongest — a luminous intelligence, a command of language ranging from colloquial ease to a sombre eloquence, a suppleness of rhythm to match the flexibility and subtlety of the emotions and themes unfolded and developed as the work moves to its appointed climax.

When reading a poem written in the first person we must never unreflectingly assume that the poet is pouring out an autobiographical confession or issuing a spiritual bulletin. The fact that the protagonist of 'Church Going' and Larkin himself share certain beliefs and sentiments gives us no warrant for supposing that Larkin is describing with photographic accuracy his normal behaviour when he visits a church. Such lines as:

> Hatless, I take off
> My cycle-clips in awkward reverence . . .

> Back at the door
> I sign the book, donate an Irish sixpence

have attracted some facile ridicule. The man who performs these and similar actions is a *persona* invented by Larkin for dramatic purposes and designed to be a mouthpiece or a medium capable of expressing a variety of complex attitudes. The gawkiness and clumsiness ascribed to this character in the opening stanzas are deliberately exaggerated so that they may contrast all the more effectively with the dark splendour of the peroration.

Unfortunately, in order to bring off this shrewd theatrical stroke, Larkin has sacrificed the chance of making his hero a credible figure. At the beginning of the poem he is so ignorant or scornful of ecclesiastical terminology that he talks slightingly and vaguely of

> some brass and stuff
> Up at the holy end;

yet a few lines further on he reveals an acquaintance with such terms as pyx and rood-lofts. Moreover, it is hard to believe that the oaf who blunders about in the first two stanzas could ever command the dignity of utterance and the reverential humility of mind with which he becomes endowed in the closing stanzas. Human beings are bundles of contradictions, but this does not mean that we can swallow every wild inconsistency in the portrayal of character. The trouble is that Larkin is neither drawing a faithful picture of himself nor creating an acceptable imaginary figure. We are not listening to the dramatic monologue of a man at war with himself, but being fobbed off with a dialogue between an intelligent, serious ventriloquist and his pert, brash dummy.

Having acknowledged this defect, we can then savour the poem's merits: the effortless gradation of tone, the shift from one emotional key to another, the unerring growth of the argument as the poem proceeds. As an example of Larkin's control of language one may turn to the fourth stanza, in which, after the deliberately casual informality of the first three stanzas, he visualizes a time when churches will all be ruins, and shunned, it may be, as unlucky places:

> Or, after dark, will dubious women come
> To make their children touch a particular stone;
> Pick simples for a cancer; or on some
> Advised night see walking a dead one?
> Power of some sort or other will go on
> In games, in riddles, seemingly at random;
> But superstition, like belief, must die,
> And what remains when disbelief has gone?
> Grass, weedy pavement, brambles, buttress, sky.

The one blemish on this stanza is the word *dubious*, its suggestion of sexual irregularity being alien to the spirit of the poem, and of this passage. Otherwise it is hard to detect any fault or weakness in the stanza: the darkening of the tone and the tautening of the rhythm mime to perfection the gravity of thought and solemnity of mood which have suddenly oppressed and overshadowed the poem. In its concluding lines, after the uneasy jocularity of:

> For, though I've no idea
> What this accoutred frowsty barn is worth,
> It pleases me to stand in silence here,

Larkin, setting aside all the stage properties, and speaking in his own voice without equivocation or defensive irony, permits his verse to attain a splendid weightiness and grandeur as he meditates on man's awareness of mortality:

> A serious house on serious earth it is,
> In whose bleak air all our compulsions meet,
> Are recognised, and robed as destinies.
> And that much never can be obsolete,
> Since someone will forever be surprising
> A hunger in himself to be more serious,
> And gravitating with it to this ground,
> Which, he once heard, was proper to grow wise in,
> If only that so many dead lie round.

One charge commonly levelled at Larkin is that he is a negative poet, afraid of all strong emotions, shrinking from sexual responsibility, and almost welcoming defeat.[1] These elements are undeniably to be found in such poems as 'Reasons for Attendance', 'Skin', and 'No Road', where he envisages the falling into disuse of a road between himself and another person, and faces the certainty of time's

> Drafting a world where no such road will run
> From you to me;
> To watch that world come up like a cold sun,
> Rewarding others, is my liberty.
> Not to prevent it is my will's fulfilment.
> Willing it, my ailment.

---

[1] In 'Wedding Wind', a beautiful affirmation of belief in life and in sexual fulfilment, Larkin speaks through the lips of a bride after her wedding-night, not in his own person.

He has learned to wait without expectancy because

> Only one ship is seeking us, a black-
> Sailed unfamiliar, towing at her back
> A huge and birdless silence. In her wake
> No waters breed or break.[1]

To blame Larkin for this bleak wanhope is to misinterpret the nature of poetry. A poet owes complete fidelity to the truth as he perceives it, however dispiriting or shameful it may be. It is a commonplace that poetry may be born of suffering, degradation, vice, and despair: Larkin has proved that a man who sees life as neither tragic nor heroic but rather as a grey, muddled, unsatisfactory affair can fashion poetry out of the drabbest, most unpromising material — the boredom, the inadequacy, the pointlessness, the nagging anxiety of suburban life in our day.

The second charge, a corollary of the first, is that by confining himself to a closed circle of emotions, and to a limited intellectual range, Larkin has stunted the growth of his inner life and of his art, condemning himself to a self-inflicted provincialism of the mind and of the sensibility. It is true that the poems which have appeared since the publication of *The Less Deceived* (1955) have explored no fresh territory; and it may be that Larkin is one of those very good (but not major) poets whose art steadily becomes more exact, discriminating, and assured without undergoing any radical transformation or spectacular development. 'The Whitsun Weddings' and 'An Arundel Tomb', to name two examples of his recent work, are proof enough that his grave observation of life preserves its old firmness and dry compassion. In 'At First', a tiny poem of crystalline delicacy and strength, he reminds us that while

> Lambs that learn to walk in snow
> When their bleating clouds the air
> Meet a vast unwelcome, know
> Nothing but a sunless glare

it will not always be winter:

[1] 'Next, Please'.

As they wait beside the ewe,
Her fleeces wetly caked, there lies
Hidden round them, waiting too,
Earth's immeasurable surprise.
They could not grasp it if they knew,
What so soon will wake and grow
Utterly unlike the snow.

Nor can we forecast what the future holds for a poet who has endured 'a wretched width of cold' with unfailing dignity and self-awareness.

Charles Tomlinson (b. 1927) has decisively rejected the assumptions and the aesthetic doctrines which animate the poetry of Philip Larkin and of almost all the poets whose work appeared in *New Lines*. In his review of this anthology he laments the general failure of these poets to pass beyond the contemplation of their own limited feelings and mental habits, their inability to face the challenge of the mysterious world that lies outside their immediate personal experience:

A poet's sense of objectivity, however, of that which is beyond himself and beyond his mental conceit of himself, and his capacity to realise that objectivity within the artefact is the gauge of his artistry and the first prerequisite of all artistic genius.[1]

Donald Davie's answer to these criticisms drew from Tomlinson the following rejoinder:

It is his contention that only by means of a 'self-imposed loss of nerve' can poetry be renewed after the verbal debauchery of the forties. It is mine that it can only be renewed by poets whose sensory organisation is alive, who are aware to the fingertips of the universe around them and who have broken through that suburban mental ratio which too many of the movement poets attempt to impose on their experience.[2]

Tomlinson believes that since 1939 English poetry has deliberately retreated into a provincial complacency, neglecting to cultivate the

[1] Charles Tomlinson, 'The Middlebrow Muse'. *Essays in Criticism*, VII, 2 (April 1957), p. 215.
[2] *Essays in Criticism*, VII. 4 (October 1957), p. 460.

territory won by Yeats, Pound, and Eliot, and preening itself upon its insular mediocrity. In his essay 'Poetry Today' he allows merit to a handful of poets over sixty — Ezra Pound (an American), Hugh MacDiarmid (a Scot), Austin Clarke (an Irishman), and Robert Graves (an Anglo-Irishman). Turning to the poetry of younger writers, he reserves his praise for Keith Douglas, who was killed in the war, and admits that in the post-war years a few poets 'have written individual poems of distinction', his verdict on Larkin being that his work shows real promise and some pleasant accomplishment.[1]

According to Tomlinson, the urgent task of English poets is to extend the achievement of Yeats, Pound, and Eliot, in order that English verse may emerge from its present provincial backwater and rejoin the main stream of European literature. It is not astonishing that his poems should have won more acclaim in the U.S.A. than in his native country, where it is no longer fashionable to regard French Symbolism as a fruitful study for young poets, and where a wholehearted admiration for modern American poetry is still uncommon and mildly suspect.

Tomlinson's most ambitious attempt to create an English equivalent of French Symbolist verse is a poem in six sections entitled *Antecedents*, the scene being 'chiefly the Paris of Jules Laforgue and Stéphane Mallarmé'. Only a reader familiar with nineteenth-century cultural history and with Symbolist poetry is competent to appraise the subtleties of the poem's argument, for Tomlinson relies upon direct and concealed quotation as well as upon multiple allusion, leaving the reverberating echoes and the spaces between the images to compose the meaning of the poem. It is impossible to summarize the poem but one can convey something of its quality by a quotation from section II, 'Praeludium':

[1] This essay is to be found in *The Modern Age*, vol. 7 of *The Pelican Guide to English Literature*, ed. Boris Ford, pp. 458–72. The few poets in question are Anne Ridler, F. T. Prince, Ronald Bottrall, Norman MacCaig, William Soutar, Patrick Kavanagh, and Donald Davie. The work of Bottrall, Soutar, and Kavanagh falls outside the scope of this book, since all three had made their mark before 1939.

'Art is a keyboard
For transitions', said Mallarmé: 'between something and nothing.'
The music persisted
'And when I heard it' (Charles Baudelaire, the
Slow horn pouring through dusk an orange twilight)
'I grew insatiate.' We had our laureates, they
Their full orchestra and its various music. To that
                                                    Enter

On an ice-drift
A white bear, the grand Chancellor
From Analyse, uncertain
Of whom he should bow to, or whether
No one is present. It started with Byron, and
Liszt, says Heine, bowed to the ladies. But Jules . . .
Outside,

    De la musique avant toute chose
The thin horns gone glacial
And behind blinds, partitioning Paris
Into the rose-stained mist,
He bows to the looking-glass. Sunsets.

The whole poem is a disdainful riposte to what he regards as the
chauvinistic parochialism of Larkin and of Amis; an assertion that
poetry is a learned art; an aristocratic statement of faith in the tradition of European literature.

Respect for the work of art, a belief in the need to fashion a
rigorous poetic, a scrupulous concern for linguistic order and
alertness are among the main tenets of Tomlinson's aesthetic creed;
he is strongly opposed to anything that may dissolve the formal
strength or blur the clarity of the artefact. Thus, in a review of
Richard Eberhart's *Collected Poems*, he censures Eberhart because
'we are, as it were, invited at too many points to approve the
integrity of the poet rather than the integrity of his art',[1] and he
discerns in the poems of Vladimir Nabokov a debilitating facility:
'By and large, words come to him too easily for us to believe that he

[1] *Critical Quarterly*, vol. II, No. 4 (Winter 1960), p. 476.

has ever known that resonant silence from which the deeper poetry emerges.'[1]

His poetry is no less bracingly austere than his critical judgement. Speaking of 'the energising weather which is a result of the combination of sun and frost', he names this weather as one of the elements that make up the moral landscape of his verse. The curtness of his rhythms, the severe richness of his vocabulary, the paucity of rhyme, and the hard, precise outlines of his poems all reinforce the impression that we are in a winter landscape — crystalline, invigorating, and pure. In 'Tramontana at Lerici' he defines the nature of his work, even as he describes the operation of the freezing wind:

> Leaf-dapples sharpen. Emboldened by this clarity
> The minds of artificers would turn prismatic,
> Running on lace perforated in crisp wafers
> That could cut like steel. Constitutions,
> Drafted under this fecund chill, would be annulled
> For the strictness of their equity, the moderation of their pity.

Tomlinson's imagination is strongly visual, as one might suspect from his review of two volumes by Emma Swan, whom he praises because

she has learned that lesson, from the experiments of Cummings and Williams, of letting the look of the poem on the page prompt and regulate *through the eye* the precise tone of voice. Most of us have yet to find out about this aesthetic experience, the secret of which is bound up with the speed at which, word by word and cadence by cadence, the elements of the poem are permitted to come into view.[1]

In poem after poem he stares intently at a landscape or at an object, not merely seeking to render its sensuous appearance or to catch an impressionistic likeness, but willing it to yield its inner significance. He frequently produces an effect of great solidity and precision:

> The heads, impenetrable
> And the slow bulk

[1] *New Statesman*, 28 April 1961, p. 674.

Soundless and stooping,
A white darkness — burdened
Only by sun, and not
By the matchwood yoke — [1]

Above, piercing the empty blue,
A gull would convey whiteness
Through the sole space which lacks it.[2]

A few of the poems are inspired by painters as diverse as Li Ch'eng, Vermeer, Van Gogh, and Cézanne; a passage from Constable's *The History of Landscape Painting* is the starting-point for a long meditation on the nature of art:

                    Art
          Is complete when it is human. It is human
      Once the looped pigments, the pin-heads of light
         Securing space under their deft restrictions
    Convince, as the index of a possible passion,
          As the adequate gauge, both of the passion
    And its object. The artist lies
          For the improvement of truth. Believe him.[3]

Much as we may admire the strictness and the accuracy of such passages, we must grant that Tomlinson's poetry lacks musical richness and ease. *Antecedents* is a far more difficult poem to enjoy than *The Waste Land*, for several reasons, one being that Eliot's command of rhythm and of melodic variety guides us over the roughest and most unfamiliar terrain, whereas Tomlinson's clipped, terse language makes no concession to human weakness. His versification is a precision instrument designed to register the subtle movements of his intelligence and of his sensibility, but it affords very little sensuous pleasure. Like Schoenberg's music, his poetry is seldom contaminated by anything so vulgar as a delicious or memorable tune.

The most damaging charge brought against Tomlinson is that in his preoccupation with aesthetic experience he has become too

---

[1] 'Oxen: Ploughing at Fiesole'.   [2] 'Icos'.
[3] 'A Meditation on John Constable'.

remote from the hopes and fears of ordinary people, too distant
from the world where men hunger and suffer. The charge is mis-
conceived. It is true that almost all poets of the first order have in
the end felt bound to make some overt statement about the moral
nature of man, and about his obligations as a political animal; to
adopt as their themes the elemental passions of men and women;
to pass beyond a contemplation of planes and surfaces and the
shifting of light upon the facets of the visible world. Yet the first
duty of an artist (though not the last) is a concentrated devotion to
the work in hand, even if this entails a measure of withdrawal and of
detachment which hostile critics can stigmatize as indifference to
society or as bloodless aestheticism. It is clear that, for Tomlinson,
a man is most richly and fully human when he is practising his art
with all the intensity and discipline of which he is capable, and that
he mistrusts the humanity which is a specious cloak for sentimental
weakness or flaccid emotionalism. Nor (if one must make the
shallow antithesis of art and life) does Tomlinson ignore the claims
of life. In 'Farewell to Van Gogh' he acknowledges that even a great
painter cannot permanently alter the universe which, for a moment,
he may have illuminated and transformed:

> Stone by stone
> Your rhetoric is dispersed until the earth
> Becomes once more the earth, the leaves
> A sharp partition against cooling blue.

His fine poem 'On the Hall at Stowey' displays a deep concern for
the quality of our living, a denunciation of all that is lazy or un-
heeding in our maintenance of civilized standards, a bitterness at our
failure to save from decay a building which human love and
endeavour had preserved inviolate for five centuries:

> Five centuries. And we? What we had not
> Made ugly, we had laid waste —
> Left (I should say) the office to nature
> Whose blind battery, best fitted to perform it,
> Outdoes us, completes by persistence

> All that our negligence fails in. Saddened,
> Yet angered beyond sadness, where the road
> Doubled upon itself I halted, for a moment
> Facing the empty house and its laden barns.

Tomlinson's first full-length collection of poems, *Seeing is Believing*, appeared in England in 1960, and in the same year he brought out his *Versions from Fyodor Tyutchev*, with an Introduction by Henry Gifford. Tyutchev (1803–73), who influenced the leading Russian poets of three generations — the Symbolists, Blok, and Pasternak — and who, in the words of Valery Bryusov, 'stands as the great master and initiator of the poetry of allusions', is obviously a congenial figure to Tomlinson. Yet one may ask why a poet so gifted as Tomlinson should devote his energies to translation rather than to original poetry. The answer may be that he is thereby deliberately asserting his belief in the great tradition of modern European poetry, paying tribute to a unique precursor of that tradition, and striking a blow at the provincialism which he takes to be the bane of contemporary English poetry. For the provincial poet is, by definition, one who shuts his mind to what is happening outside his own cultural environment, who fears or mistrusts alien modes of experience, who does not care how foreign poets are tackling their problems or exploiting the resources of their language. Complete fidelity to the promptings of his inner voice, and sincerity of feeling, are what he most prizes; and since a poem must be, to quote Larkin again, 'its own sole freshly-created universe', he is likely to find the process of translation thoroughly repugnant. Casual allusions to foreign poems or poets are bad enough, but a translation is one vast systematic allusion to another man's work, a mere refurbishing of another man's unique imaginative vision.

The traditional poet believes that his native poetry enriches itself by drawing upon the literature of other lands, and that translation is one of the most valuable ways by which cultures may be cross-fertilized. Nor does he accept the doctrine that a poem's chief use is to give a sincere account of a poet's innermost feelings — what matters, above all, is the integrity of the artefact, the completed poem. Hence a translation is no less valid than an original poem, may indeed be a way of enlarging our vision, of learning to respect the achievement of others, of destroying that parochial self-regard and complacency which tether us to the little world of pleasant minor poetry.

Of all contemporary poets, the most defiantly traditional is Donald Davie (b. 1922) who, despite his defence of *New Lines* against Charles Tomlinson, is much closer to Tomlinson in his aesthetic principles than to most of his fellow-contributors to the anthology.[1] He believes, with Tomlinson, that Ezra Pound is a great poet; joins with him in deploring the insular philistinism of Larkin and of Amis (though he admires their verse); and shares with him the belief that English poetry since the war has beaten a sad retreat from the major tradition established by Pound, Eliot, and Yeats, that tradition which Robert Graves has described less approvingly, in his Inaugural Lecture as Professor of Poetry at Oxford, as 'the foul tidal basin of modernism'.

Davie counters any charge of pedantry and academicism by reiterating that poetry is a learned art, and that artifice is an essential element in the writing of poems. In the course of a controversy with Robert Graves, he rejects what Graves calls 'Robert Frost's splendidly provincial definition of poetry — "what gets lost in translation" '[2] and refutes the doctrine that poetry cannot be transplanted from its indigenous soil:

It seems to me more reasonable to suppose that the greatest poetry is that which best survives translation, than that it is poetry which is least translatable. It is more reasonable, also more to the credit of poetry, if poetry is an exploration of universal truth, not just the exploitation of the idiosyncrasies of one language out of all the languages of mankind.[3]

Davie is acutely conscious of the historical situation at any given time, and of the poet's responsibility for preserving the purity and the vigour of his native language. He judges a poet, in part, by the

---

[1] In his article 'Remembering the Movement', which appeared in *Prospect* (Summer 1959), pp. 13–16, Davie tacitly agrees with Tomlinson's main criticisms of *New Lines*.
[2] Letter in the *Times Literary Supplement*, 9 August 1957, p. 483.
[3] Letter in the *Times Literary Supplement*, 18 October 1957, p. 625.

example he sets, by his effect on his successors, by what he does to strengthen or to corrupt his native poetic tradition. Davie's concern with the moral significance of poetry for society comes out very strongly in the following passage:

I should suppose . . . that the poetic tradition is in a healthy state when the poor poetry of a period is not vicious but merely dull; and that when the tradition is sick, the opposite is true. The quality of the poor or minor poetry of an age is thus a matter of more urgent importance to society as a whole than the quality of its major poetry. For it is the use of language by a slender talent which is the true register of the health or sickness of the language as such.[1]

His sense of history makes him aware that a poet, however gifted he may be, is inescapably a man of his epoch, limited and moulded by his inheritance. Thus, in his view, Hopkins cannot successfully take Shakespearean liberties with words and syntax, because Victorian English is much less fluid and malleable than Jacobean English; which accounts for the Sandow-like distortion that we find in Hopkins when he ignores the historical development of the language and the stage to which it has evolved in his day.[2]

He believes that Malraux's concept of *le Musée Imaginaire* is valid for poetry as well as for the visual arts, and that the modern poet must make a deliberate choice between a variety of styles and modes, or condemn himself to the writing of minor, even provincial, poetry. The poet must grow ever more self-conscious, ever more aware of his bewilderingly diverse cultural heritage.

Although Davie has plumped for the post-Symbolist tradition as the richest source for a contemporary poet, in his verse and prose alike he frequently aims at a neo-Augustan lucidity and exactness. The very title of his first book of criticism, *Purity of Diction in English Verse*, underlines one aspect of this concern;[3] in *Articulate*

[1] See Davie's comment on Tomlinson's review of *New Lines*, in *Essays in Criticism*, VII, 3 (July 1957), pp. 343–4.
[2] See the chapter 'Hopkins as a Decadent Critic' in *Purity of Diction in English Verse*, pp. 160–82.
[3] For Pope's views on poetic diction see his *Second Epistle of the Second Book of Horace*, 157–79.

Energy he examines the function of what he calls true syntax in poetry, demonstrating how post-Symbolist technique may weaken this syntax by dissolving the firm structure of a poem in musical suggestiveness. In his anthology, *The Late Augustans*, he reveals his sympathy for a number of poets who flourished between the death of Pope and the publication of the *Lyrical Ballads*, a period often dismissed as an age when stiffness, dullness, and artificiality had blighted English poetry. His rational conservatism about metre, his admiration of Ben Jonson, Pope, and Samuel Johnson, his insistence on what is reasonable and universal, his scepticism about organic form, are other signs of his Augustan predilections, which lead him to trample upon the toadstool growth of squelchy neo-Romantic heresies and to mistrust all that is rankly luxuriant and undisciplined:

> And Cherry ripe, indeed ripe, ripe, I cry.
> Let orchards flourish in the poet's soul
> And bear their feelings that are mastered by
> Maturing rhythms, to compose a whole.
>
> But how the shameful grapes and olives swell,
> Excrescent from no cornucopia, tart,
> Too near to oozing to be handled well:
> Ripe, ripe, they cry, and perish in my heart.[1]

It would, however, be false to regard Davie merely as an academic poet who has revived certain Augustan modes of sensibility. His early poems have, admittedly, an air of eighteenth-century pastiche, with their poised elegance, manipulation of antithesis, and formal, polished diction:

> A pasticheur of late-Augustan styles,
> I too have sung the sofa and the hare,
> Made nightmares ride upon a private air,
> And hearths, extinguished, send a chill for miles.[2]

The mannered irony and wit of this early verse, and its playful, condescending tone, can be extremely tiresome:

[1] 'Cherry Ripe: On a Painting by Juan Gris'.   [2] 'Homage to William Cowper'.

You round upon me, generously keen:
The man, you say, is patently sincere.
Because he is so eloquent, you mean?
That test was never patented, my dear.[1]

When Bradbury sang 'The Roast Beef of Old England'
And Watts, 'How doth the little busy bee',
Then Doddridge blessed the pikes of Cumberland
And plunging sapphics damned eternally.

Said Watts the fox: 'Your red meat is uncouth.
We'll keep the bleeding purchase out of sight.
Arminian honey for the age's tooth!
With so much sweetness, who will ask for light?'[2]

The quizzical mockery, the learning, the allusiveness, and the intellectual superiority are paraded negligently but ostentatiously: 'Doctors will wear scarlet' is a perilous injunction for poets.

Yet there are a few admirable poems in this vein, such as 'On Bertrand Russell's "Portraits from Memory"', in which Davie analyses the dangers for a poet of working in Cambridge, England, where the heavy Fenland soil and the bright chatter of Academe are equally maleficent:

I wonder still which of the hemispheres
Infects the other in this grassy globe;
The chumbling moth of Madingley, that blears
The labourer's lamp, destroys the scarlet robe.

It was the Muse that could not make her home
In that too thin and yet too sluggish air,
Too volatile to live among the loam,
Her sheaves too heavy for the talkers there.

An even more accomplished example of his early verse is 'The Fountain', which takes as its starting-point an observation by Bishop Berkeley:

Feathers up fast, and steeples; then in clods
Thuds into its first basin; thence as surf

[1] 'The Evangelist'.   [2] 'Dissent: A Fable'.

Smokes up and hangs; irregularly slops
Into its second, tattered like a shawl;
There, chill as rain, stipples a danker green,
Where urgent tritons lob their heavy jets.

For Berkeley this was human thought, that mounts
From bland assumptions to inquiring skies,
There glints with wit, fumes into fancies, plays
With its negations, and at last descends,
As by a law of nature, to its bowl
Of thus enlightened but still common sense.

We who have no such confidence must gaze
With all the more affection on these forms,
These spires, these plumes, these calm reflections, these
Similitudes of surf and turf and shawl,
Graceful returns upon acceptances.
We ask of fountains only that they play,

Though that was not what Berkeley meant at all.

This poem, like the most finely-tempered verse of Johnson and of
Goldsmith, delights us by the elegance of its melodic line no less
than by the firmness of its intellectual structure. Davie takes a
notion of an eighteenth-century philosopher, plays with it and holds
it up to the light so that it may glitter, as the waters of the fountain
glint and fume in the sunlight. We enjoy these stanzas partly because it is always satisfying to watch the graceful unfolding of an
ingenious argument; but the poem affords a more than intellectual
pleasure. The precise observation of physical appearances and the
sensuous vivacity of the images lend colour, sharpness of contour,
and physical immediacy to what might otherwise be nothing but a
clever piece of versified wit. These images both define the shape of
the poetic argument and are, at the same time, the very shade and
texture of that argument.[1]

Even in the early poems there are signs that Davie is determined
not to remain a 'late-Augustan pasticheur'. He knows that Augustan

[1] It would be instructive to compare this poem with the fine 'Roman Fountain' by
Louise Bogan.

satire, which cleansed the air two centuries ago, is powerless now:

> I might have been as pitiless as Pope
> But to no purpose; in a tragic age
> We share the hatred but we lack the hope
> By pinning follies to reform the age.[1]

'At Knaresborough', which begins by acknowledging Davie's Yorkshire background:

> 'Broad acres, sir'. You hear them in my talk,

ends with the significant phrase 'I must be moving on'. In 'Limited Achievement', where the ostensible subject is Piranesi, *Prisons*, Plate VI, Davie seems to be glancing obliquely at his own verse and inquiring whether, like Piranesi's engravings, it always exhibits 'the same few dismal properties':

> Those were his true proclivities? Perhaps.
> Successful in his single narrow track,
> He branches out, but only to collapse,
> Imprisoned in his own unhappy knack,
>
> Which, when unfailing, fails him most, perhaps.

More strikingly still, certain poems in his second volume, *A Winter Talent* (1957), have passed beyond the boundaries marked out in the earlier collection, *Brides of Reason* (1955). The polemical hostility towards Romanticism has given way to the more searching appraisal of 'Dream Forest', where he names as types of ideal virtue Brutus, Pushkin, and Strindberg:

> Classic, romantic, realist,
> These have I set up.

The smooth versification and the flaking irony have yielded to a new gravity, a steady reflectiveness, which inform such poems as 'Obiter Dicta', 'Under St. Paul's', 'The Wind at Penistone', and 'Time Passing, Beloved':

> What will become of us? Time
> Passing, beloved, and we in a sealed

[1] 'Too Late for Satire'.

Assurance unassailed
By memory. How can it end,
This siege of a shore that no misgivings have steeled,
No doubts defend?

Even the wit is no longer a dazzling juxtaposition of conceits, an erudite interlocking of cross-references, or a fireworks display. In 'Hearing Russian Spoken' one notices that Davie is now using the serious pun as a means of exploring a number of interrelated moral problems, and that his Augustan standards have acquired a sombre weightiness and resolution. The complex word-play in this poem is not a stylistic device but the most appropriate means of ordering the painful and perplexing material which Davie is contemplating with a fine, scrupulous honesty:

Unsettled again and hearing Russian spoken
I think of brokenness perversely planned
By Dostoievsky's debauchees; recall
The 'visible brokenness' that is the token
Of the true believer; and connect it all
With speaking a language I cannot command.

If broken means unmusical I speak
Even in English brokenly, a man
Wretched enough, yet one who cannot borrow
Their hunger for indignity nor, weak,
Abet my weakness, drink to drown a sorrow
Or write in metres that I cannot scan.

Davie holds that a poet must maintain professional standards of competence, and that the ability to master a variety of metrical forms is one proof of technical proficiency. This proficiency, however, far from being a question of manipulating words with a mechanical dexterity and of observing a few codified rules of prosody, is revealed in such matters as the control of rhythm and of tone, the variation of texture, the power to sustain a long melodic line, the employment of syntactical devices to alter the tempo of the verse — in short, the art of orchestration which shapes a sequence of words into a musical pattern. He has found the kind of mastery which he desires in the Italian *canzone*, in Spenser, in the French Symbolists, in Valéry and in Ezra Pound. A recent poem, 'To a Brother in the Mystery: Circa 1290', which has obvious affinities with Browning's monologues, shows Davie's unobtrusive skill in handling the heroic couplet, into which he has introduced so many subtle variations of pace and stress that all danger of stiffness and of monotony is averted. This is one example of the certainty and ease which he brings to the practice of his art; *The Forests of Lithuania* (1959), an adaptation of Mickiewicz's long narrative poem *Pan Tadeusz*, demonstrates the variety and the resourcefulness of his versification on a larger scale. Perhaps the most impressive portion of this work is the lengthy description of Lithuania's vast impenetrable forest, swarming with foliage and animal life; the language takes on a richness and density that correspond to the physical characteristics of the forest and its inhabitants:

> Once past
> The manageable tangles,
> The rampart rises — logs,
> Roots, stumps, which a quagmire defends —
> And water, and nets
> Of rank weeds and ant-hills, and knots
> Of snakes, and the wasp's and the hornet's
> Nests. And then small meres
> Grass-choked yet unplumbable, thought
> To harbour devils, hold water
> Rust-spotted, emitting a thick
> And stinking steam . . .
>
> All around,
> Treed that they may command
> The land's approaches, wait
> Their[1] ministers of state
> The lynx and wolverine;
> Beside them where they reign
> Fed on their broken meats

[1] *Their* refers to the buffalo, bison, and bear who rule the forest.

> The two court favourites
> Eagle and falcon skulk;
> Boar, wolf and antlered elk
> Each in suburban fief
> Owe vassalage.

The grinding, erudite Foreword to the poem, which shows what a dangerous model Ezra Pound can be, ends with a noble and characteristic declaration:

> And Europe's heart
> Is wherever community happens in any age.

For Davie is passionately concerned about our European heritage and, indeed, about civilizations other than our own. In his latest work, *A Sequence for Francis Parkman*, he meditates on the making of America, on the contrast between the Old World and the New:

> Man with man
> Is all our history; American,
> You met with spirits. Neither white nor red
> The melancholy, disinherited
> Spirit of mid-America, but this,
> The manifested copiousness, the bounties.[1]

It may be argued that Davie's self-conscious artistry, his harping on tradition, his doctrine of the Imaginary Museum, are signs that, lacking true poetic creativeness, he has taken refuge in an Alexandrian eclecticism and cosmopolitanism.[2] He is, in my judgement, a poet whose emotional range is continually growing wider and deeper, whose art is steadily maturing, and who is better equipped

---

[1] These are the final lines of the last poem in the sequence 'A Letter to Curtis Bradford'.

[2] Robert Graves, in his letter to the *Times Literary Supplement*, 9 August 1957, p. 483, refers to poets who 'prove their modernism by inhabiting imaginary museums of foreign literary and dramatic tradition. The exhibits remain unassimilated . . . but they enable the museum-man to write MAJOR poems of truly contemporary malaise.' Graves goes on to defend his own defiant provincialism: 'Yet if, as Mr. Davie argues, the languages of poetry are necessarily national, need this defiant provincialism always imply ignorance? May it not also mean that the poet has taken some trouble to investigate the literature of cultures historically associated with his own, and been at pains to refine, by contrast, what is peculiarly and metropolitanly English?'

than almost any of his contemporaries to write the kind of major verse that Keats has in mind when he declares: 'A long poem is a test of invention which I take to be the Polar star of poetry, as fancy is the sails, and imagination the rudder.'[1]

The conflict between provincialism and tradition, at which I have glanced in this chapter, is likely to recur in every age and to remain unresolved. We can study one engagement in this perennial war by reading Blake's annotations to the *Discourses* of Sir Joshua Reynolds. When Reynolds asserts:

The mind is but a barren soil; a soil which is soon exhausted, and will produce no crop, or only one, unless it be constantly fertilized and enriched with foreign matter

Blake contemptuously answers:

The mind that could have produced this Sentence must have been a Pitiful, a Pitiable, Imbecility. I always thought that the Human Mind was the most Prolific of All Things and Inexhaustible. I certainly do Thank God that I am not like Reynolds.

It is fashionable to regard Blake's pronouncements, however wrong-headed, as Everlasting Gospel truth, but reason and experience alike suggest that he is employing a misleading analogy and ignoring facts when he refuses to believe

that Rafael taught Mich. Angelo or that Mich. Angelo taught Rafael, any more than I believe that the Rose teaches the Lilly how to grow, or the Apple tree teaches the Pear tree how to bear Fruit. I do not believe the tales of Anecdote writers when they militate against Individual Character.

Those of us who believe the traditional view of poetry to be more catholic, liberal, and just than the provincial, must beware of judging a poet by his theories instead of by his poems. What matters about Larkin is the goodness of his verse, not the inadequacy of his doctrine; and the example of Thomas Hardy may remind us that a provincial poet can write poems of the first order. One of our greatest traditional poets, Alexander Pope, seems to have set the

[1] Letter to Benjamin Bailey, 8 October 1817.

highest store upon 'the language of the heart'.[1] Thomas Hardy, who at first sight appears to be diametrically opposed to Pope in every conceivable way, quotes with approval a judgement by Sir Leslie Stephen which Pope might have endorsed, a judgement that may reconcile the conflicting values of Provincialism and Tradition:

The ultimate aim of the poet should be to touch our hearts by showing his own, and not to exhibit his learning, or his fine taste, or his skill in mimicking the notes of his predecessors.[2]

[1] For Pope's use of this phrase in verse and in prose see G. Tillotson, *Pope and Human Nature* (Clarendon Press, 1958), p. 58.
[2] 'Gray and his School', in *Hours in a Library*, vol. IV. I owe this quotation to Geoffrey Grigson, *The Victorians*, p. 205. Grigson mentions Hardy's approval in the Notes, p. 327.

V

THE MEANING OF A LANDSCAPE

IT is hard to imagine three poets of our century more strikingly dissimilar than W. B. Yeats, D. H. Lawrence, and T. S. Eliot, yet all three are united in taking a religious view of the world. Eliot has summed up his own position by referring us to T. E. Hulme's dictum:

I hold the religious conception of ultimate values to be right, the humanist wrong.[1]

Yeats and Lawrence are equally explicit on this matter. For Yeats declares:

I am very religious, and deprived by Huxley and Tyndall, whom I detested, of the simple-minded religion of my childhood, I had made a new religion, almost an infallible Church of poetic tradition,[2]

while D. H. Lawrence, in a letter to Ernest Collings dated 24 February 1913, unequivocally asserts his belief in the holiness of art, in the sacredness of the artist's vocation:

I always feel as if I stood naked for the fire of Almighty God to go through me — and it's rather an awful feeling. One has to be so terribly religious to be an artist.

Since these men differ so violently in their temperaments as well as in their metaphysical, moral, political, and artistic creeds, we may be tempted to wonder whether we can assign any precise meaning to the term *religious*. It would be absurd to pretend that we can draw up any confession of faith to which all religious men would sub-

[1] Quoted by T. S. Eliot in 'Second Thoughts About Humanism', *Selected Essays* (Faber, 2nd ed. 1934), p. 452.
[2] W. B. Yeats, *Autobiographies* (Macmillan, 1955), p. 115.

scribe, or that by some ingenious juggling with verbal formulas we can reconcile widely divergent beliefs. It is, however, possible to note certain characteristic attitudes of mind which may justly be called religious, and to distinguish the religious from the irreligious man.

The religious man believes that the universe is governed by spiritual laws and controlled by a divine purpose; and that at the heart of the universe there lies a mystery of which human beings may be aware but which they can never hope to solve. The irreligious man acknowledges that the universe is immensely complicated but dislikes the connotations of the word *mystery*. Since he does not assume that there is any divine purpose, or sacred enigma, concealed at the heart of things, he judges that human reason is capable both of analysing the properties of matter and of energy and of discovering the answers to such problems as the origins of life.

There are corresponding disagreements about the nature of human beings. According to the religious view, man is created to worship the divine and to attain spiritual illumination. The sexual act has a religious significance, being fraught with enormous consequences for good or for ill. Concepts such as sin, guilt, sacrifice, rebirth, and redemption are pointers to certain basic facts about the nature of man and of the universe; legend, myth, ritual, and the arts give access to truths which the reason is powerless to apprehend. W. B. Yeats returns to this theme again and again:

When I try to put all into a phrase I say, 'Man can embody truth but he cannot know it.' . . . You can refute Hegel but not the Saint or the Song of Sixpence.[1]

Europe belongs to Dante and the witches' sabbath, not to Newton.[2]

For the irreligious mind, this view of the world is a refusal to face the facts, a desperate attempt to find comfort by pretending that there is a supernatural realm where our sorrows and imperfections

[1] Letter to Lady Elizabeth Pelham, 4 January 1939. *The Letters of W. B. Yeats*, ed. Allan Wade (Hart-Davis, 1954), p. 922.
[2] Letter to Olivia Shakespear, 9 March 1933. Ibid., p. 807.

are redeemed. Man painfully makes his own moral standards in a universe where no divine pattern is revealed, no divine sanctions exist. Sexual passion is neither a barrier to spiritual perfection, nor a sacramental gift that hints by analogy at the nature of divine love, but a powerful instinct with which we must come to terms. The notions of sin and of guilt are symptoms of a psychological failure to adjust ourselves to our environment, while the concepts of sacrifice and of redemption are atavistic survivals, powerful still but declining in strength as we learn to accept ourselves for what we are — unique creatures, limited and mortal, whose intelligence and adaptability have enabled us to survive in a morally neutral universe.

The third main difference between the religious and the irreligious world-pictures lies in their attitudes towards death. The religious man holds that life on earth is meaningful only in the context of eternity, and that communion between the living and the dead is a spiritual reality. This belief in a life beyond the grave seems, to the irreligious, a pathetic desire for survival, an attempt to find a palliative for the universal fear of death. We die utterly, and with the death of the body everything ceases, nor can we begin to speculate about non-existence:

> What words can say to me the words have said
> Out there where nothing happens since you are
> No longer there for things to happen to
> And there's no way of telling what is true
> You cannot find me any image for
> Our knowledge of our ignorance of the dead.[1]

The four poets whom I propose to consider in this chapter — Jack Clemo, F. T. Prince, R. S. Thomas, and Thomas Blackburn — all hold a religious view of life. The work of almost all English religious poets, whatever their formal beliefs may be, is permeated with Christian feeling and based upon Christian modes of thought, and these four poets conform to this common pattern. None of them is a devotional writer; one of them is certainly not an orthodox Christian; and another of them subscribes to dogmas which most

[1] Burns Singer, *Sonnets for a Dying Man*, XXIII.

Christians would regard as so lopsided as to smack of heresy. Yet, despite their doctrinal variety, all employ Christian concepts and reveal a Christian sensibility.

The most extraordinary of these four poets is Jack Clemo, who still lives with his mother in the four-roomed granite cottage on Goonamarris Slip in which he was born in 1916.[1] The son of an illiterate clay-worker who was drowned at sea in the First World War, Clemo has endured blow after blow, any of which would have crushed the majority of poets. He suffered his first attack of blindness when he was five; his formal education was ended by another attack at the age of thirteen; at eighteen his hearing began to show signs of damage, and for much of his adult life he has been stone-deaf. More than once he has regained the use of his faculties, and he refuses to learn Braille, since he believes that his bodily torments are sent by God as a trial of faith and as a mark of salvation. Indeed, the mainspring of his life is his belief in the Calvinist doctrine of Election.

Clemo has recorded his spiritual development in *Confession of a Rebel* (1949), where he observes that something of his religious outlook 'is implied in Kierkegaard's philosophy and in the work of modern Calvinists like Barth and Niebuhr, but I had reached it independently before I read any of their books'.[2] To talk of literary influences on such a man is scarcely relevant: Clemo's own terminology gives us a more helpful clue, when he tells us that 'the walls of our front room became adorned with the portraits of Browning, Spurgeon and T. F. Powys — the three men whose spiritual affinities with me were most obvious'.[3] We may add to this list the names of Coventry Patmore, Nietzsche, Thomas Hardy, and D. H. Lawrence — men whose writings have left a profound mark upon him, even if he has later experienced a revulsion against them.

Much of his verse is concerned with the relationship between religion and sex which, as he admits, has been a dominant theme in

[1] I take all the biographical facts about Clemo from Charles Causley's Introduction to Clemo's volume of poems, *The Map of Clay*.
[2] Jack R. Clemo, *Confession of a Rebel* (Chatto, 1949), p. 233.
[3] Ibid., p. 244.

his life. His admirably direct account of the matter lays stress upon the joy which his experiences have yielded:

... this unusual blend of Calvinism and erotic mysticism — the alternating stresses of dogma and sex from which all my education was derived — has brought much happiness into a life that would otherwise have been a very dark one.[1]

The second recurrent motif in his work is the conflict between Grace and Nature, as a result of which

a man's spiritual life passes from the control of the general Mood of Providence, which operates only through the laws of Nature, to the control of the Galilean Mood, the Will of Christ which subdues or adapts the tendencies of Nature when they impede the purposes of grace.[1]

The poems in which these themes are worked out are set in the weird, desolate landscape of the Cornish clay-pits where Clemo has spent all his life, and whence he draws the harsh, relentless imagery of his best verse.

In 'The Burnt Bush' the poet climbs with a girl to a dump where they find a bush:

> A fang of Nature from the cold
> And clay-purged sand: denied a clump,
>   She put forth one gorse-stump.

The girl lights a match and fires the bush; the pair then climb down to the fresher air:

> Fresh too was my desire.
> I looked upon her laughing play
> There in the gully's winding way:
> A dry cool breeze had bared her clay.
> Rain fosters sap and fashions mire,
>   But dry clay prompts the fire.
>
> She fired the gorse — fired too
> One gnarled old bush of Adam's seed
> Which in a cleft of naked need

[1] Ibid., p. ix.

Within my soul had fouled indeed
White purity, and as it grew
  Spread doubts in scent and hue.

Her hand held mine — and then
The flame leapt in and burnt the bush:
My soul knew smoke and fire, then hush
Of clay delivered from the push
Of Nature's sap: now in God's ken
  I stand unsoiled again.

This is, in some ways, a clumsy poem, but the repetitive images, the Biblical connotations of the burning bush, the unashamed reference to the soul, which a more sophisticated poet would hesitate to make, all combine to lend these verses a naked urgency and spiritual force.

Clemo is aware of the dark, cruel side of sexuality. In 'The Excavator', which is primarily a poem about the relationship of beauty to Christian worship, Clemo meditates upon one aspect of the excavator:

That broken-mouthed gargoyle
Whose iron jaws bite the soil,
Snapping with sadist kisses in the soft
White breasts of rocks, and ripping the sleek belly
Of sprawling clay-mounds, lifting as pounded jelly
Flower-roots and bush tufts with the reeking sand.
I fondle and understand
In lonely worship this malicious tool.

There is no need to comment on the Freudian significance of the embarrassingly explicit imagery: Clemo records that he wrote this poem on Sunday, 28 September 1946, partly as a result of reading the evidence given at the trial of Neville Heath, the sadistic murderer.[1]

Clemo's most remarkable and finely-disciplined love-poem is 'A Calvinist in Love', where even sensuality grows in a harsh soil and despises all that is warm, soft, and abundant:

[1] *Confession of a Rebel*, pp. 239–40.

This bare clay-pit is truest setting
    For love like ours:
    No bed of flowers
But sand-ledge for our petting. . . .

This truculent gale, this pang of winter
    Awake our joy,
    For they employ
Moods that made Calvary splinter. . . .

Our love is full-grown Dogma's offspring,
    Election's child,
    Making the wild
Heats of our blood an offering.

Even more original and impressive are those poems which spring from Clemo's renunciation of poetry in obedience to the claims of Dogma.[1] Just as Baudelaire would slash at a flower to punish the insolence of Nature, so Clemo wishes to trample on the foxgloves and blackberries which ensnare him and insult God:

I have no friends but things inanimate,
And taste no mood of God save Dogma's power.[2]

The protagonist of 'The Clay-Tip Worker' rejoices to pour sand, mud, and rock on the soil, thereby condemning it to ugliness and sterility:

Praise God, the earth is maimed,
And there will be no daisies in that field
Next spring; it will not yield
A single bloom or grass blade: I shall see
In symbol potently
Christ's Kingdom there restored:
One patch of Poetry reclaimed
By Dogma: one more triumph for our Lord.

The excavator, apart from being the cruel raper of the earth, is also a Christian symbol,

---

[1] See *Confession of a Rebel*, pp. 221-2. Hopkins made a similar sacrifice.
[2] 'The Traitor Child'.

> A Cross that lacks the symmetry
> Of those in churches, but is more
> Like His Whose stooping tore
> The vitals from the world's foul secrecy.

This ambivalent view of the excavator is difficult to justify, even if we can accept imaginatively Clemo's thoroughgoing Calvinism. Indeed the whole poem, 'The Excavator', is packed with too many concepts to be entirely successful, and as Clemo launches his attack on Art and Nature the language becomes strained and grandiloquent. Only in the concluding lines does the argumentative rhetoric give way to the stark intensity of poetry, as Clemo finds the terrible courage to praise God for

> Thy meaner moods, so long unprized;
> The motions of that twisted, dark,
> Deliberate crucial Will
> I feel deep-grinding still
> Under the dripping clay with which I am baptized.

The main weakness in Clemo's poetry is a verbal inflation that is a legacy of late nineteenth-century bankrupt Romanticism. The purity of Clemo's vision of himself as a clay phoenix is spoiled by the melodramatic language, the reverberating emotional clichés:

> Let my peak be smitten, then, I offer still
> No sufferer's creed from a sealed gallery.
> My soul foreknows its destined thrill
> Beneath the ashes and the oncoming moon,
> My phoenix-vision rising from the scorched heart.[1]

To remark on this technical inadequacy is not to deny the power of his religious faith or to belittle the courage which has sustained him through the years of darkness and of silence. Instead of dwelling on his failures we should be grateful for the handful of poems in which Clemo has fused his experience of suffering, his certainty of Christ's redeeming grace, his passionate response to the lunar strangeness of

[1] 'Clay Phoenix'.

the Cornish clay-pits, into a fully-achieved work of art. He has seen
Christ in the clay-pit, and made a true poem of his vision:

> I see His blood
> In rusty stains on pit-props, waggon-frames
> Bristling with nails, not leaves. There were no leaves
> Upon His chosen Tree,
> No parasitic flowering over shames
> Of Eden's primal infidelity.
>
> Just splintered wood and nails
> Were fairest blossoming for Him Who speaks
> Where mica-silt outbreaks
> Like water from the side of His own clay
> In that strange day
> When He was pierced.[1]

There could hardly be a more dramatic contrast to the poetry of
Jack Clemo than that of F. T. Prince (b. 1912) who, after receiving
his education in South Africa and at Oxford, and after his military
service in the war, began to follow an academic career in England.
Prince, who is a fine Shakespearean scholar and a Miltonist, and
Professor of English at Southampton University, has published
only two volumes of verse, *Poems* (1938) and *Soldiers Bathing*
(1954). Although his early poems, which some discriminating
critics regard as his most accomplished, lie beyond the scope of this
inquiry, it may be useful to make a few observations on their nature
and quality. Some of them are baffling, not because they are loosely
constructed, muddled, or careless, but because one senses, behind
their enigmatic strength, an unwillingness to do more than hint at
the reserves of pent-up emotion that the poet is reluctant to disclose
or unleash. The distinction of the writing, the exactness of the
epithets, the rippling, muscular strength of the language, the
fastidious rhythmical control, are everywhere unmistakable, whether
in the delicate precision of

[1] 'Christ in the Clay-Pit'.

In the frosty morning that his motions flatter
He kindles and where the winter's in the wood
I watch you dance him out on delicate shanks.
And lashes fall on a dark eye,
He sheds a silvery mane, he shapes
His thin nostrils like a fop's.[1]

the sonorous magnificence of

And barracks, fortresses in need of no vest save light, light
That to me is breath, food and drink, I live by effects
                of light, I live
To catch it, to break it, as an orator plays off
Against each other and his theme his casual gems, and
                so with light
Twisted in strings, plucked, crossed or knotted, or crumbled
As it may be allowed to be by leaves
Or clanged back by lakes and rocks or otherwise beaten
Or else split and spread like a feast of honey, dripping
Through delightful voids and creeping along long
                fractures, brimming
Carved canals, bowls and lachrymatories with pearls. . . .[2]

or the Yeatsian sensuousness and nobility of

I wish that when you call for supper, when
You sit down, guests and serving-men
May seem light-bearers planted on the stair,
Lights in the roof, lights everywhere:
So that as if you were a salamander
Your sensuality may wander
In a community of flames, and breathe
Contentment, savouring wine and wreath.[3]

The post-war volume, *Soldiers Bathing*, contains, besides the
title-poem, three early poems, translations from St. John of the
Cross, and a section entitled 'Love Poems', eight poems in this
group being composed in the manner of the seventeenth-century

[1] 'To a Man on his Horse'.
[2] 'An Epistle to a Patron'.   [3] 'To a Friend on his Marriage'.

K

Metaphysical poets. Whether pastiche is a defensible mode of poetry remains an open question. Donald Davie has argued that those who wander in the Imaginary Museum can scarcely avoid breaking the formal perfection of their verse by introducing into it some deliberate archaism, some element of pastiche. Eliot's adaptation of Laforgue and of the late-Elizabethan dramatic poets is familiar to every reader of modern verse; we know that Eliot and Pound adopted Gautier's *Émaux et Camées* as a remedy against the dilution of *vers libre*, Amygism, Lee Masterism, general floppiness; Charles Tomlinson's note on Section V of *Antecedents* indicates how difficult life can be for the highly self-conscious literary artist:

In rendering this from *Derniers Vers*, one cannot avoid the tone of (early) Eliot because Eliot himself has not avoided the tone of Laforgue.

This note suggests that Tomlinson is reluctant to embrace pastiche as a method of solving his problems: no such doubts inhibit that splendid Australian poet, A. D. Hope, who unashamedly writes poems of dazzling bravura in the manner of the mid-seventeenth and early eighteenth centuries. Even Robert Graves, that derider of the museum man, has proved his ability as a *pasticheur*. In his novel *Seven Days in New Crete*, which is set in the remote future, he invents a character named Quant, a philologist who, desiring to write a poem in that long-extinct language, English, forges a seventeenth-century love-poem. Graves reprints this enchanting forgery ('The Chink') in his next book of verse, without a word of explanation.

Strangely enough, the most succinct argument against pastiche comes from Ezra Pound, as reported by T. S. Eliot:

I remember that Pound once induced me to destroy what I thought an excellent set of couplets; for, said he, 'Pope has done this so well that you cannot do it better; and if you mean this as a burlesque, you had better suppress it, for you cannot parody Pope unless you can write better verse than Pope — and you can't.'[1]

[1] Ezra Pound, *Selected Poems*, edited with an introduction by T. S. Eliot (Faber, 1928), p. xxi.

Bearing this caution in mind, we may nevertheless admire Prince's ingenious handling of metre and of diction in these eight poems. He displays a cunning skill in mimicking certain characteristic features of the Metaphysical style — those daring, intricate contortions of the poetic argument, the sudden variations in rhythm, the disturbing changes of pace, the elaborate conceits, the bare simplicity of diction mingled with the use of recondite images drawn from an unusual branch of learning or from some incongruous field of activity. Certain of his conceits are worthy of John Donne, even if others are more reminiscent of John Cleveland. He catches the very accents and the rhythmical subtlety of Donne in the first poem, 'The Inn':

> Royal marriages were celebrated so,
> Before the year's intrigues began.
> A royal woman and a man
> Were joined like puppets to beget a love
> Imputed by the plot, and set to move
> Apart, together, as you come, I go
> To the unknown the way I do not know.
>
> That's in your arms, where now you know, and why.

Every poem boasts this kind of felicity, and we must allow that Prince has brought off a feat of considerable virtuosity. Yet without falling into the heresy of depreciating artifice, and of extolling sincerity as the chief poetic virtue, we are surely justified in feeling a profound dissatisfaction with a sequence of love-poems composed in an antique mode. It is significant that the most successful of these poems is the last one, 'The Question', in which he is furthest from mere pastiche; in which he is no longer making a brilliant archaeological reconstruction of a buried sensibility, but learning from Donne, as Yeats once had learned, a new concentration and richness:

> And so we too came where the rest have come,
> To where each dreamed, each drew, the other home
> From all distractions to the other's breast,
> Where each had found, each was, the wild bird's nest.

For that we came, and knew that we must know
The thing we knew of but we did not know.

We said then, What if this were now no more
Than a faint shade of what we dreamed before?
If love should here find little joy or none,
And done, it were as if it were not done,
Would we not love still? What if none can know
The thing we know of but we do not know?

For we know nothing but that, long ago,
We learnt to love God whom we cannot know.
I touch your eyelids that one day must close,
Your lips as perishable as a rose:
And say that all must fade, before we know
The thing we know of but we do not know.

Much as Prince may be indebted in this poem to his study of the
Metaphysicals, its note of tenderness, its tinge of Romantic longing,
and its peculiar fusion of human with divine love are deeply
personal and individual. There are other hints in the sequence of
Prince's growing concern with religious values; his translations
from St. John of the Cross may be a further sign of his turning
towards Roman Catholic mysticism; certain passages from 'The
Old Age of Michelangelo' suggest that he is much perplexed by the
nature of human love, and conscious of the despair in which it may
issue unless it is grounded in the Will of God:

I am naked in that sea of love
Which is an infinite savage glowing sea,
Where I must sink or swim. Cold, burning with sorrow,
I am naked in that sea and know
The sad foam of the restless flood
Which floats the soul or kills, and I have swum there
These fifty years and more,
And never have I burned and frozen
More than I have for you,
Messer Tommaso . . .

And the light fades from the sky, the dream dies in the stone
Slowly, I finish nothing I begin, and in my evening
Last torments and last light, torn hesitations
Between desire and fear, between desire and my disdain
— Emerging into dusky rooms, high halls, rich architecture
And the tawny roofs of Rome. For this love discovers only
The world's desert and death, the dusty prison
Where we have shut ourselves, or the sky shuts us.

The title-poem, 'Soldiers Bathing', is not only Prince's master-piece but the one poem directly inspired by the Second World War which can stand comparison with the best work of Owen and of Rosenberg. The man who has suffered 'the experience of war's horrible extreme', the lover of Italian art, the scholar aware of the European heritage in its glory and tragedy, the devout Catholic, and the accomplished poet, have united to achieve a poem of unfaltering grandeur and profound compassion. The language, although more open in texture and more relaxed than in the early poems, retains its former distinction; and whereas in his first volume Prince's subject-matter is often private and impenetrable, he is dealing here with a major public theme.

The poem opens with a scene of idyllic simplicity:

The sea at evening moves across the sand.
Under a reddening sky I watch the freedom of a band
Of soldiers who belong to me. Stripped bare
For bathing in the sea, they shout and run in the warm air;
Their flesh, worn by the trade of war, revives
And my mind towards the meaning of it strives.

Then, after observing the sweetness of the human body grown fragile and luminous after bathing, Prince recalls

Michelangelo's cartoon
Of soldiers bathing, breaking off before they were half done
At some sortie of the enemy, an episode
Of the Pisan wars with Florence. I remember how he showed
Their muscular limbs that clamber from the water,
And heads that turn across the shoulder, eager for the slaughter,

Forgetful of their bodies that are bare,
And hot to buckle on and use the weapons lying there.
— And I think too of the theme another found
When, shadowing men's bodies on a sinister red ground,
Another Florentine, Pollaiuolo,
Painted a naked battle: warriors, straddled, hacked the foe,
Dug their bare toes into the ground and slew
The brother-naked man who lay between their feet and drew
His lips back from his teeth in a grimace.
They were Italians who knew war's sorrow and disgrace
And showed the thing suspended, stripped: a theme
Born out of the experience of war's horrible extreme
Beneath a sky where even the air flows
With *lacrimae Christi*. For that rage, that bitterness, those blows,
That hatred of the slain, what could it be
But indirectly or directly a commentary
On the Crucifixion? And the picture burns
With indignation and pity and despair by turns,
Because it is the obverse of the scene
Where Christ hangs murdered, stripped, upon the Cross. I mean,
That is the explanation of its rage.

The poem ends, not with a simple reflection about the wickedness and horror of war, but with a subtle acceptance of evil as something strange, even beautiful. In his early poem 'Words from Edmund Burke' Prince uses a curious phrase:

                    and the wound now
Opens the red west, gains ground.

This image reappears in the last two lines of 'Soldiers Bathing', where it has been transformed into a symbol of great imaginative power. At the beginning of the poem we see a band of ordinary soldiers bathing on a beach; the reference half-way through the poem to *lacrimae Christi* prepares us for the final transfiguration of this sea-shore into a supernatural landscape where the Christian drama of the Fall and of Redemption is enacted:

        These dry themselves and dress,
Combing their hair, forget the fear and shame of nakedness.

Because to love is frightening we prefer
The freedom of our crimes. Yet, as I drink the dusky air,
I feel a strange delight that fills me full,
Strange gratitude, as if evil itself were beautiful,
And kiss the wound in thought, while in the west
I watch a streak of red that might have issued from Christ's breast.

Jack Clemo inhabits, physically and imaginatively, the world of
the Cornish clay-pits; F. T. Prince, tethered to no particular time
or place, moves from one epoch to another in the spiritual history
of Europe; R. S. Thomas's poetic landscape is the border country
between England and Wales. Thomas (b. 1913) is of Welsh
ancestry and, being stirred by the movement to revive Welsh
literature, taught himself, as an adult, the language of his forebears.
He is a country priest who was rector of Manafon from 1942–1954,
when he moved to a parish in another part of Wales.

Contemporary poets sometimes lament the fact that they are
isolated figures deprived of any secure place in society, the odd men
out in the anonymous mass who crowd together in the great wen
of suburbia. A priest in his parish knows that he is a member of a
community and is constantly aware of his responsibility for others
(it is worth noting that, in 'Soldiers Bathing', F. T. Prince feels this
sense of responsibility — 'soldiers who belong to me'). He is
brought face to face with birth, marriage, and death, with poverty,
pain, and courage, so that he is never far from the basic material of
poetry. If he is a country priest he may, while celebrating the liturgy
of his church, observe also the cycle of the seasons and listen to the
counterpoint of the natural against the divine order as the pagan
year and the Christian year turn, with the revolving earth, in their
separate but allied rhythms. The verse of our country clergy, from
Herbert and Herrick through Crabbe and Charles Tennyson-
Turner down to Andrew Young, has made its distinctive contribution to our literature: its main characteristics are a keen, unsenti-
mental observation of rural life, of men's customs, behaviour, and
beliefs no less than of birds, beasts, and flowers; a natural piety
which rejoices in the fruitfulness of the earth; a sense of Nature's

inexhaustible profusion and of the brief span which is allotted to men.

The verse of R. S. Thomas, the latest poet in this long and honourable line, besides possessing all these qualities, is distinguished by a rare harshness and pungency of concept and of phrase. Almost all his poems circle round two or three themes, to which he returns over and over again, seeking to become ever more lucid and articulate, paring away the surplus flesh of epithet and of explanation, stripping his language to the bone. These recurrent themes are: the life of the hill farmers who struggle to gain a bare living from the barren soil of the Welsh borders; his relationship as a priest to his parishioners and to the rest of his fellow-countrymen; the significance of the Christian faith, and the condition of man in the mid-twentieth century. His three main collections of verse, *Song at the Year's Turning* (1955),[1] *Poetry for Supper* (1958), and *Tares* (1961), are best regarded as a set of symphonic variations upon these allied themes.

Thomas is unfailingly aware that life on these lonely farms is hard and bitter, that ceaseless toil, poverty, and lack of education breed narrowness, ignorance, stupidity, and despair in the local farmers:

> This man swaying dully before us
> Is a muck farmer, to use his own words;
>   ... His rare smile
> Cracked as the windows of his stone house
> Sagging under its weight of moss,
> Falls on us palely like the wan moon
> That cannot pierce the thin cloud
> Of March. His speech is a rank garden,
> Where thought is choked in the wild tangle
> Of vain phrases.
>   Leave him, then, crazed and alone
> To pleach his dreams with his rough hands.
> Our ways have crossed and tend now apart;

[1] This volume contains nineteen new poems, the rest being reprinted from *The Stones of the Field* (1946), *An Acre of Land* (1952), and *The Minister* (1953).

> Ours to end in a field wisely sown,
> His in the mixen of his warped heart.[1]

Even if, for a moment, the beauty of the landscape and the bodily grace of a young farmer cause Thomas to forget the harsh underlying realities of life in these hills, he soon shakes off the comforting day-dream:

> Yes, I forgot the mixen,
> Its crude colour and tart smell . . .
> I sang him early in the fields
> With dew embroidered, but forgot
> The mixen clinging to his heel,
> Its brand under the ripped coat,
> The mixen slurring his strong speech.
> I made him comely but too rich;
> The mixen sours the dawn's gold.[2]

The tourist or the passing stranger who sees only an idyllic pastoral landscape cannot perceive the sickness and the decay that lurk behind the painted backcloth:

> Too far for you to see
> The fluke and the foot-rot and the fat maggot
> Gnawing the skin from the small bones,
> The sheep are grazing at Bwlch-y-Fedwen,
> Arranged romantically in the usual manner
> On a bleak background of bald stone. . . .

> Too far, too far to see
> The set of his eyes and the slow phthisis
> Wasting his frame under the ripped coat,
> There's a man still farming at Ty'n-y-Fawnog,
> Contributing grimly to the accepted pattern,
> The embryo music dead in his throat.[3]

Thomas has written a number of poems about Iago Prytherch, who stands for all the poor sheep-farmers of the district, a Welsh John Doe:

[1] 'The Muck Farmer'.   [2] 'The Mixen'.   [3] 'The Welsh Hill Country'.

> Who pens a few sheep in a gap of cloud.
> Docking mangels, chipping the green skin
> From the yellow bones with a half-witted grin
> Of satisfaction . . .
> So are his days spent, his spittled mirth
> Rarer than the sun that cracks the cheeks
> Of the gaunt sky perhaps once in a week.
> And then at night see him fixed in his chair
> Motionless, except when he leans to gob in the fire.[1]

Repulsive though this man may be to 'the refined/But affected sense', Thomas admires him for his ability to endure and pities him for the bleakness of his life. Yet this is to oversimplify the subtle complex of emotions which Prytherch arouses in the poet's mind. In 'Green Categories' Thomas contrasts the world made by Kant's systematizing intellect with the world known to the five senses of Prytherch:

> Here all is sure:
> Things exist rooted in the flesh,
> Stone, tree and flower. Even while you sleep
> In your low room, the dark moor exerts
> Its pressure on the timbers. Space and time
> Are not the mathematics that your will
> Imposes, but a green calendar
> Your heart observes;

The Welsh peasant and the German metaphysician speak, in every sense of the phrase, a different language:

> Yet at night together
> In your small garden, fenced from the wild moor's
> Constant aggression, you could have been at one,
> Sharing your faith over a star's blue fire.

One of his best meditations on this theme is 'Iago Prytherch', where Thomas recognizes that his poems are attempts to find an answer to the perplexities which crowd into his mind as he observes the life of the hill-farmers, so remote and different from his own:

[1] 'A Peasant'.

Fun? Pity? No word can describe
My true feelings. I passed and saw you
Labouring there, your dark figure
Marring the simple geometry
Of the square fields with its gaunt question.
My poems were made in its long shadow
Falling coldly across the page.

There is no answer, except an awareness of the humanity which all men have in common; and although Thomas never ignores the huge gulf separating the educated and the uneducated, or lapses into sentimental humbug about the virtues of the untutored heart, he acknowledges the fact that men are equal because all share the same essential needs. This comes out most forcibly in 'Affinity', most dramatically in 'The Hill Farmer Speaks':

The dirt is under my cracked nails;
The tale of my life is smirched with dung;
The phlegm rattles. But what I am saying
Over the grasses rough with dew
Is, Listen, listen, I am a man like you.

Thomas has recorded in a number of poems his attitude towards his own parishioners, towards Welsh Nonconformity, and towards the mass of his countrymen who belong neither to his Church nor to the Dissenting Chapels. He feels a bewildered, helpless anger at the general indifference to all that softens and enriches human intercourse, yet he is not blind to the instinctive animal vigour which courses through the graceless men of Wales, or to the pattern made by the sensual movement of their lives:

Men of the hills, wantoners, men of Wales,
With your sheep and your pigs and your ponies,
        your sweaty females,
How I have hated you for your irreverence, your scorn even
Of the refinements of art and the mysteries of the Church. . . .

You are lean and spare, yet your strength is a mockery
Of the pale words in the black Book,

And why should you come like sparrows for prayer crumbs,
Whose hands can dabble in the world's blood?

I have taxed your ignorance of rhyme and sonnet,
Your want of deference to the painter's skill,
But I know, as I listen, that your speech has in it
The source of all poetry, clear as a rill
Bubbling from your lips; and what brushwork could equal
The artistry of your dwelling on the bare hill?[1]

In 'Valediction' the note is far more bitter, for he portrays the farmer as a coarsened brute who has lost all kinship with the life of the soil and failed to attain man's potential stature:

You stopped your ears to the soft influence
Of birds, preferring the dull tone
Of the thick blood, the loud, unlovely rattle
Of mucous in the throat, the shallow stream
Of neighbours' trivial talk.
                For this I leave you
Alone in your harsh acres, herding pennies
Into a sock to serve you for a pillow
Through the long night that waits upon your span.

Thomas observes with a cold distaste the prevalence of mercenary calculation made even nastier by the cant of Welsh Nonconformity:

Who put that crease in your soul,
Davies, ready this fine morning
For the staid chapel, where the Book's frown
Sobers the sunlight? Who taught you to pray
And scheme at once . . . ?[2]

He confesses to a slow growth of hatred over the years

For men of the Welsh race
Who brood with dark face
Over their thin navel
To learn what to sell;

[1] 'A Priest to his People'.   [2] 'Chapel Deacon'.

although this hatred is tempered by love for

> those other
> Castaways on a sea
> Of grass, who call to me,
> Clinging to their doomed farms.[1]

Morgan, the Calvinist minister of his radio-play, *The Minister*, died worn out by his fanatical struggle against the inhuman force of Nature and the power of sin. Thomas is spared this doom by the warmth of his compassion and by the wider generosity of his faith, which is profoundly Christian but not sectarian. His verdict on the sour, sterile inheritance of Welsh Calvinism is uncompromisingly severe:

> Is there no passion in Wales? There is none
> Except in the racked hearts of men like Morgan,
> Condemned to wither and starve in the cramped cell
> Of thought their fathers made them.
> Protestantism — the adroit castrator
> Of art; the bitter negation
> Of song and dance and the heart's innocent joy —
> You have botched our flesh and left us only the soul's
> Terrible impotence in a warm world.[2]

Coupled with this rejection of the life-denying elements in Protestantism, there runs through Thomas's work a reverent love for the bleak, harsh land of Wales and for its people. A ramshackle Welsh village is, like every place in the world, part of the Divine Economy, and is seen by Thomas in that light:

> Stay, then, village, for round you spins
> On slow axis a world as vast
> And meaningful as any poised
> By great Plato's solitary mind.[3]

This most reticent of poets writes very little about his personal beliefs and inner life, or even about the major doctrines of Christianity. There are one or two poems, such as 'Judgment Day' and

---

[1] 'Those Others'.   [2] *The Minister*.   [3] 'The Village'.

'Earth', in which his probing scalpel lays bare the wretchedness of
his heart and the coldness of his faith; we are given a few meditations
on the Crucifixion, notably 'Pisces', 'The Musician', and, finest of
all, the richly austere 'In a Country Church', where nothing is heard
by the worshipper but the wind's song and the dry whisper of bats'
wings:

> Was he balked by silence? He kneeled long,
> And saw love in a dark crown
> Of thorns blazing, and a winter tree
> Golden with fruit of a man's body.

He knows that God is not bound by a sacred book or even by His
divinely-appointed Church, and reminds us that on the cruel, barren
hillsides of Wales there was love as well as hate, and that

> Among the fields
> Sometimes the spirit, enchained
>
> So long by the gross flesh, raised
> Suddenly there its wild note of praise.[1]

He sees Prytherch as a priest ministering at his

> stone altar on which the light's
> Bread is broken at dusk and dawn

and admits that he must turn to Prytherch as a penitent seeking
absolution,

> And come now with the first stars
> Big on my lids westward to find
> With the slow lifting up of your hand
> No welcome, only forgiveness.[2]

Thomas has watched the modern world, with its tractors and
television sets, invade the old order of the hillside community, and
he believes that, although it has brought certain material comforts,
'the cold brain of the machine' will destroy the traditional dignity of
the Welsh race. He is aware also of the grimmer threat which hangs
over all humanity now that, for the first time, man has acquired the

[1] 'The Cry'.   [2] 'Absolution'.

power to wipe out his own kind and even to make barren for ever the surface of the earth. Thomas utters no melodramatic warnings, no denunciations of man's wickedness, but he reminds us of the prospect before us. In the past, he says to the farmer,

> you waited till the ground was cool,
> The enemy gone, and led your cattle
> To the black fields, where slow but surely
> Green blades were brandished, the old triumph
> Of nature over the brief violence
> Of man. You will not do so again.[1]

The apparent simplicity and directness of Thomas's poems should not delude us into believing that they are naïve or artless. His curt tone, deliberate skirting of the regular iambic pentameter, reluctance to use full rhyme, and unwillingness to read nineteenth-century verse lest its emphatic rhythms should corrupt his sense of metre,[2] are all part and parcel of the exact, frugal craftsmanship which goes to the making of these poems. The territory which Thomas has chosen to cultivate may be strait and rocky, but he knows that beyond the Welsh border-country there stretches the world of European culture. The occasional unforced reference to Athens, Florence, Plato, Chaucer, Shelley, Coleridge, and Nietzsche is a sign that he has ready access to this more spacious world; one of his most incisive poems is called 'On a Line in Sandburg'; a memory of Kreisler's playing the violin suggests an analogy with the Crucifixion. The quietness of the verse may disguise from the casual reader the touches of sudden vividness, the stabs of piercing insight, that chequer the unemphatic calm of a sombre world in which the brightest light is yielded by the glint of wintry sun on ice, the brilliance of snow, and the gleam of blood. Much of his work has the quality of those lines by Robert Bridges which Yeats so greatly admired:[3]

> A glitter of pleasure
> And a dark tomb.

[1] 'To the Farmer'.
[2] See John Betjeman's Introduction to *Song at the Year's Turning*, p. 14.
[3] See W. B. Yeats's Introduction to *Oxford Book of Modern Verse*, p. xvii.

Half-a-dozen examples may serve to illustrate not only these characteristics of his verse, but also the telling economy of his metaphors and his mastery of the quickening epithet:

> I remember also the trapped wind
> Tearing the curtains, and the wild light's
> Frequent hysteria upon the floor.[1]

> It was the dark
> Silting the veins of that sick man
> I left stranded upon the vast
> And lonely shore of his bleak bed.[2]

> And yet their skulls,
> Ripening over so many prayers,
> Toppled into the same grave
> With oafs and yokels.[3]

> The buds swarming for the last time
> In boughs over the earth's hive.[4]

> The fox drags its wounded belly
> Over the snow, the crimson seeds
> Of blood burst with a mild explosion,
> Soft as excrement, bold as roses.[5]

> . . . he has lost all
> Property but the grey ice
> Of a face splintered by life's stone.[6]

> For Twm was true to his fate,
> That wound solitary as a brook through the crimson heather,
> Trodden only by sheep, where youth and age
> Met in the circle of a buzzard's flight
> Round the blue axle of heaven; and a fortnight gone
> Was the shy soul from the festering flesh and bone
> When they found him there, entombed in the lucid weather.[7]

An exacting critic, surveying the progress of Thomas's poetry from *The Stones of the Field* (1946) to *Tares* (1961), might argue that

[1] 'Death of a Peasant'. [2] 'Evans'. [3] 'The Country Clergy'.
[4] 'Fable'. [5] 'January'. [6] 'Hireling'. [7] 'The Airy Tomb'.

there has been comparatively little development; and that, as with Larkin, while the artistry has grown more refined and the sensibility more firmly disciplined, the emotional range has not greatly widened. Is there no danger that the curt reticence, the laconic compassion, will harden into a mannerism; has the time perhaps not come for Thomas to administer the last rites to Iago Prytherch? One answer is that half the poems in the two latest volumes are not specifically about the Welsh landscape or the Welsh people, although a lifetime's devotion to these themes cannot but colour everything that he writes. A second, more general, answer is that of all our post-war poets Thomas comes nearest to satisfying the criterion established by Yeats: 'As you know, all my art theories depend upon just this — rooting of mythology in the earth.'[1] For Thomas's faith is rooted in the soil of Wales, and also in the earth, which is our element, our planet, and our home. In a recent poem, 'Here', after tracing man's evolution, Thomas reminds us that we are what our crimes have made us and that if we reject the hope of heaven we are left only with the earth:

> I am a man now.
> Pass your hand over my brow,
> You can feel the place where the brains grow. . . .
>
> Why are my hands this way
> That they will not do as I say?
> Does no God hear when I pray?
>
> I have nowhere to go.
> The swift satellites show
> The clock of my whole being is slow.
>
> It is too late to start
> For destinations not of the heart.
> I must stay here with my hurt.

Jack Clemo, F. T. Prince, and R. S. Thomas, although they belong to different churches, are all Christian writers. Thomas

[1] *W. B. Yeats and T. Sturge Moore: Their Correspondence*, ed. Ursula Bridge (Routledge, 1953), p. 114.

L

Blackburn (b. 1916) is, like them, a religious poet, but it is not easy to discover the precise nature of his beliefs, either from his five volumes of poems or from his survey of contemporary poetry, *The Price of an Eye*. In early Victorian England, when Sir James Stephen was appointed Regius Professor of Modern History at Cambridge, 'Dr. Corrie, the Master of Jesus College, wagged his head at Archdeacon Hardwick. "Who would have thought we should have seen a live Gnostic walking about the streets of Cambridge? You know, my friend, in healthier times he would have been burnt".'[1] I am not sufficiently well versed in the niceties of Christian dogma to determine whether or not Blackburn is a Gnostic, but one can imagine him in the fourth century A.D. as the expounder of a daring heresy or as a devotee of one of those mystery religions which tried to synthesize the doctrines of the Church with the ceremonies and the esoteric teaching of remote Asiatic cults. Mistrusting all that is purely rational and cerebral, fascinated by myth and legend, preoccupied with suffering, evil, and mystical ecstasy, Blackburn holds that the task of poetry is to explore 'all those strange intentions and dynamics of the psyche, which every seer has been telling us about since the first cave-man scratched an outline on stone or buried his dead facing the sun-rise'.[2]

This is an ambitious undertaking, and it must be confessed that most of Blackburn's early poetry is weird stuff. In his first small collection, *The Outer Darkness* (1951), poems on traditional Christian themes lie cheek by jowl with a sequence called 'The Beast', in which religious and erotic motifs intertwine most curiously. This is melodramatic, hot-house poetry, the luxuriant, steaming images threatening to overpower us with their heady odours, the warm chromaticism of the verse cloying us with its over-sweet ripeness. The anthology *Springtime*[3] (1953) includes a sequence by Blackburn entitled 'The Black Way' and dedicated to Aleister Crowley, a grubby high-priest of Black Magic who rejoiced

[1] Noel Annan, *Leslie Stephen*, pp. 43–44.
[2] Thomas Blackburn, *45–60. An Anthology of English Poetry*, p. 19.
[3] *Springtime*, ed. G. S. Fraser and Iain Fletcher.

in the appellation of The Beast.[1] The prevailing obsession with darkness, evil, and damnation, like the conjuring up of a fantastic world in which Beauty and the Beast belong to the same order of reality as Lazarus and Jesus, is a symptom of something morbid and decadent in Blackburn's early work.

In his next volume, *The Holy Stone* (1954), Blackburn is already moving away from the heavy opulence of his first book. The poem on Pasiphae[2] is a sign that Blackburn is still enthralled by what is monstrous, sinister, and ecstatic in sexual and in religious experience; but the firmness of the writing, the bare simplicity and compassion of the final lines, keep the poem free from any taint of perverse gloating:

> White on the salted margin she lies down,
> 'Darkness, now take me, now, Darkness'; she sighs.
> Slowly it breeds upon her, throbs, grows full,
> The spirit carnal in a panting bull,
> Straddles her body with its heavy thighs. . . .
>
> I like to think they took her home to rest,
> Wiped her quite clean and fed her, till that day,
> Matted with ochre fur, the man-beast lay
> And whimpered naked on her childish breast.

Blackburn is no longer drawn towards the shuddering contemplation of perversity and of evil; his concern now is with spiritual exploration, with the mystery of birth and death, with such puzzles as the problem of identity, the reality of the visible world, the significance of time:

> Because our situation is elsewhere
> We do but grow into our vanishing.
> No act in time the actors can assuage;
> Their words are in the margin of the page.[3]
>
> Do you not feel your time unfolding strange
> Green shoots, indifferent to this shadow play,

[1] Blackburn has not included this sequence in any collection of his poems.
[2] This poem was originally the first section of 'The Maze'. It is reprinted as a separate poem, 'Pasiphae', in *A Smell of Burning* (1961).
[3] 'The Margin'.

> Deeper inbreathings that increase their range
> Until the clock's white face is burnt away
> And wait with some impatience on your change,
> Naked and wet and gasping; the next day.[1]

Although Blackburn is beginning in *The Holy Stone* to formulate his unique vision of the world, he has not yet discovered his own voice. Throughout this volume, and indeed to a lesser degree in the two succeeding volumes, we encounter images, cadences, rhythms, and even phrases lifted from W. B. Yeats. This is not a question of feeble imitation; nor is it a case of deliberate, sophisticated pastiche: it is almost as though Blackburn were possessed by Yeats's daimon and compelled, willy-nilly, to speak with his accents.

In the Fire (1956) marks another stage forward in Blackburn's poetic development. The Yeatsian echoes are still very strong, the fondness for bold rhythms, melodramatic imagery, and gong-like resonance is still pronounced; but Blackburn is moving towards a new lucidity of thought and a more resolute control of speech. 'The Clockwork' is an attempt to invest a political theme with a metaphysical and spiritual import, an effort to leave the realm of myth for the world of everyday experience or, rather, to endow our mundane actions with a transcendental significance. It is a poem in memory of Sophie Scholl and of those other German students who were executed for resistance to the Nazi régime. The clock-face symbolizes the world of mortality, of brutal calculation, that mechanistic universe from which William Blake struggled to set men free. Unlike the Nazis, who are prisoners of this metallic cage, Sophie Scholl escapes into a world of eternity where time is meaningless:

> No wonder that the clock-face laughed
> And every law of strain and stress
> To see that foolish woman roll
> Her body into emptiness;
> Could she not read her time of day?
> 'I read between the lines', she said,

[1] 'Intimations'.

'Those letters will not burn away
Though all my history book is dead.'
And there, as the appalling wheels
Her mortal circumstance unwound,
Stared through the clockwork and the blood,
And closed her lips and made no sound.

The one blot on these lines is the phrase 'appalling wheels': too
great a reliance on evocative, high-sounding adjectives is a deleterious legacy of Romanticism and a vice to which Blackburn
frequently succumbs.

The finest poem in the volume, 'The Unabiding', resumes the
main themes of 'The Margin', 'Intimations', and 'The Clockwork',
employing once again the images of clock-hand and of shadow-
play, and introducing the image of the double bed which recurs in
later poems, in order to emphasize that our consummation and our
destiny lie beyond time:

It is by vanishing that we draw near,
Though every step is grief, the scholars say.

To grasp the full force of these two last lines, one must turn back to
the first stanza in which Blackburn states the poem's theme:

Grief is the word that separate letters make,
By reading them with care, you rightly say,
A scholar's accurate heart must bend and break.
Because they read unclouded their vile day,
Ophelia, Lear and Timon all go mad.
Yes, but their dying makes the audience glad,
Who see their separate letters burn away
First in a sentence then a paragraph
And lastly the whole bonfire of the play.
You read each letter but have failed to catch
How discourse underneath their shadow-play
Persists beyond the burning of each match;
Though every word is grief, the scholars say.

In *The Next Word* (1958) Blackburn reaches his full poetic
maturity, giving us a series of poems on linked themes: the nature

of human identity; the relation between suffering and imaginative vision; the pleasures, shames, and inadequacies of carnal love; the need for sacrifice; and the desire for grace. 'The Lucky Marriage', a poem as cunningly organized as Larkin's 'Church-Going', even though its emotional pulse beats considerably faster, begins with a gay, light-hearted review of those fairy-tales in which Cinderella marries the prince or the kitchen boy weds the princess. Gradually, by a barely perceptible transition, the tone of the poem darkens as we are led to explore the meaning of personality, the significance of sexual passion, the rôle of suffering and rejection in the growth of spiritual insight:

> I mean the elder son and cherished sister
> Know but the surface of each common day;
> It takes the cunning eye of the rejected
> To dip beneath that skin of shadow-play
> And come into the meaning of a landscape.

The poem's abundant rhythmical *élan* and lyrical freedom ensure that we shall respond to the difficult argument without having to pause and stumble over its complexities; it is Blackburn's ability, here and in other poems, to sustain a melodic flow, to convey a sense of musical delight, which marks him as a poet of high accomplishment. In the final stanza, Blackburn recapitulates the several themes of the poem and we may recognize among them fragments of themes from earlier poems:

> And yet all images for this completion
> Somehow byepass its real ghostliness
> Which can't be measured by a sweating finger,
> Or any salt and carnal nakedness.
> Although two heads upon a single pillow
> May be the metaphor that serves it best,
> No lying down within a single moment
> Will give the outward going any rest;
> It's only when we reach beyond our pronouns
> And come into ourselves that we are blest.
> Is this the meaning of the lucky marriage

Which lasts forever, it is often said,
Between the goose-girl and the kitchen servant,
Who have no wedding ring or mutual bed?

In this volume one can still detect echoes of W. B. Yeats, although his accents have grown fainter and are no longer predominant. The last couplet of 'Old Man':

Although such dying comes most hard,
Follow we must; we must discard

may owe something to Yeats's 'Meeting':

But such as he for such as me —
Could we both discard
This beggarly habiliment —
Had found a sweeter word.

'The Arrow and the Target', 'The School of Babylon', 'The Next Word', 'In Canaan', and 'The Pronouns' have a Yeatsian lilt and fiery exultation; the refrain of 'The Holly Tree':

oh, Holly Tree,
Quicken my heart with your dark thorn

recalls one of Yeats's most haunting cadences:

O honey-bees,
Come build in the empty house of the stare.[1]

Yet in 'The Holly Tree' we find a sense of guilt, a renunciation of the flesh and a Christian longing for grace which sharply distinguish it from any poem by Yeats. Blackburn has at last found his own voice and in the process has learned to relate his old preoccupation with legend, myth, and fairy-tale to the moral and spiritual problems of all human beings.

The final stage of his poetic development is reached in *A Smell of Burning* (1961). A few of the poems in *The Next Word*, notably 'Hospital for Defectives', suggested that he was moving towards a new mode of speech in which the oracular cloudiness and ritual

[1] 'The Stare's Nest by my Window'.

declamation would be laid aside for a no less complex but more direct utterance. This promise is largely fulfilled in *A Smell of Burning*; and four of his earlier poems printed at the end of this volume conveniently illustrate the progress of his art. In one of them, 'Cnossos', he meditates on a theme which has never ceased to haunt him: the wounds and the terrors of childhood. Blackburn characteristically turns to legend in order to discover the significance of his pain and bewilderment, and grasps at two images which recur again and again in his poems — fire and the maze. If, he says, I

> search through creaking woods these Autumn days
> To trace a smell of burning to their tinder
> And find it is my heart that is ablaze,
> I know my road's returning to the centre,
> And think of Theseus in the Cretan Maze.

In 'A Smell of Burning', which is concerned with a similar theme, there is less self-dramatization and more self-knowledge; the emphatic rhythms clang less monotonously, giving way to a more flexible speech-pattern, and instead of dwelling on an unvaryingly tragic note Blackburn can now assimilate into his verse an ironical reflectiveness, even a dark, sardonic humour:

> After each savage, hysterical episode,
> So common with us, my mother would sniff the air
> And murmur, 'Nurse, would you look at the upstairs fire,
> I smell burning, something's alight somewhere' . . .
> But what mattered then was a trick of dodging flame,
> And keeping some breath alive in the heat of it.
> I have it still that inbred dodging trick;
> But always — when fire beset — I see them turning,
> My parents, to name elsewhere their sour fire reak,
> And touch myself and know what's really burning.

In his earlier poems Blackburn apparently finds certain themes, such as sexual jealousy and conflict between man and woman, too raw and painful to contemplate unless he keeps them at a safe distance, ringed within a fence of legend or elevated to the status of

myth. In 'Othello's Dream' and 'Dialogue' he identifies himself
with Shakespearean characters so that he may come to terms with
his towering rage and anguish. Even in 'At the Door', the impotent
fury seems to work itself out as part of a dream, or against the backcloth of a stage setting. But in 'Café Talk', and still more strikingly
in 'An Aftermath', he attempts neither to evade nor to mythologize
these intimate human relationships and perplexities. 'An Aftermath'
etches with a sharp intensity the bewildered terror of a child who
has witnessed a savage quarrel between her parents, their unconvincing pretence that nothing has happened, and the scene at the
child's bedtime the next evening:

> As bedtime came, he sensed her terror grow;
> Would it rise again, the petroleum sea, and pluck
> Their features away in its savage undertow;
> Must she ride their beaten minds down gulfs of shock?
> She undergoes, he thought, what we've undergone —
> Remembering, himself a child, how the house would rock —
> Will this circle of revenants never, never be done,
> Must ever the haunted ones to haunt come back?
> He turned and saw his daughter was asleep,
> His wife beside her in the faint blue air;
> It seems as well as furies of the deep,
> Moments of clarity we also share.

The reference to the furies is not a decorative classical allusion
paraded with a flourish to dignify a domestic brawl or to raise the
emotional temperature, but an image perfectly appropriate to the
theme of violence, hatred, and remorse. The poem is an answer to
the prayer at the end of 'Cnossos':

> O may I also leave the Maze and childhood,
> And come to Athens and my present day.

It is easy to draw up a formidable list of Blackburn's faults: the
looseness of phrasing, the jaunty carelessness of execution, which
crop up even in his latest volume; the elements of Yeatsian rhodomontade in his bardic utterances; his tendency to lapse into

Romantic argot, to boom away like a florid actor posturing in a costume drama; the wearisome reiteration of strident rhythms; the mechanical fluency which swells over into grandiloquence; the recourse to Myth as a facile means of making an oracular pronouncement. These blemishes are enough to repel the fastidious critic who regards intellectual rigour, a precise use of language, and emotional subtlety as the prime virtues of poetry. In my view, the rhythmical energy and melodic inventiveness of Blackburn's verse more than compensate for the lapses of taste and of judgement in his gaudier poems. His best work is free of these defects, and we can trace a steady development of his art over the past decade, a discarding of all that is meretricious and exhibitionist, a finer lucidity, a richer imaginative understanding, a maturing wisdom. He has, in his poetry, escaped from that labyrinth of images against which Yeats has warned us;[1] and he has recorded with memorable insight the parallel struggle of the human spirit to drag itself away from the nightmare of being trapped in its own darkness, to escape from the labyrinth of desire and mortality into peace and light

> Beyond the 'I am I' where 'I am you',
> Divine Volition, and your will is peace.[2]

However widely they may differ in their religious beliefs, Clemo, Prince, Thomas, and Blackburn are united in dwelling on the darker facets of human life; all accept the need for suffering and for sacrifice as the inescapable prelude to spiritual regeneration:

> Yet who is ever turned towards that journey
> Till deprivations riddle through the heart?
> And so I praise the goose-girl and the scullion
> Beside a midden or a refuse cart.[3]

Only by starting on this painful journey can we thread our way out of the maze and come into the meaning of the landscape.

[1] W. B. Yeats, *Autobiographies*, p. 225.
[2] 'The Journey', from Blackburn's first volume, *The Outer Darkness*.
[3] Thomas Blackburn, 'The Lucky Marriage'.

VI

METAPHYSICS AND MYTHOLOGIES

WHEN we talk of metaphysical poetry, we may be referring to poetry whose concern is to scrutinize or to solve various problems which have engaged the attention of metaphysicians for centuries past: the one and the many, unity-in-duality, the relationship of body, mind, and spirit, transience and permanence, mortality and immortality, the nature of the universe, the limits of free will, the exercise of moral choice, and a score of allied questions. Or we may use the term to describe the poetry written by a group of English poets in the early seventeenth century, and more recent verse which, in its deployment of imagery, handling of rhythm, and control of tone, owes much to Donne and to his followers.

There may well be poetry which is metaphysical in one of these senses only — Shelley is an obvious example of a poet who is preoccupied with the fundamental problems of metaphysics, and who yet has no stylistic affinities with the school of Donne. But frequently the two senses of the phrase will overlap or coincide. A poet whose mind is at full stretch, in an endeavour to resolve teasing perplexities and to make subtle philosophical distinctions, will often find the devices of the Metaphysical school peculiarly appropriate for his purposes. The most famous of these devices is the conceit, which is not primarily a fantastic ornament, a piece of verbal ingenuity, or a riotous manifestation of Baroque energy, but a means of keeping the warring elements of the poem in a state of perpetual tension without disturbing the poem's precarious equilibrium or shattering its emotional coherence.

Unlike the religious poet who assumes that there is a region in the universe which man cannot hope to penetrate, and a divine mystery which defies rational analysis, the metaphysical poet does not necessarily adopt the hypothesis of a reserved area whose sanctity he must acknowledge. He will not lighten his burden of moral and intellectual responsibility by calling on the aid of an omnipotent Providence, nor will he postulate any limits to the bounds of human speculation. The strain on the metaphysical poet is therefore likely to be greater than on his religious counterpart who, recognizing the weakness and the inadequacy of his own nature, looks elsewhere for sustenance. Some metaphysical poets, unable to bear the tension, have sought relief by surrendering to the claims of the divine: one thinks of Donne's turning from Apollo to the Christian God; and of Marvell's devoting his last twenty years to the Puritan cause, abandoning the exquisite poise of his earlier verse for the rough vigour of his propagandist street ballads. In our more sophisticated world one possible answer is for a poet to fashion an elaborate, self-contained myth as a means of reducing the bewildering diversity of experience into a harmonious unity. Thus Edwin Muir, although he saw everywhere in Rome symbols of the Incarnation and enjoyed a new tranquillity of mind in his last few years, was probably not an orthodox Christian, and as he lay dying said to his wife, Willa Muir, 'There are no absolutes'.

The four poets whom I propose to discuss in this chapter are all metaphysical poets in the first sense of the term: the verse of Norman MacCaig and of Thom Gunn bears also the unmistakable imprint of the Metaphysical style, while a similar, though fainter, imprint is visible in the work of Roy Fuller and of Ted Hughes; all except MacCaig have felt the need to draw on traditional mythology or to invent a new mythology of their own, either as a way out of the metaphysical impasse, or as a means of enriching their response to the world.

It is fascinating, though idle, to speculate on the direction which Auden's poetry would have taken had he remained in England during the war, or served overseas in the armed forces and then returned to live in his native land. The other leading poets of the 'thirties have gone their separate ways, and of their slightly younger contemporaries only Roy Fuller (b. 1912) has carried over into the nineteen-fifties and early nineteen-sixties the kind of concern with social values, the blend of Marxist historicism and Freudian analysis, which lent the verse of Auden and his coevals so pungent and curious a flavour. Too wary and sceptical even in his youth to believe that the redemption of society was at hand, Fuller has grown steadily more and more disillusioned as he contemplates the world in which we live. I quoted in my first chapter the ironical poem 'On Reading a Soviet Novel', which appeared in *Counterparts* (1954); five years earlier in his first post-war volume, *Epitaphs and Occasions* (1949), he strikes a similar note in several of the poems, notably 'Fathers and Sons', 'Hymn', and 'The Civilization', in which human history is portrayed as a meaningless cycle of frenzy, war, exhaustion, and a return to frenzy. Even when man appears to have won a victory, the triumph is hollow and transitory:

> When the hero's task was done
> And the beast lay underground,
> In the time that he had won
> From the fates that pushed him round
>
> He had space to contemplate
> How the peasants still were bled
> And that in the salvaged state
> Worms continued at the head.[1]

Yet disappointed in his hopes though he may be, Fuller has not retreated into mysticism, turned into an embittered right-wing propagandist, or lapsed into a cynical indifference. Throughout an epoch of fanaticism, tyranny, and superstition he has struggled to preserve the values held by left-wing intellectuals and agnostics in the days when Marxists offered a hope of a just society and Freudians promised to eradicate the cancer of sin and guilt.

Fuller is one of the most versatile and resourceful of post-war poets, a commentator on a wide variety of subjects, who enjoys ranging over an enormous field of interests. Such versatility may be a source of strength or of weakness; it may be a sign that a poet is

[1] 'The Hero'.

great enough to make poetry out of the most unpromising material, and that for him every object, every word, is charged with poetry, as one feels when reading Shakespeare or Pope; it may, on the contrary, indicate that the poet's imagination works at a low pressure, and that any feeble triviality is enough to start him prattling away in verse. In a mood of despondency Fuller admits the possibility that he is a poetaster with nothing to affirm:

> In this the thirty-ninth year of my age,
> Back from historic shores, it seems as though
> Any old subject fits into my verse;
> Whatever I put down is code for no.[1]

It is true that any incident, object, image, or stray thought may be the starting-point for one of Fuller's poems: among the themes treated in his verse are an advertisement for PEARCE DUFF'S CUSTARD in red neon letters, a lungworm, a spider in the bath, a performing dog, a kind of sweet called a jelly baby, a film of the 1936 Olympic games, a shop-girl arranging the window of a store, and a Freudian interpretation of Shakespeare. What saves his verse from being negative or trivial is the sharpness of his intelligence, and the zest with which he pursues his researches into the odd region where his fancy has led him. He has the omnivorous appetite for out-of-the way information that one finds in the early novels and essays of Aldous Huxley, and he shares Huxley's pleasure in communicating to his readers some recondite discovery, some faintly sinister fact, some disquieting observation about human behaviour or social custom. It is worth remembering that Fuller is not only a good poet but an admirable novelist, who brings to the writing of poetry the novelist's determination to make sense of the world in which men and women earn their daily bread, and to trace the patterns of life in the social community of which we are all members, whether we like it or not. He is an observer, a moralist, who, lacking any faith in a life after death or in a divine purpose, believes that man must come to terms with himself and his environment, in an

---

[1] 'Poem to Pay for a Pen'.

effort to solve the immensely complex problems which have been engendered by his struggle with nature in the course of his evolution.

If we examine the seven volumes which Fuller has so far published we shall find that a few themes continually recur. Since these themes are interrelated, our best plan is to take these volumes one by one, to note the entry of these themes, and to trace their reappearance, often in modified forms, in later volumes. In this way it should be possible to show that although his verse is multifarious in its subject-matter, tones, and moods, Fuller has persisted in his attempts to find an answer to the questions which have haunted him for over twenty years.

We need not linger over *Poems* (1939), a typical volume of the period, filled with unhappy echoes of Auden and containing the obligatory poem in memory of a friend killed in Spain. It is worth noting that Fuller is already fascinated by the sonnet-form; that one poem is called 'Variations on a Theme by Donne'; and that in one or two poems Fuller is already experimenting with the device of counterpointing the flat against the grandiloquent, the curt and matter-of-fact against the terrifying and the mythical.

With *The Middle of a War* (1942), Fuller is beginning to fashion a style of his own, although such poems as 'August 1940' and 'October 1940' are still completely overshadowed by Auden, and one phrase in the title-poem is so Audenesque that it sticks out like a cuckoo in the nest — 'The ridiculous empires break like biscuits'. But in this volume we meet for the first time the clear annunciation of those themes which we shall encounter in every subsequent volume: the calm, ironical scrutiny of the self; an inquiry into the nature of art and into its relevance for society; a meditation on the structure, the discontents, and the wretchedness of society; a sense of foreboding as he contemplates the course of history and the destiny of man, a dying species in a universe which is indifferent to him. He has already learned how to vary his tone of voice in order to achieve the required effect, and we can detect throughout this volume the expert craftsmanship which is so characteristic and pleasurable a feature of his work. 'January 1940' is a good example of this. Fuller wants to emphasize the freakishness of poets and he does this by using subtly belittling words, by evoking grotesque images, and by writing very short sentences arranged in irregular couplets, thereby forcing the reader to emphasize a rhyme-word at an inappropriate moment:

> Water inflated the belly
> Of Hart Crane, and of Shelley.
> Coleridge was a dope.
> Southwell died on a rope.
> Byron had a round white foot.
> Smart and Cowper were put
> Away. Lawrence was a fidget.
> Keats was almost a midget.

When he wants to suggest that this kind of abnormality is a pre-requisite of artistic genius, he makes a skilful transition to a tone from which all mockery is excluded, and he does this by slightly modifying the metre, by altering the pace of the verse and by darkening its texture:

> I envy not only their talents
> And fertile lack of balance
> But the appearance of choice
> In their sad and fatal voice.

Two of the most incisive expressions of Fuller's misgivings about man and his future occur in a nightmarish poem 'The Growth of Crime' and in 'Harbour Ferry'. In the first of these poems, a sailor in bed with a whore hears voices whispering to him:

> Each one has only his little world
> Of sensuousness and memory
> And endeavours with the ghastly shell,
> The savage skin, the cruel eye,
> To save it: in that animal's
> Rank den and bed of love it dies.

In 'Harbour Ferry' he envisages the destruction of man, the coming of the time when our species has vanished from the face of the earth:

> ... the forces
> Controlling lion nature
> Look out of the eyes and speak:
> *Can you believe in a future*
> *Left only to rock and creature?*

This profound unease about man's nature and about the fate which lies in store for humanity pervades the entire volume. Indeed it is difficult to understand how anybody who denies the providence of God can escape sorrow and despair when he reflects that the beauty, the variety, the excitement, and the fascination of the world are meaningless, and that man is only a complex animal whose very cleverness makes him mutilate himself and destroy all that he has built. Fuller is too honest a writer to shrink from following his beliefs to their logical ends, and in all his poetry he accepts uncomplainingly the inevitability of defeat, while extracting all the pleasure and consolation he can from the absorbing struggle.

During his spell in the Forces, Roy Fuller was stationed for a while in East Africa. Living in this magnificent region — with its tropical coast-lines, its enormous plains and forests where lion and rhinoceros still wander untamed, its green hills, and its primitive tribes — appears to have liberated new energies in Fuller, to have extended the range of his verse and to have suffused it with a colour and a melody which, though partially discarded in his next two volumes, illuminate and enrich his most recent poems. Aldous Huxley has argued that nobody who has lived in the tropics is likely to accept the Wordsworthian doctrine that Man and Nature are indissolubly wedded in spiritual harmony, and Fuller seems to have experienced with unusual intensity the feeling that the natural world and the animal kingdom are utterly alien to man. After describing the giraffes most precisely and vividly, he records his conclusions as they move away:

> So as they put more ground between us I
> Saw evidence that these were animals with
> Perhaps no wish for intercourse, or no
> Capacity.

M

> Above the falling sun
> Like visible winds the clouds are streaked and spun,
> And cold and dark now bring the image of
> Those creatures walking without pain or love.[1]

In 'Crustaceans' he observes with a fascinated disgust the monstrous'
obscene otherness of crabs on the beach;[2] in 'The Plains', however,
the sight of a lion, 'loose, suede, yellow', accompanied by 'a pair of
squint hyenas', both reminds him of our history:

> The archetypal myths
> Stirred in my mind

and serves as an emblem of our condition:

> The animals gallop, spring, are beautiful,
> And at the end of every day is night.

But he returns again in 'October 1942' to his belief that the animals
yield no clues which may help us to solve the riddle of human
existence:

> For what can be explained? The animals
> Are what you make of them, are words, are visions,
> And really they are moving in dimensions
> Impertinent for us to use or watch at all.

There are two or three fine poems about the relationship of
European civilization to the tribal life of the Africans, about the
way in which our commercial values are destroying a primitive
mode of life and turning a cruel, superstitious, but meaningful
ritual of behaviour into a motiveless, degrading existence in shanty-
towns. A few lines from 'The Green Hills of Africa' illustrate some
of Fuller's characteristic qualities:

> The girls run up the slope,
> Their oiled and shaven heads like caramels.

[1] 'The Giraffes', from *A Lost Season* (1944).
[2] In a later poem, 'Meditation', printed in his first post-war volume, *Epitaphs and Occasions*, he draws on his memory of these crabs:

> While outside the demon scientists and rulers of the land
> Pile up the bombs like busy crabs pile balls of sand.

> Behind them is the village, its corrugated
> Iron and, like a wicked habit, the store.
> The villagers cough, the sacking blows from the naked
> Skin of a child, a white scum on his lips.
> The youths come down in feathers from the summit.
> And over them all a gigantic frescoed sky.

One notes here the brilliant descriptive touch about the girls' heads; the acute social observation; the economy with which he contrasts the old and the new ways of life; the sense of the world as a place in which human beings play out their lives against an enormous mythical background. Perhaps the counterpointing of the old and the new, the splendour and the squalor, is a shade too mechanical and slick; the propriety of comparing a store to a wicked habit is dubious. I suspect that this is merely a reminiscence of Auden, and that *wicked*, like *improbable* and *appalling*, is a vogue-word which in the early nineteen-forties was an essential part of every fashionable poet's wardrobe.

A Lost Season also contains a number of poems about the inner significance of the war and of the daily news

> That glares authentically between the bars
> Of style and lies . . .

>   . . . it says the human features
> Are mutilated, have a dreadful lack.

> It half convinces me that some great faculty,
> Like hands, has been eternally lost and all
> Our virtues now are the high and horrible
> Ones of a streaming wound which heals in evil.[1]

There are certain other poems which both recapitulate the themes of his earlier work and foreshadow the ways in which his later verse was to develop. Thus, in 'A Wry Smile' which, like 'The Middle of a War', is a poem of self-scrutiny, we can detect a note of quizzical, deprecating mockery levelled at his own image in the mirror — a note that re-echoes throughout his next three volumes. 'Winter in

[1] 'October 1942'.

England', a poem about man's predicament in a world torn by fear
and hatred, is a sonnet-sequence, a form which Fuller was again to
adopt in two of his most ambitious poems, 'Mythological Sonnets'
and 'Meredithian Sonnets'. 'The Emotion of Fiction' is a discourse
on the nature of art and of myth, a topic to which Fuller returns
over and over again in the post-war years.

In his first two post-war volumes, *Epitaphs and Occasions* (1949)
and *Counterparts* (1954), Fuller has eliminated much of the freedom
and spaciousness that characterize his East African poems. His verse
is now tighter and more constricted, the tone is drier, the humour is
wry, the smile is painful, as though he has bitten a juicy fruit and
found it unpleasantly tart. The elegance of his versification, his
reliance upon antithesis and paradox, his recourse to a defensive
irony and disdain as a means of keeping weariness at bay and of
scrutinizing and checking his reserves of pent-up emotion, are signs
that he has said farewell to his youth, put his Muse on short rations
and armed himself with sharp weapons in order to withstand a long,
dreary siege.

The 'Dedicatory Poem' in *Epitaphs and Occasions* sets the tone
for these two volumes: political disillusion, lack of faith in the
future, a gnawing fear that his creative powers are decaying, coupled
with a conviction that the most urgent task of poetry is to speak the
truth. Fuller's resolve to obey this duty and to endure bravely the
evil days to come lends these post-war collections a stern dignity:

> And let the poetry be soon forgotten
> In which the human animal seems rotten.
> But, time, keep through whatever wretched ages
> May be in store, the few courageous pages.
>
> Reader, remember that behind the worst
> There was of all resolves the writer's first,
> The one neglected for its imagery —
> To be as truthful as reality.[1]

In 'Poem to Pay for a Pen', Fuller acknowledges that art may do
more than mirror reality, that it

[1] 'Tailpiece'.

Resolves and then transcends the mortal pain.

His deft commentaries on the artistic process and on individual writers such as Chekhov, Dorothy Wordsworth, Emily Dickinson, Gide, Ibsen, and Proust, may be a means of seeking a cure for his despondency at the wretchedness of the times. He finds little reassurance in scrutinizing himself or the political scene: in a number of autobiographical poems he records his wavering faith in Marxism, his misgivings about the future of mankind, and his own tragi-comic inability to act or to make decisions. One such poem comes dangerously near self-parody:

> A strange dog trots into the drive, sniffs, turns
> And pees against a mudguard of my car.
> I see this through the window, past *The Times*,
> And drop my toast and impotently glare.[1]

'The Divided Life Re-Lived', 'Meditation', 'Poem to Pay for a Pen', 'Translation', and 'The Fifties' convey a deep-rooted weary despair at the spectacle of human stupidity and fanaticism:

> I do not know which are the most obscene:
> Poets profoundly sceptic, scared, unread;
> The leaders monolithic in their mania;
> Or the unteachable mass, as good as dead.[2]

Fuller seems to rally in 'Poet and Reader', the last poem of *Counterparts*, where he suavely defends himself against the charge of being gloomy and morbid, and in his next volume, *Brutus's Orchard* (1957), he casts off the oppressive mood which weighs on him so heavily in the two previous collections. Although the Metaphysical tautness and wit remain a marked feature of his style, the sense of exhaustion and of defeat, the note of sour distaste, the faint nausea at the acrid stench of the world have vanished. The structure of the verse is still as beautifully articulate as ever, but the bones of his poetic argument are now decked with warm, sensuous flesh. Even a study of the lungworm, instead of giving rise to a bitter grimace

---

[1] 'Inaction'.   [2] 'Poem to Pay for a Pen'.

at its disgusting cycle of existence, fills the poet with a puzzled
wonder at this fantastic series of mutations. The lungworm itself
points the moral:

> What does this mean? The individual,
> > Nature, mutation, strife?
> I feel, though I am simple, still the whole
> > Is complex; and that life —
> A huge, doomed throbbing — has a wiry soul
> > That must escape the knife.[1]

While Fuller does not hope for very much from the future, 'now
the state of nations/Threatens a burnt-out strain', he accepts the
possibility, in 'The Ides of March' and in 'Expostulation and Inadequate Reply', that by making a firm choice and practising the
virtue of endurance, man will survive this cold age of anxiety and

> > find the new,
> Delicate but sure republic of the crocus,
> The warm fraternal winds, the growing strength
> Of wheat and apple's equal luxury.[2]

Yet Fuller holds that even if we avoid nuclear annihilation we are a
dying species on a planet doomed to perish. It is a measure of his
new-found energy and surging vitality that the prospect evokes
some of the most lyrical poetry he has ever given us:

> When this race has vanished, who
> Will observe the silvered yew
> Springing out of pits of dark
> In the breathings of the park,
> Or the calculable rise
> Of the strangely blazing skies
> Signalling a prince's woe?[3]

Even the vision of man's history as a momentary episode in the
enormous time-span of the universe takes on a grandeur which

[1] 'Autobiography of a Lungworm'.
[2] 'Expostulation and Inadequate Reply'.   [3] 'Night Piece'.

recalls the sombre yet magnificent cosmic pessimism of *The City of Dreadful Night*:

> Ages piled on the planet's flank that freeze
> With inconceivable immobility;
> And far back in the wastes the tiny span
> Of the erect and big-brained Primate, man.[1]

In the 'Mythological Sonnets' which end this volume, and in the 'Meredithian Sonnets', published in his *Collected Poems* (1962), Fuller passes beyond the borders of metaphysical speculation into the realms of myth. Just as his wartime sojourn in East Africa released certain potentialities, so this journey into mythological territory has irradiated his verse with a new lustre and melodic richness. The old wit and alert social observation are still there:

> The worker columns ebb across the bridges,
> Leaving the centre for the few ablaze.
> In bars, fox terriers watch their masters raise
> Glass to moustache. . . .
> > So this is the thing it is,
> He says aloud, to live in mortal cities —
> Haunted by trivial music, stomach tensed.[2]

But more striking is the mingled horror, awe, and exultation with which he roams through the mythological landscapes, celebrating the enormous power of sex. He moves backwards and forwards through time, encompassing the modern world, Greek legends, and Stone Age man; and he reminds us that, far from being fanciful tales, the myths are pointers to the history of our race and symbolic representations of our innermost desires:

> But could mere images make even now
> Ears drum with lust, the chest run secret shame?
> The myths are here: it was our father's name
> The maiden shrieked in horror as she turned
> To wrinkled bark; our dearest flesh that burned
> Straddling her legs inside the wooden cow.[3]

[1] 'To Posterity?'.
[2] 'Meredithian Sonnets', I.   [3] 'Mythological Sonnets', XVII.

Fuller's verse is so unfailingly lively, intelligent, and resourceful, and is composed with such masterly skill, that it seems churlish to end on a note of critical dissatisfaction. Yet, surveying his poetry as a whole, one is conscious that his world is limited, fragmentary, and evanescent. The spider in the bath, the lungworm, the African warriors, the mythical heroes, are, like Fuller's own image in the mirror, insubstantial creatures lacking a dimension: their lives, however fascinating to an observer, are brief and shadowy, fading into darkness, deprived of any ultimate significance. But even though he may not command that unifying vision of life which we ask of a major writer, we have cause to be grateful to a man who has practised his art and maintained his standards with such resolution and skill through the war years and the dreary post-war decades. None of his contemporaries has covered a wider range of subject-matter or written a greater number of incisive short poems which yield a comparable pleasure and linger so long in the memory.

Unlike Roy Fuller, who has attempted to survey the ramifications of contemporary society and to diagnose the sickness of man as a political animal, Norman MacCaig seldom makes any reference to current affairs or hazards a generalization about the state of the world. He concentrates his attention upon certain basic metaphysical problems, such as the nature of identity, the relationship of the perceiver and the perceived, the power of the mind to endow a landscape or an object with shape and meaning. Even in his love poems he is intent on analysing the mode of love's operation, the ways in which it can transform a person's inner life, either by creating order, unity, and peace out of chaos, or by shattering the principle of harmony in the mind so that chaos is come again. The self in its relations with one other individual; the self in its perception of the visible world and in its consciousness of the universe: these themes occur in poem after poem.

MacCaig (b. 1910) is a Scot who, after taking a degree in Classics at the University of Edinburgh, his native city, became and has remained a schoolmaster (it is likely that an English poet of comparable talent would soon have found a niche in the literary world of London). He was one of the contributors to *The New Apocalypse* and to *The White Horseman*, anthologies designed to display the wares of the self-styled Apocalyptics, a group of poets who enjoyed a brief notoriety in the nineteen-forties and whose stock today is extremely low. MacCaig's first two collections of verse are so greatly inferior to his three subsequent volumes, *Riding Lights* (1955), *The Sinai Sort* (1957), and *A Common Grace* (1960), that we can ignore them completely and devote ourselves to his mature work.[1]

He is, in both senses of the term, a metaphysical poet. His wit, his reliance upon the conceit, his delight in playing with paradox and antithesis, his fondness for a close-knit argument as he teases out the thread of a subtle philosophical disquisition, his skill in maintaining a perilous equilibrium while dancing along the knife-edge of a daring speculation — all these are signs that he has studied to good effect the practice of the Metaphysical poets. There is no question of pastiche in his vocabulary, in his images, in his rhythms, or in the texture of his verse; but he owes much to his reading of the Metaphysicals and he has clearly fallen under the spell of John Donne, being one of those whom, to quote Mario Praz, 'the rhythm of thought itself attracts by virtue of its own peculiar convolutions'. His characteristic approach to experience is succinctly defined in the last stanza of 'Summer Farm':

> Self under self, a pile of selves I stand
> Threaded on time, and with metaphysic hand
> Lift the farm like a lid and see
> Farm within farm, and in the centre, me.

Some of MacCaig's most beautiful poems are descriptions of a landscape or a seascape. He portrays with a vivid immediacy the exact physical contours of a scene and of the objects in that scene, evoking their sensuous qualities with an unfailing accuracy. Yet even in his most direct transcriptions of the visible world he is never content merely to reproduce a physical likeness: he wants to make us aware that the simplest objects are part of a marvellously com-

---

[1] A fourth volume, *A Round of Applause* (1962), appeared after this chapter was written.

plex system of interrelationships, which we can explore by means of
our five senses and by letting our minds play upon this elaborate
network. What might degenerate into a pretentious and arid piece
of scholastic logic-chopping is saved from this disaster by the alertness of MacCaig's observation and by the vivacity of his five senses.
He is, moreover, no bookish recluse, but a man who knows and
loves the countryside, who has fished the lochs and rivers, climbed
the mountains, and studied the wild life of his native Scotland.

The enchanting wit, the melodic ease, the rhythmical subtlety of
these descriptive poems do not readily lend themselves to analysis.
There comes a point when criticism can no more anatomize the
felicities of language than it can dissect the shape of a tune. One
either responds or fails to respond to lines such as these:

> Long islands at their cables ride
> The double talk of the split tide
> > And a low black rock pokes out
> > From caves of green its dripping snout.[1]

> That blueness is what pine-tips, weathered thus
> And backed with only pine-tips, make of air,
> Region of compromise which they two share.
> Their growth exceeds them, leaking inches up
> Till the stain fails in air too luminous.[2]

> Clouds overhead swim winsomely their white
> Cherubic hull-shapes on a race of light
> Where boats might sail as truthfully as these
> That swoop and dip in the half-dowsing seas.

> The seas half-dowse the houses that race still
> And stand headlong. Foam rushes by the sill
> And spurts as roses up till gables fret
> With foam as lace as roses, whitely wet.[3]

In 'Moor Burns' MacCaig attempts to convey the total impact of a
landscape on all his senses and to evoke the sensuous confusion that
drifts through his memory: paradoxically, he must employ language

[1] 'Clachtoll'.
[2] 'Bloom on Pine-Trees in August'.   [3] 'Regatta, Plockton'.

with a more than usual accuracy in order that his memory of confusion may be precise:

> Sound, so remembered, so can tangle wit
>
> That senses in confusion speak more clear,
> Sight being sound and light being born of water.
> And with remembering I am scarcely here
>
> As though space also were translated.

One finds in 'Half-built Boat in a Hayfield' a similar deliberate
intermingling of land and sea, the effect being to enhance the distinctive qualities of the objects described and yet at the same time,
in the true Metaphysical vein, to fuse them into a rich synthesis:

> Rye-grass was silk and sea, whose rippling was
> Too suave to rock it. Solid in the sun,
> Its stiff ribs ached for voyages not begun.

Occasionally he sketches not only the visual elements of a scene
but gives us a synoptic view of a landscape, in which stone, plant,
water, beast, fish, and bird are caught up in earth's diurnal course,
obedient to savage, inhuman rhythms:

> Prowling like cats on levels of the air
> These buzzards mew, or pounce: one vole the less,
> One alteration more in time, or space.
> But nothing's happened, all is in control
> Unless you are the buzzard or the vole.[1]

'Spate in Winter Midnight' delineates with remarkable economy and
strength the way in which the noise of the streams in flood binds
together in a common panic the wild life of the countryside. One
notes admiringly that MacCaig's art can encompass the immensity,
the mythical grandeur of Nature — 'Troys of bracken and Babel
towers of rocks' — and yet limn with the delicacy of a miniaturist
the heraldic figure of the sleeping adder:

> Through Troys of bracken and Babel towers of rocks
> Shrinks now the looting fox,

[1] 'Treeless Landscape'.

Fearful to touch the thudding ground
And flattened to it by the mastering sound.
And roebuck stilt and leap sideways; their skin
Twitches like water on the fear within.

Black hills are slashed white with this falling grace
Whose violence buckles space
To a sheet-iron thunder. This
Is noise made universe, whose still centre is
Where the cold adder sleeps in his small bed,
Curled neatly round his neat and evil head.

It is hard to illustrate the nature and the quality of MacCaig's
love-poetry by means of short extracts, because any abbreviation of
his slowly unfolding, ruthlessly exploratory argument, diminishes
its forensic impact. His love-poems never describe the physical
characteristics of the beloved; they seldom portray her moral
features; nor do they attempt to suggest the range of emotions
awakened by the sexual act, to sketch the lineaments of gratified
desire. They are, primarily, metaphysical inquiries into the essence
of love, and into the painful intricacies of a unique relationship
between two people.

MacCaig sees love as a force charged with supernatural energy
that can transfigure a mode of life, or even bring into existence what
formerly slept in embryo or in chaos. Love may do

> What the day does when it holds up a morning

and the world's darkness is buried at daybreak:

> Last night has buried all its ancestors
> And we're gravediggers too. Give me my answer
> And see it clap and crow that new hour in
> That sends my dead men bundling off together.[1]

He seldom strikes this note of confident affirmation: although love
may lend substance to what has been shadow and unreality, the
world thus created is one of tension, ambiguous meaning, doubt,

[1] 'Be Easy'.

whose mode of action is a desperate striving to clutch at an elusive joy. He frequently uses cosmic imagery, less in order to hint at the supernatural intensity of sexual passion than as a means of asserting that lovers are a sort of universe. The following passages yield the characteristic flavour of his love-poetry:

> For mile and moment are no larger than
> Each other is; and that is less than what
> Divides one thought of you from another thought;
> And that is nothing — space to hold a man
> It must be, though, since taking your thought from me
> Leaves me and nothing; for I'm a fantasy
> Your thoughts unghost into reality.[1]

> No parliament of beasts or flowers
> Utters laws more fierce than ours
> By which we burn the sun and kill
> The dark with darkness; all to prove,
> One useless moment, that death will
> Go blindfold by our dying love.[2]

>   ... I make
> A knot of seasons where time's end is one
> With his beginning, and for your graceless sake
> Sit, a small chaos awaiting your word; for none
> That I can speak has power unless you, too,
> Utter what makes a world of me and you.[3]

> Else I'd be off into the half of space —
> And that's nowhere — to search for you with my
> Wild undiscovering light. But you are here
> Fast in the shadow love heaves in the sky:
> And these unnatural stars you brighten shine
>   To show you are half mine.[4]

The danger of this method, which leans so heavily on the riddling paradox, is that the ingenuity of the conceits, the tortuous progression of the argument, may stifle the emotional life of the poem.

[1] 'Information'.   [2] 'Sad Cunning'.
[3] 'In No Time at All'.   [4] 'Shadow of Love'.

In 'Particular You' the metaphysical discourse on particulars and universals is counterpoised by the bodily presence of a real woman:

> ... and universals gather where
> Your hands lie still or light falls on your hair.

In 'Growing Down' MacCaig seems fascinated by the theory which finds language more and more metaphorical as it is traced back in the past, rather than by the woman who transfigures the cold air of 'the little room inside the skull'; while in 'Poem for a Goodbye' we admire the dexterity with which he has twisted the Metaphysical true-love knot, but do not care much about the lovers' ultimate reunion. In his best love-poems, however, among which I should include 'Gifts', with its candid, dignified avowal of pain and unhappiness, and the serene 'Two Ways of It', we find a noble gravity, a concentrated passion, and an urgent resolve to illuminate the most perplexing facets of the love relationship. Because of these qualities, he shares with Robert Graves the distinction of having written the finest love-poems in the language since the death of Yeats. The poem 'Too Bright a Day', short though it is, may prove that this is not extravagant praise:

> I live invisible (in my whole sky
> That is the light of where you are)
> Calling the night to welcome my
> Sad and procrastinating star,
> Which will not leave, as it must do,
> Its short conjunction here with you.
>
> Light so engrossing cannot show
> More than itself. I fade in it
> And have no shadow even to throw.
> But when I leave you, I'll commit
> Such darkness on myself you'll stare
> At the great conflagration there.

Perhaps MacCaig's most original poems are those in which he speculates on certain key problems of metaphysics, without either relaxing the rigour of the argument or letting his verse become slack and arid. The nature of time, of existence, and of identity, the meaning of chaos, the omnipresence of mortality which involves every creature and every inanimate object — such are the themes on which he composes his variations. In 'Ego' he surveys the stars, water, a tree, a rose, and tries to relate them all to his own mode of being, for

> ... they prefigure to my human mind
> Categories only of a human kind.

MacCaig rephrases an old philosophical commonplace, and then gives it a sudden twist, revivifying his argument with the shock of surprise that is one of poetry's most effective weapons:

> Tree
> And star are ways of finding out what I
> Mean in a text composed of earth and sky.
>
> What reason to believe this, any more
> Than that I am myself a metaphor
> That's noticed in the researches of a rose
> And self-instructs a star? Time only knows
> Creation's mad cross-purposes and will
> Destroy the evidence to keep them secret still.

When snow 'Stages pure newness on the uncurtained land', it may bring a similar revelation that every object exists in its own right. MacCaig continues the theatrical metaphor in the poem's last three lines:

> And the hill we've looked out of existence comes
> Vivid in its own language; and this tree
> Stands self-explained, its own soliloquy.[1]

MacCaig lacks Wordsworthian piety nor has he any feeling of warm sympathy with Nature, any belief in her reconciling, beneficent power; but his poetry takes on a Wordsworthian solidity and depth when he acknowledges himself to be part of a universal process into which everything is drawn, and which overwhelms all

'Explicit Snow'.

creation. Wherever man looks he discovers his identity with all that
exists in the cosmos:

> ... He
> Stares, in the end, at his own face, and shame
> Of his deep flaw, mortality,
> Shines in the star, and from the tree the same
> Pity is shed that weakens him when he knows
> That he is going where even the stone goes.[1]

The 'cold Latinities of cloud' have a message which the human
interpreter can translate:

> Take their cool word; death and desire will sigh
> Your own name through the world's wild imagery.[2]

All things obey the laws of gravity and of time; all things are
uncertain and ambiguous, even the meaning of the Word, which,
for MacCaig, has not been made Flesh:

> The lark from his tall spire at last
> Tumbles, his gay ascension past:
> And into pits of suns suns fall
> Till nothing's left centrifugal.[3]

> The recording mind goes down. The day goes down.
> The mountain spills down its own side, the bird
> Becomes a purse of maggots. Yet they mean
> And are the ambiguities of the Word,
> That vanishing-point beyond which Chaos sits
> Warming his timeless wits.[4]

MacCaig's territory may not be large, but it is densely populated
with good poems which are memorable for their alert Metaphysical
wit, their sensuous energy, the closeness of their texture and the
elegance of their pattern. He owes much to Donne, and something to
Yeats; in one or two poems — 'Blue Chair in a Sunny Day' and
'Country Bedroom' — there are echoes of Wallace Stevens:

[1] 'By Comparison'.   [2] 'Landscape in Cloud'.
[3] 'Gravity'.   [4] 'Advices of Time'.

It must have been the moon, because it was.
Because it was, it must have been a shadow
Uglily collapsing on the floor.[1]

He owes even more to the keenness of his senses and to his innate philosophical turn of mind; but his greatest debt is to his native country: for his sense of being rooted in Scotland, with its tradition of metaphysical inquiry, its sombre, rich scenery, its pride in its ancient culture, has given his poetry an integrity of purpose, an air of aristocratic breeding, an austere but exhilarating strength, that distinguish it from the work of all but a few of his English contemporaries.

Ted Hughes (b. 1930) was almost completely unknown in England until he won the First Publication Award in a contest sponsored by the New York City Poetry Center, the judges being W. H. Auden, Stephen Spender, and Marianne Moore. Faber and Faber then published the prize-winning poems in a volume entitled *The Hawk in the Rain* (1957), which most reviewers welcomed with enthusiastic praise. The appearance of a second collection, *Lupercal* (1960), reinforced the general belief that Hughes was a poet of marked talent.

Some critics have detected in his work the influence of Donne which, to my eyes, is microscopically small. In *The Hawk in the Rain* one can hear echoes of the Jacobean dramatists, with their sullen, smouldering passion; and at times Hughes resembles an early seventeenth-century Malcontent projecting his baffled fury upon the universe at large. The title-poem recalls Hopkins:

and I,

Bloodily grabbed dazed last-moment-counting
Morsel in the earth's mouth, strain towards the master-
Fulcrum of violence where the hawk hangs still.

'Complaint' exhibits some ill-digested reminiscences of Dylan Thomas raving about the process of generation:

[1] 'Country Bedroom'.

Though that Jack Horner's hedge-scratched pig-splitting arm,
Grubbing his get among your lilies, was a comet
That plunged through the flowery whorl to your womb-root,
And grew a man's face on its burning head.

By 1960, the year of *Lupercal*'s publication, Hughes had forged a style which is entirely his own, and had thoroughly assimilated whatever elements he may have acquired from his reading of other poets during his apprenticeship.

The most obvious feature of his early verse is the extraordinary vehemence of the language. Hughes studs his poems with verbs, adjectives, and nouns denoting powerful muscular activity or fierce sensual reactions. He is a bruiser who pummels his readers with the harshest, most solid words in order to batter them into submission. It is significant that in 'Famous Poet' the failure of poetic talent is described as an inability 'to concoct/The old heroic bang'.

Some critics of this first volume accused him of cultivating brutality, partly for its own sake, partly as a smoke-screen to hide a radical absence of purpose, an immature moral judgement. In their view the only instrument which he knows how to manipulate is 'the master-fulcrum of violence'. Unfair though this judgement is, particularly in the light of his second volume, the emphasis on violence in *The Hawk in the Rain* is disquieting and omnipresent.

Hughes is fascinated by animals, and by those strains in man's nature which link him to the beasts. He writes with a savage intensity about a jaguar:

a jaguar hurrying enraged
Through prison darkness after the drills of his eyes

On a short fierce fuse.[1]

He evokes the hysteria latent in a caged bird:

In a cage of wire-ribs
The size of a man's head, the macaw bristles in a staring
Combustion, suffers the stoking devils of his eyes.[2]

[1] 'The Jaguar'.
[2] 'Macaw and Little Miss'.

The image used to describe the genesis of a poem is 'a sudden sharp hot stink of fox';[1] the encounter of two men meeting for the first time is a clash of wild beasts, who hate each other

> As dog and wolf because their blood before
> They are aware has bristled into their hackles.[2]

Allied to this theme of primeval ferocity is the theme of sexual violence: they are sometimes conjoined in a single poem. The girl in 'Macaw and Little Miss' rouses the bird to fury because of her sexual frustration, which also begets turbulent erotic dreams:

> The spun glass of her body bared and so gleam-still
> Her brimming eyes do not tremble or spill
>   The dream where the warrior comes, lightning and iron,
>   Smashing and burning and rending towards her loin.

Hughes portrays with an affable contempt the secretary of thirty who scurries away from sex 'like a starling under the bellies of bulls',[3] but one can hardly blame her for ducking away from sexual passion as depicted by Hughes: a blind descent into a maelstrom of darkness, leading not to mutual tenderness and enrichment but to vacancy and isolation:

> Desire's a vicious separator in spite
>   Of its twisting women round men:
> Cold-chisels two selfs single as it welds hot
>   Iron of their separates to one.[4]

The first of his mythical characters, Fallgrief, grinds out his contemptuous philosophy of sex:

> Whilst I am this muck of man in this
> Muck of existence, I shall not seek more
> Than a muck of a woman.[5]

When the theme is love, as distinct from desire, the notion of suppressed violence pervades the poem: in 'Parlour-Piece' love is

---

[1] 'The Thought Fox'.   [2] 'Law in the Country of the Cats'.
[3] 'Secretary'.   [4] 'Incompatibilities'.   [5] 'Fallgrief's Girl-Friends'.

fire and flood held in check; in 'The Dove Breeder' it is a hawk
destroying pedigree doves. 'A Modest Proposal', after developing
for two stanzas the image of the lovers as two wolves madly hunger-
ing for each other, introduces a new image of a great lord riding by,
with two great-eyed greyhounds at his stirrup. Is he meant to symbolize the glory of love? If so, the wolves are scarcely capable of
recognizing him in that rôle, since to them he is either their prey or
their killer. The image is a striking piece of embroidery, but it
disturbs the poem's coherence. When love is not goaded by violence
the result is 'Song', a decorative, plangent, but unconvincing
literary exercise.

The series of poems on death in battle and the last poem in the
book, 'The Martyrdom of Bishop Farrar', illustrate other aspects of
this preoccupation with violence and suffering. Pain and death seem,
for Hughes, to be machines that are designed to wring every drop
of significance out of life; or levers that raise our unsatisfactory
daily existence to a mythical, heroic level. As an epigraph to his
poem on Farrar, he quotes the Bishop's words as he was chained to
the stake by Bloody Mary's executioners: 'If I flinch from the pain
of the burning, believe not the doctrine that I have preached.'
Greatly as one must admire such fortitude in the agony of death,
one cannot accept his defiant message as an adequate philosophy of
life.

Even in *The Hawk in the Rain* there were signs that Hughes would
soon break away from this brooding obsession with violence as the
most rewarding theme of poetry, and that he might reduce the
volume of his thunderous rhetoric. In 'Griefs for Dead Soldiers' he
recognizes what the heroic bang may mean in terms of human pain
to the widow of a man fallen in battle:

> She cannot build her sorrow into a monument
> And walk away from it.

In 'The Man Seeking Experience Enquires his Way of a Drop of
Water', the man grandiloquently interrogates a drop of water as
though, having lodged in

> The abattoir of the tiger's artery,
> The slum of the dog's bowel

it could reveal the secret of the universe. But

> This droplet was clear simple water still.
> It no more responded than the hour-old child
> Does to finger-toy or coy baby-talk.

In his second volume, *Lupercal*, Ted Hughes has purged his poetry of the blemishes which disfigured *The Hawk in the Rain*. The old preoccupation with birds and beasts of prey is still apparent: in the first half-dozen poems we find references to the hyena, the vulture, the owl, the crow, the stoat, the leopard, the anaconda, the shrew, the wolf, the hawk, and the fox. He writes of a tomcat who

> Grallochs odd dogs on the quiet,
> Will take the head clean off your simple pullet.

As he watches thrushes catching worms, he marvels at their 'bullet and automatic/Purpose', and passes on to make a curious observation about this kind of purpose:

> ... Mozart's brain had it, and the shark's mouth
> That hungers down the blood-smell even to a leak of its own
> Side and devouring of itself.

There is, however, no longer any morbid dwelling upon the details of some brutal incident, no desperate immersion in animal violence as a means of renewing one's energy. Instead, Hughes contemplates with a steady mind, and a saturnine humour, the nature and function of violence in the universe. His language is no longer frenetic and clogged with words huddling upon one another, but firm, muscular, taut as whipcord. A notable example of his new-found control and economy is 'Hawk Roosting', where the hawk is the principle of violence personified:

> My feet are locked upon the rough bark.
> It took the whole of Creation
> To produce my foot, my each feather:
> Now I hold Creation in my foot

Or fly up, and revolve it all slowly —
I kill where I please because it is all mine.
There is no sophistry in my body:
My manners are tearing off heads . . .

The sun is behind me.
Nothing has changed since I began.
My eye has permitted no change.
I am going to keep things like this.

One may, nevertheless, still feel a tinge of disquiet after reading *Lupercal*. We do not expect a poet to tag a neat moral on to every poem, nor do we ask that he should express a pious horror at the rending ferocity of the animal kingdom. But when a poet continually reverts to the theme of feral impulse and, by comparing the working of Mozart's genius with a shark's hunger for blood, suggests that blind instinct is the mainspring of action in the world of men and of beasts, we may reasonably demand that he should unfold the metaphysical implications of his imagery. What principle, if any, informs the moral and the spiritual order of creation, assuming that such an order exists? Does a divine providence govern the universe, and what is the meaning of the violence which ravages the realm of Nature? These are the kinds of problems that a poet must face if he is writing serious metaphysical poetry. Ted Hughes plots with notable skill the curve of violence in the cosmos, but makes scarcely any attempt to elucidate the significance of his graph. There are times when he seems almost to admire power for its own sake, to revere the ruthless killers simply because they are infallible engines of slaughter, purposeful and devoid of hypocrisy. Shakespeare's vision of the world in *Troilus and Cressida* is akin to that of Ted Hughes:

Then everything includes itself in power,
Power into will, will into appetite;
And appetite, an universal wolf.[1]

For Shakespeare, however, this disaster comes only when the principle of degree is violated, when men no longer observe

[1] *Troilus and Cressida*, I. iii.

Insisture, course, proportion, season, form,
Office, and custom, in all line of order.

In the world of Ted Hughes there seems to be no coherent paradigm
by which disorder can be measured and judged:

'Tis all in peeces, all cohaerence gone;
All just supply, and all Relation.[1]

An unsympathetic reader of *The Hawk in the Rain* and *Lupercal*
might argue that this cool appraisal of violence is a form of nihilism;
my own view is that Hughes is basically a Stoic. In common speech
we talk of stoical courage or of stoical indifference to pain, and we
certainly find in Hughes an admiration for sheer guts, for the
qualities of toughness, endurance, fortitude. He celebrates 'Dick
Straightup', unweakened by eighty winters, who toppled, dead
drunk, into the gutter:

... and, throughout
A night searched by shouts and lamps, froze,
Grew to the road with welts of ice. He was chipped out at dawn
Warm as a pie and snoring.

He likens the retired colonel — 'face pulped scarlet with kept
rage'[2] — to the last English wolf, and he clearly relishes the courage
that sustains an outlawed, outmoded creature as he pits his strength
and cunning against the murderous pack. In a fine poem, 'November', he marvels at the strong trust which sleeps in a tramp lying
bundled in a ditch, and salutes the dead creatures hanging on the
gamekeeper's gibbet

In the drilling rain. Some still had their shape,
Had their pride with it; hung, chins on chests,
Patient to outwait these worst days that beat
Their crowns bare and dripped from their feet.

More significant than this admiration for what we loosely term
the stoic virtues, is the strain of philosophical Stoicism which we

---

[1] John Donne, *An Anatomie of the World: The first Anniversary*, 213–14.
[2] 'The Retired Colonel'.

find in Hughes, the dignified acceptance of the universe as a whole.[1] His deliberate submission to the rhythmical process of birth, growth, and decay comes out most movingly in 'Relic', where the finding of a jawbone at the sea's edge recalls the endless cycle of life and death:

> Nothing touches but, clutching, devours. And the jaws,
> Before they are satisfied or their stretched purpose
> Slacken, go down jaws; go gnawn bare. Jaws
> Eat and are finished and the jawbone comes to the beach.

His poems about animals, birds, and insects owe their weight and solidity to the fact that he can survey, without flinching, the most grotesque forms of life, revering them no matter what their nature may be, however repulsive they are, however alien to our human modes of existence. He feels for them an intuitive sympathy which enables him to convey the inner quality of their being, without any trace of sentimental anthropomorphic glibness.[2] No poet of his generation evokes more powerfully the otherness of the beasts, or is more keenly aware of their remote unchanging world. The terrifying savagery of pike; the comic pathos of the bull-frog; the strange amphibious nature of the otter; the bulk of the bull Moses 'in the locked black of his powers' — all these are faithfully portrayed by Hughes in verse that is firm and rich in tactile strength. Nor does he ever forget the life that claws and slays beneath the placid surface of appearances. In the lily-pond's bed,

> Prehistoric bedragonned times
> Crawl that darkness with Latin names,

[1] I do not want to draw a forced parallel between Wordsworth and Hughes, but some poems in *Lupercal* have a Wordsworthian gravity. It is interesting to recall that Wordsworth came to know Seneca more deeply than he knew any other philosopher.

[2] Vernon Scannell, in his poem 'Ruminant', pays a humorous tribute to Hughes and to his sympathy with the world of animals. Observing a cow, he knows that

> It is the anthropomorphic fallacy
> Which puts brown speculation in those eyes.
> But I am taken in . . .
> Almost, it seems, she might be contemplating
> Composing a long poem about Ted Hughes.

Have evolved no improvements there,
Jaws for heads, the set stare.[1]

He can observe this monstrous realm with scarcely a hint of per-
turbation because he has adopted that Stoical attitude which is given
its most famous expression in English poetry by George Chapman:

A man to join himself with th' Universe
In his main sway, and make (in all things fit)
One with that All, and go on, round as it:
Not plucking from the whole his wretched part,
And into straits, or into nought revert,
Wishing the complete Universe might be
Subject to such a rag of it as he;
But to consider great Necessity.[2]

One can trace in *Lupercal* an increased maturity as well as an
advance in technical prowess. 'A Woman Unconscious' is tinged
with a new compassion, which recognizes that the death of a woman
in hospital is as fraught with pain and significance as the holocaust
of millions by an atomic bomb. 'Pennines in April' is an extended
Metaphysical conceit, admirably sustained for three stanzas with a
lithe intelligence and grace. Such poems are a proof that Hughes is
enlarging his emotional range and breaking away from his narrow
concentration on the destructive element.

When critics accuse a poet of being unmusical, they lay themselves
open to ridicule. One thinks of Coleridge's judgement on Tennyson:
'The misfortune is that he has begun to write verses without very
well understanding what metre is.'[3] Yvor Winters, after making
some shrewd thrusts at T. S. Eliot's critical theories, rashly affirms
that 'the meter of *The Waste Land* . . . is a broken blank verse inter-
spersed with bad free verse and rimed doggerel'.[4] I therefore feel a
certain trepidation in remarking that, to my ear, the verse of Ted
Hughes seems deficient in orchestral colour and melodic variety.
Moreover, by abandoning the use of regular metrical forms, he has

[1] 'To Paint a Water Lily'.
[2] George Chapman, *The Revenge of Bussy D'Ambois*, Act IV, Sc. i.
[3] *Table Talk*, 24 April 1833.   [4] Yvor Winters, *In Defense of Reason*, p. 500.

thrown away the chance of counterpointing speech rhythms against his chosen pattern, and has thus eliminated a device which has traditionally enabled poets to augment their technical resources and to achieve certain memorable and subtle triumphs peculiar to the art of poetry. It is foolish to dogmatize about poetic technique; and one should always bear in mind Johnson's defence of Pope against those who judge his versification 'by principles rather than perception'.[1] I can only say that seldom, when reading Hughes, have I experienced the sense of musical delight which Coleridge held to be the chief distinguishing mark of a poet.

In the process of hammering out his striking images, Hughes occasionally sacrifices poetic logic and coherence. An example of this fault occurs in the last two and a half lines of 'Snowdrop':

> She, too, pursues her ends,
> Brutal as the stars of this month,
> Her pale head heavy as metal.

The emphasis on the heaviness of the snowdrop's head, and the implied comparison with a metal bell, are brilliant strokes of insight, which makes it all the more unfortunate that the image in the last line but one is so crudely bludgeoning. One may attempt to justify the description of the snowdrop as *brutal* by arguing that Hughes wants to stress the unrelenting force exercised by the snowdrop as it pierces the hard earth; even so, *brutal* is an ill-chosen word, since it bears connotations of savagery, coarseness, ignorance. I suspect that he is simply resorting to shock tactics; but to outrage the decorum of language by attaching a lunatic epithet to a commonplace noun is a flashy trick unworthy of a serious artist. There is even less justification for attributing brutality to the stars; and why the stars of any one month should be especially designated as brutal remains a mystery.

If my criticisms of Ted Hughes are well-founded, it is a poor reflection on contemporary standards of taste that his achievement, which is genuine and considerable, should have been hailed in

[1] *Lives of the Poets*, iii, p. 248. Quoted by G. Tillotson, *Pope and Human Nature*, p. 185.

wildly extravagant terms. He is, luckily, too hard-headed a York-shireman to lap up all the adulatory reviews, and he has written enough good poems to justify the hope that, like George Chapman, he will celebrate in major verse the heroic vision of royal man.

Thom Gunn (b. 1929) is, unlike Ted Hughes, not greatly per-plexed or fascinated by the problem of violence in the universe, his concern being with the nature of the aggressive will, that may seek its gratification by subduing others, by taming the lawlessness of Nature, or by imposing metaphysical order on the flux of exis-tence. In his first volume, *Fighting Terms* (1954), various poems de-scribe sexual relationships in a series of metaphors drawn from armed combat or from military strategy. The opening poem in the book, 'Carnal Knowledge', is melodramatically self-regarding, and callously direct, the poet's virility being flaunted:

> Even in bed I pose: desire may grow
> More circumstantial and less circumspect
> Each night, but an acute girl would suspect
> That my self is not like my body, bare.
> I wonder if you know, or, knowing, care?
> You know I know you know I know you know.

This riddling, ingenious refrain, which alternates with

> I know you know I know you know I know

is curtailed in the last stanza when the poet sends the girl packing:

> Your intellectual protests are a bore
> And even now I pose, so now go, for
> I know you know.

Other poems in this vein, 'To his Cynical Mistress' and 'The Beach Head', are written with an assurance, a verve, and an insolent wit that partially disguise their coldness and their unpleasant flavour, but they are contrived and faintly rebarbative. Gunn is usually at his least satisfactory when he invents mythical heroes: 'Lofty in the Palais de Danse', although a *tour de force*, wobbles alarmingly between a dry self-analysis and a Shropshire Lad brooding on death and doom; while 'A Village Edmund' unintentionally lapses into uproarious farce. Young Edmund, 'randy and rowdy and rough', picks up a mawkish girl:

> And she lay down and obeyed his every whim.
>
> When it was over he pulled his trousers on.
> 'Demon lovers must go', he coldly said.

This exit line could come straight from a sequence between the regal Margot Dumont and Groucho Marx.

His most impressive poems have always been those in which he develops a philosophical theme, thereby giving full scope to his enormous poetic talents, the chief of these being lucidity of thought, the power of controlling the ramifications of an elaborate metaphor, the tautness and poise of his Metaphysical wit, and a poetic language that is swift-moving, weighty, supple, and incisive. Even in this first volume the maturity and the range of his imagination are astonishing for a poet in his early twenties. The difficult, severely compressed 'Helen's Rape', the love-poem 'Without a Counterpart', which owes much to Robert Graves's 'The Terraced Valley', 'Lazarus not Raised', and 'Lerici' are among the poems which merit careful study. 'A Mirror for Poets', a masterly, learned evocation of Tudor England, foreshadows one of the main themes in Gunn's later poetry: the resolve to take upon himself the full burden of human experience, to flinch neither from action nor from speculation:

> In street, in tavern, happening would cry
> 'I am myself, but part of something greater,
> Find poets what that is, do not pass by
> For feel my fingers in your pia mater.
> I am a cruelly insistent friend
> You cannot smile at me and make an end.'[1]

In 'The Court Revolt' Gunn faces

> A problem which is problem of us all:
> His human flames of energy had no place.

[1] Gunn explores a similar theme, more elaborately and at greater length, in 'Merlin in the Cave: He Speculates Without a Book', a poem in *The Sense of Movement*.

'Looking Glass' signals the first appearance of a motif which recurs many times in the two succeeding volumes:

> I am the gardener now myself, and know,
> Though I am free to leave the path and tear
> Ripe from the branch the yellows and the reds,
> I am responsible for order here.

The very early work of exceptionally talented writers often yields a unique flavour which fades as they grow older .The poems in *The Sense of Movement* (1957) may, therefore, have lost something of the sharp tang that made *Fighting Terms* so exciting and memorable a first volume; but the verse in this second collection is more weighty, mature and harmonious.

One group of poems explores the operation of the assertive will: the first poem in the book, 'On the Move', sets the tone for many of the other pieces in this volume. The Boys of the poem, who have some affinities with Lofty and the Village Edmund, clearly owe much to Marlon Brando's film, *The Wild Ones*:

> On motorcycles, up the road, they come:
> Small, black, as flies hanging in heat, the Boys,
> Until the distance throws them forth, their hum
> Bulges to thunder held by calf and thigh.

Gunn develops a complex metaphysical argument through a series of images which are exact symbols for certain emotional states and intellectual concepts. The Boys, to put the matter crudely, stand for all who impose their hard wills upon the natural world, and Gunn admires this gratuitous act, no matter what the consequences or lack of consequences may be:

> Much that is natural, to the will must yield.
> Men manufacture both machine and soul,
> And use what they imperfectly control
> To dare a future from the taken routes.

He has ordered his imagery with so firm an exactitude that we feel no sense of strain in the parallel drawn by Gunn, and prolonged for several stanzas, between the motorcycle and the human soul. The power to unravel an elaborate argument by means of linked metaphors and counterpointed images is seldom found except in metaphysical poetry of the first order. The concluding stanza has the decisive finality and effortless perfection of phrasing which only a poet of the front rank can command:

> A minute holds them, who have come to go:
> The self-defined, astride the created will
> They burst away; the towns they travel through
> Are home for neither bird nor holiness,
> For birds and saints complete their purposes.
> At worst, one is in motion; and at best,
> Reaching no absolute, in which to rest,
> One is always nearer by not keeping still.

'The Unsettled Motorcyclist's Vision of his Death' resumes the debate between nature and the will of man:

> My human will cannot submit
> To nature, though brought out of it.

The motorcyclist, even in death, is superior to the stagnant marsh and to the tubers, swelling and twisting without volition:

> Cell after cell the plants convert
> My special richness in the dirt:
> All that they get, they get by chance.

> And multiply in ignorance.

On several occasions, notably in 'Elvis Presley', 'Merlin in the Cave', and 'A Map of the City' (this latter poem being printed in his third volume, *My Sad Captains*), Gunn refers to chance as an alluring but hostile instrument that man must seize and bend to his own purposes. The random element in life mesmerizes him: he praises the modern city, amorphous, broken, unfinished, precisely because its rhythms are alien to those of nature. There is something perverse, yet compelling, in his total acceptance of the metropolis:

> She presses you with her hard ornaments,
> Arcades, late movie shows, the piled lit windows
> Of surplus stores. Here she is loveliest;
> Extreme, material, and the work of man.[1]

An allied theme which haunts Gunn is the nature of identity, of the divided self, and of separateness. Scattered throughout his work are poems where, in imagery that is often raw and painful, he explores these related problems — 'Human Condition', 'The Secret Sharer', 'The Allegory of the Wolf Boy', 'The Beaters', and 'The Monster'. In 'A Plan of Self-Subjection' and 'During an Absence' we can sense the perplexity of a man who wants to discover the truth about his condition and about his suffering, however much it may hurt him to probe the distempered wound. In these two poems the close texture of the verse, its concentrated intellectual passion, and the fidelity with which the rhythmical pauses and stresses mirror the fluctuating moods of the emotional argument, are strongly reminiscent of Donne. The opening of 'A Plan of Self-Subjection' conveys something of the poem's quality:

> A fragment of weak flesh that circles round
> Between the sky and the hot crust of hell,
> I circle because I have found
> That tracing circles is a useful spell
> Against contentment, which comes on by stealth;
> Because I have found that from the heaven sun
> Can scorch like hell itself,
> I end my circle where I had begun.

A stanza from 'During an Absence', although it loses much by being divorced from its context, may at least indicate the luminous severity, the masculine terseness of Gunn's art. The play to which the second line refers is *Romeo and Juliet*: the poem is an intricate metaphysical commentary on the tragedy's inner meaning, and a set of variations on its basic images:

> No, if there were bright things to fasten on
> There'd be no likeness to the play.

[1] 'In Praise of Cities'.

> But under a self-generated glare
> Any bad end has possibility,
> The means endurance. I declare
> I know how hard upon the ground it shone.

In 'A Plan of Self-Subjection', while naming Alexander, Mark Antony, and Coriolanus as the characters 'whom I most admire', Gunn acknowledges that 'I stay myself'. In the lines 'To Yvor Winters, 1955', he lays aside this romantic hero-worship in favour of a calm resolve to persist in the long struggle waged by the deliberate human will against the forces of negation. The middle stanza of this poem has a superb dignity and balance:

> Continual temptation waits on each
> To renounce his empire over thought and speech,
> Till he submit his passive faculties
> To evening, come where no resistance is;
> The unmotivated sadness of the air
> Filling the human with his own despair.
> Where now lies power to hold the evening back?
> Implicit in the grey is total black:
> Denial of the discriminating brain
> Brings the neurotic vision, and the vein
> Of necromancy. All as relative
> For mind as for the sense, we have to live
> In a half-world, not ours nor history's,
> And learn the false from half-true premisses.

Gunn has always stressed the need for mastery of others and of one's environment, even though it may involve isolation and the trampling underfoot of human sympathy; his fear has been that, in the act of love,

> If once he acted as participant
> He would be mastered, the inhabitant
> Of someone else's world, mere shred to fit.[1]

Now, in his latest volume, *My Sad Captains* (1961), he recognizes what this worship of the will may entail. The epigraph to *The Sense*

[1] 'The Corridor'.

of Movement was the proud affirmation from *Cinna*: 'Je le suis, je veux l'être'; the epigraph to the first part of this new collection is more hesitant:

The will is infinite and the execution confined, the desire is boundless and the act a slave to limit.

Troilus and Cressida

'Innocence' explicitly shows that the cult of courage, endurance, loyalty, and skill may end in a Nazi's watching, unmoved, a Russian partisan being burned alive. In the book's first two poems he faces the possibility that the exercise of the lonely inviolate will may issue in the acceptance of nothingness. As he turns from his study of Caravaggio's painting, set in the shadowy recess of Santa Maria del Popolo, and itself composed of shadows, he tries, by recalling other paintings of Caravaggio, and certain episodes in his life, to resolve the enigma of the gesture made by 'Saul becoming Paul'. Baffled, he moves away into the interior of the church, where he observes the old women kneeling and finds in their weary posture a hint of the painter's meaning:

> Their poor arms are too tired for more than this
> — For the large gesture of solitary man,
> Resisting, by embracing, nothingness.[1]

The next poem, 'The Annihilation of Nothing', takes us one stage further on the metaphysical journey. Gunn is eager to embrace nothingness:

> Stripped to indifference at the turns of time,
> Whose end I knew, I woke without desire,
> And welcomed zero as a paradigm.

But he finds that Nothing cannot exist, that this abstract concept is only chance, change, and flux, which man must endow with contour and purpose. What might have been an arid philosophical exercise, or a mere riddling paradox, becomes a true poem, precise yet suggestive, the pattern being at once logical and musical:

[1] 'In Santa Maria del Popolo'.

o

> It is despair that nothing cannot be
> Flares in the mind and leaves a smoky mark
> Of dread.
> > Look upward. Neither firm nor free,
>
> Purposeless matter hovers in the dark.

'From the Highest Camp' records a similar awareness of negation, the images here being drawn not from the cosmos but from the bright region of the Himalayan peaks:

> The abominable endures, existing where
> Nothing else can: it is — unfed, unwarmed —
> Born of rejection, of the boundless snow.

By concentrating on those poems in which Gunn wrestles with the burden of responsibility, the exercise of the will, the definition of the self, the creation of one's own touchstone in a world where traditional values have decayed, I have done scant justice to the variety of his art and to the range of his subject-matter. He can write a harsh, curt ballad ('St. Martin and the Beggar'), a tender meditation for the Virgin ('Jesus and His Mother'), a series of witty aphorisms about French literature, and two of the coolest, frankest poems in the language about casual lust, both entitled 'Modes of Pleasure'.

Nor has he been content to go on repeating his previous triumphs, the poems in the second part of *My Sad Captains* all being written in syllabic metre that is a far cry from the elaborate formal patterns of his earlier verse (although 'Vox Humana', the last poem in *The Sense of Movement*, foreshadows these syllabic experiments). Presumably Gunn wants to avoid the dangers of monotony and agrees with Hopkins in his belief that perfection must be broken up by violence. The epigraph to Part II, taken from Scott Fitzgerald's *The Last Tycoon*, prepares us for the perspicuity, the clean-washed freshness of these poems:

I looked back as we crossed the crest of the foothills — with the air so clear you could see the leaves on Sunset Mountains two miles away. It's startling to you sometimes — just air, unobstructed, uncomplicated air.

The first poem, 'Waking in a Newly-Built House', sets the tone for what is to follow:

> There is a tangible remoteness
> of the air about me, its clean chill
> ordering every room of the hill-
> top house, and convoking absences.

Some readers have found the tentative delicacy of these poems more to their liking than the emphatic resonance of Gunn's earlier work. My feeling is that they represent a necessary stage in his poetic development; my hope is that they are a prelude to verse whose richness of imagery and complexity of orchestration will surpass anything he has so far achieved.

One of the main flaws in Gunn's work is that it lacks any satisfactory social framework or terms of reference. The myth of toughness is a poor substitute for traditional religious beliefs and codes of conduct, nor is it possible to confer heroic stature on such shoddy figures as Lofty, Young Edmund, the Boys, and the Black Jackets. Even if, in his later poems, Gunn surveys these heroes with an ironical eye, his attitude to them remains equivocal. The example of Cavafy is enough to prove that one can fashion poetry out of the most unpromising thematic material, but his homosexual encounters, his irony, his sun-warmed hedonism, and his sense of Alexandrian history are rooted in a way of life which, however morally offensive it may be, is mature, civilized, and dignified, unlike the random existence of Gunn's fallen rakes, the surly violence and dingy self-pity of his moronic adolescents. The characteristic artist of this milieu is 'Blackie, The Electric Rembrandt'; the red-haired boy who hears 'Leather creak softly round his neck and chin' recalls his initiation into the gang:

> And one especially of the rites.
> For on his shoulders they had put tattoos:
> The group's name on the left, The Knights,
> And on the right the slogan Born to Lose.[1]

[1] 'Black Jackets'.

Gunn is reduced to celebrating a few friends and historical characters who, having withdrawn from the chaos and failure of existence,

> . . . turn with disinterested
> hard energy, like the stars.[1]

Gunn's cult of the will and his philosophy of callous sexual pleasure are efforts to fill the void left by the lack of stable relationships and of social responsibility in the world where he has chosen to set his poems. J. B. Yeats, writing to his son W. B. Yeats in 1906, comments on this very theme:

The English admiration for strong will, etc. is really part of the gospel of materialism and money making and Empire building.[2]

As you have dropped affection from the circle of your needs, have you also dropped love between man and woman? Is this the theory of the overman, if so, your demi-godship is after all but a doctrinaire demi-godship.[3]

Did you stay too long at that English School, and have you a sort of airy contempt for women? If so cast it from you, it dishonours you as a man and a poet.[4]

This disabling lack of compassionate warmth and imaginative tenderness is linked with a third deficiency in Gunn's poetry: an indifference to the minute particulars of the natural world except in so far as he can convert them into metaphysical tropes. He sees flowers, landscapes, birds, animals, and even human beings as figures to be arranged in his emblematic universe, rather than as creatures existing in their own right. He seldom tries to evoke colours, smells, tastes, and textures, or to give us sharp visual and auditory impressions; there are considerably more references to motor and to organic sensations. The affinities with Donne's verse

---

[1] 'My Sad Captains'. Gunn is probably thinking of the Shakespearean connotation of *sad*, i.e. 'resolute' and 'steadfast', as well as of the modern meaning. I owe this conjecture to J. C. A. Rathmell, in his review of *My Sad Captains*, in *The Cambridge Review*, 27 January 1962, pp. 233–34.

[2] J. B. Yeats, *Letters to his Son W. B. Yeats and Others*, ed. J. M. Hone (Faber, 1944), p. 96.

[3] Ibid., p. 97.   [4] Ibid., p. 98.

are plain;[1] but in Donne we meet a generous, full-bodied involvement in the whole range of human experience, which is absent in Gunn. He is weak precisely where his coeval, Ted Hughes, is strong: in the ability to respond to the abundant vitality of the natural world, to respect the life that proliferates in alien modes of being, strange, beautiful, and protean, defying all attempts to cage them in metaphysical categories. He seems powerless or reluctant to follow the example of the Ancient Mariner and to bless the water-snakes unaware.

These faults in Gunn's poetry, serious though they are, do not invalidate his achievement. His swift lucidity of thought and the tensile strength of his versification afford a pleasure rarely to be found in the work of his contemporaries. A deeply serious poet, he has traced, with scrupulous candour, the lineaments of truth as he perceives them. Like his heroes in 'The Byrnies', he has armoured himself against the fearful dark, the lack of presence, in the barbaric forest; and like Odysseus confronted by the ghosts in 'The Book of the Dead', he accepts the burden of pain, vigilance, and responsible action as an integral part of human life:

> . . . He knew the lack,
> And watching, without comfort, was alive
> Because he had no comfort. He turned back.

[1] See *The Songs and Sonnets of John Donne*, ed. Theodore Redpath (Methuen, 1956), especially pp. xxx–xxxi.

VII

TRAVELLERS

ENGLISH aristocrats, men of fashion, and artists from the six-teenth century onwards have been passionately devoted to travel: the Grand Tour, the hotels all over the world named after wealthy English noblemen, the creation of the French Riviera by respectable Victorians in search of private beaches are among the more spectacular manifestations of this wanderlust. Of all foreign parts it is the Mediterranean lands that English poets have known and loved most intimately. Some have been drawn there by a desire to study the region where the ancient civilizations of Greece and of Rome once flourished; a few have gone in search of the sun and of the warm blue sea; others have exiled themselves in the hope of finding a society where morals are laxer, food and wine cheaper, people less rigid and censorious than in our chillier, Puritan climate.

One can detect in the travel-poetry of the past two hundred years three strands, which are often interwoven. First, there is the desire to record strange landscapes, picturesque scenes, impressive ruins, splendid works of art. Poems inspired by this motive may be no more than the verse equivalent of the coloured picture-postcard with an X marking the sender's hotel-room; but we owe to this impulse some fine passages in Shelley, Byron, Tennyson, Browning, and a dozen minor Victorian writers. Poets may want to portray themselves against an exotic background, or to find in a landscape a counterpart of their emotional state — Byron's *Childe Harold*, Tennyson's 'Frater Ave Atque Vale', 'The Daisy', and 'In the Valley of Cauteretz' are obvious examples. Finally, poets may depict unfamiliar scenes as a way of investigating the customs, beliefs, and manners of a foreign land, or of casting an oblique light upon the habits of their own. Clough attempts this kind of exploration in *Amours de Voyage*; Pope's account of the journey through Europe undertaken by a young fop and his 'lac'd governor' is a superb piece of landscape-painting informed by a penetrating moral and aesthetic discrimination.[1] Colouring all these strands is the wish to taste new experiences, a longing given fresh impetus and fervour by the Romantic Movement, with its emphasis on escape from the present, through time and space, into other worlds:

> To travel like a bird, lightly to view
> Deserts where stone gods founder in the sand,
> Oceans embraced in a white sleep with land;
> To escape time, always to start anew.[2]

Since the Second World War foreign travel has become all the rage among sections of the community which, before 1939, would have been reluctant to venture on a channel packet. At its most glossy and superficial, travel abroad is an advertiser's ramp, the foreign affairs branch of gracious living, part of the trivial snobbery of post-war Britain, whose cults of status symbols, of U and non-U, of professional sport, and of the Royal Family are all symptoms of a deep-rooted disease in a paunchy society.

The war itself took a number of poets to regions of the world which they might otherwise never have visited. Donald Davie was on the Arctic convoys; Roy Fuller served in East Africa; Alun Lewis died in Burma; Keith Douglas fought in the Western Desert and fell in Normandy. In the post-war years travelling fellowships, visiting lectureships, contract teaching-posts in foreign universities have enabled poets to wander all over the globe. Of the five poets to be discussed in this chapter, Lawrence Durrell, Bernard Spencer, and Terence Tiller found themselves in Cairo during the war, some of their early work being printed in the periodical, *Personal Land-scape*, which was edited and produced on the spot.[3] This period of

---

[1] *The Dunciad*, Book IV, 283–322.
[2] C. Day Lewis, 'O Dreams, O Destinations', 9.
[3] *Personal Landscape: An Anthology of Exile*, containing poems originally printed in this quarterly periodical, was published in 1945, with an Introduction by Robin Fedden. The contributors include Durrell, Spencer, Tiller, Keith Douglas, G. S. Fraser, and George Seferis.

residence in Cairo seems to have been a decisive factor in their poetic evolution. D. J. Enright has spent most of his working life outside Britain, mainly in the Far East; while John Heath-Stubbs, though far less peripatetic than Enright, taught for three years in the University of Alexandria. All five have found in their change of environment a stimulus to the writing of verse: travel and exile have whetted their sensibility, sharpened their wits, modified their vision of the world and of England.

Lawrence Durrell (b. 1912) has only recently gained wide recognition as a novelist, but for the past twenty years he has poured out a stream of travel books, essays, works of fiction, and poems; and since all his writings throw light upon one another it will be helpful, when considering his poetry, to refer, from time to time, to his prose. The best introduction to the *Alexandrian Quartet* is to read the *Collected Poems*, just as the best gloss on his poems is contained in the *Alexandrian Quartet*. It is amusing, and not wholly frivolous, to ascribe individual poems to various characters in the *Quartet*, for although Durrell affirms that 'there is hardly a snatch of autobiography',[1] some of his personages, L. G. Darley, Purse-warden, and Mountolive, unmistakably reflect certain facets of their creator. After Pursewarden and his sister have danced together in Trafalgar Square, Pursewarden delights Mountolive by chanting a lewd poem of his own composition about Nelson. We know the song Pursewarden sang, because it is printed on p. 273 of the *Collected Poems*:

> The Good Lord Nelson had a swollen gland,
> Little of the scripture did he understand
> Till a woman led him to the promised land
>   Aboard the Victory, Victory O . . .
>
> Now stiff on a pillar with a phallic air
> Nelson stylites in Trafalgar Square
> Reminds the British what once they were
>   Aboard the Victory, Victory O.[2]

[1] *The Paris Review*, 22 (Autumn–Winter 1960), p. 49.
[2] 'A Ballad of the Good Lord Nelson'.

The city of Alexandria, *anus mundi* and the winepress of love, is one of the novel's recurrent themes: indeed, the characters seem to be puppets moved by the goddess-like city. Many of Durrell's poems either present in concentrated form episodes from the *Quartet*, or recall its emotional atmosphere. Whores, rumpled beds, women's perfume, scabrous incidents, eccentric characters swollen into grotesque mythical figures, reflections about sexual activity and about art: these stage-properties of the novel lie scattered thickly on the pages of the *Collected Poems*:

> Scent like a river-pilot led me there:
> Bedroom darkness spreading like a moss.[1]

This conjures up the heavy, languorous sensuality in which Justine and her lovers steep themselves; and L. G. Darley's self-indulgent remorse and regret pervade these lines from 'A Bowl of Roses':

> Now alas the writing and the roses, Melissa,
> Are nearly over: who will next remember
> Their spring remission in kept promises?

'A Portrait of Theodora' plunges us into the world of street-walkers, a topic which fascinates Durrell and about which he usually writes with a defiant grandiloquence and a pseudo-metaphysical profundity that other Anglo-Saxons reserve for their celebration of bull-fighting:

> Then in another city from the same
> Twice-used air and sheets, in the midst
> Of a parting: the same dark bedroom,
> Arctic chamber-pot and cruel iron bed,
> I saw the street-lamp unpick Theodora
> Like an old sweater, unwrinkle eyes and mouth,
> Unbandaging her youth to let me see
> The wounds I had not understood before.[2]

Of the various poems about Alexandria and the Levant, the most memorable is 'Cavafy', the old poet so constantly named in the

[1] 'Chanel'.
[2] I can think of no other contemporary English poet who would have written an 'Elegy on the Closing of the French Brothels', with its resonant lamentation: 'All the great brothels closed save Sacré Coeur!'

Quartet, who, unashamedly pagan and hedonistic, practised until the end the cult of homosexual love:

> Dilapidated taverns, dark eyes washed
> Now in the wry and loving brilliance
> Of such barbaric memories
> As held them when the dyes of passion ran.
> No cant about the sottishness of man!

Durrell has lived in many parts of the world, including Latin America, Yugoslavia, the mainland of Greece, Rhodes, Corfu, and Cyprus. He repeatedly evokes the landscape and the sensuous atmosphere of the Eastern Mediterranean in verse which, like magical spells, relies on delicacy of sound-pattern and vividness of imagery to lull and to enchant the listener. His own estimate of his descriptive powers is characteristically ebullient and revealing:

One of the things I have strongly is the defect of vision. For example I can't remember any of the wild flowers that I write about so ecstatically in the Greek islands, I have to look them up. And Dylan Thomas once told me that poets only know two kinds of birds at sight: one is a robin and the other a seagull, he said, and the rest of them he had to look up, too.[1]

His senses of touch, taste, smell, and hearing are much more acute than his visual faculties. The words that at once come to mind when one wishes to convey the quality of his verse are *flavour*, *tang*, *aroma*; the most successful lyrics are those which communicate the feel of a landscape and of an experience, or which present the image of a place whose diverse shapes, sounds, and smells are bound together in a sensuous unity by an emotional mood, by remembered legends, or by the knowledge that some great historical event took place there. The lilt and cadence of his spells are Durrell's most individual contributions to the art of poetry:

> Song for the brides of Argos
> Combing the swarms of golden hair:
> Quite quiet, quiet there . . .

[1] *The Paris Review*, 22 (Autumn–Winter 1960), pp. 49–50.

Only the drum can celebrate,
Only the adjective outlive them . . .

Tone of the frog in the empty well,
Drone of the bald bee on the cold skull,

Quiet, Quiet, Quiet.[1]

Blind Homer, the lizards still sup the heat
From the rocks, and still the spring

Noiseless as coins on hair repeats
Her diphthong after diphthong endlessly.[2]

Tread softly, for here you stand
On miracle ground, boy.
A breath would cloud this water of glass,
Honey, bush, berry and swallow.[3]

Sometimes the mood of a poem is darkened by the thought of death, by the poignant contrast between that final oblivion and the aching pleasure of being alive:

> Perhaps a single pining mandolin
> Throbs where cicadas have quarried
> To the heart of all misgiving and there
> Scratches on silence like a pet locked in.[4]

Or the awareness of a landscape's tranquillity may be given a new dimension by the memory of the past, as when Durrell watches the mule-teams above Sarajevo, now only 'a town/Peopled by sleepy eagles'. We seem to be as far from 1914 as from Homer or Alexander the Great, and the poem's final stanza hints at this remoteness:

> No history much? Perhaps. Only this ominous
> Dark beauty flowering under veils,
> Trapped in the spectrum of a dying style:
> A village like an instinct left to rust,
> Composed around the echo of a pistol-shot.[5]

---

[1] 'Nemea'.   [2] 'Blind Homer'.
[3] 'On Ithaca Standing'.   [4] 'The Tree of Idleness'.   [5] 'Sarajevo'.

Durrell has written a few poems about men of letters, the most satisfactory being 'On First Looking Into Loeb's Horace'. He finds an edition of Horace belonging to an old friend or lover, who has added comments in the margin; he then meditates on these comments as well as on Horace, occasionally being reminded of Keats, for Horace also was a poet haunted by autumn and by urns,

> Who built in the Sabine hills this forgery
> Of completeness, an orchard with a view of Rome;
> Who studiously developed his sense of death.

Durrell has reproduced in this poem something of Horace's calm severity, his measured response to the maturity of an ordered civilization: he has, for once, sustained, for more than a few lines, a note of steady gravity.

He has written also a number of poems, half autobiographical, half reflective, made up of aphorisms, cryptic asides, allusive references to literature and to private events, metaphysical speculations, reveries on sex, on art, and on growing older. Much of this verse is pretentious and dull; he is happier when responding to the stimulus of sense impressions or to the atmosphere of a place rather than when trying to construct a long philosophical argument. In the *Alexandrian Quartet* one recalls with enjoyment the duck-shoot, the fancy-dress ball, the diving among the under-water wrecks; one soon tires of those discussions about Gnosticism and the psychic wounds of sex. In the poems, also, it is clear that Durrell's true gift lies in his ability to record and so give permanence to the fleeting moments of sensuous pleasure that run through our veins like quicksilver. He is a completely pagan writer, for whom Christ is a supple, graceful figure, like a young Alexandrian shepherd,

> whose head of woman's hair
> Grew down his slender back
> Or whose soft palms were puckered where
> The nails were driven in.

The pathetic life and death of this figure have been twisted by moralists and by fanatics until He has become

> Dark consul for the Countries of the Will.
>
> Here named, there honoured, nowhere understood.[1]

Durrell reveres the spirit of place, that *deus loci* whose sacraments are the simple daily fare of the Mediterranean peasant — 'garlic and bread, the wine-can and the cup'. The poem printed last in his *Collected Poems* ends on a note of peace, for in Italy he finds all things

> refreshed again in you O spirit of place,
> Presence long since divined, delayed, and waited for,
> And here met face to face.[2]

His reputation as a poet rests on a few slight but enchanting lyrics, a handful of mature reflective poems, and one or two insolently accomplished ballads. Although he has an enormous verbal facility, a mind bubbling with recondite notions, a sensibility that is alert and quivering, his poems, for all their erratic brilliance, lack the weight and the integrity often found in the work of less well-endowed poets. In the course of an article on Henry Miller, he observes that

For the creative man the whole world of philosophic or religious ideas is simply a sort of harem from which he chooses now this pretty concubine, now that. . . . The truth is that the artist is at his most amoral when he reaches the domain of ideas.[3]

When a mathematician ridicules Durrell's cosmological scheme of the *Alexandrian Quartet*:

Dear Boy, Poppycock! The continuum is a mathematical concept and to try and make literature from such things is rubbish

Durrell airily replies:

I am simply using the continuum as one of the most important cosmological formulations of the day, to do a poetic dance upon, as it were.[4]

These high spirits and lack of solemnity are engaging, but the intellectual promiscuity, the irresponsible refusal to take seriously

---

[1] 'Christ in Brazil'.   [2] 'Deus Loci'.
[3] *Horizon*, vol. XX, No. 115 (July 1949), p. 47.
[4] *Encounter*, No. 75 (December 1959), p. 64.

the truth or falsity of any idea, are as limiting as the aestheticism of the eighteen-nineties. The emphasis on cruelty and on mutilation, so prominent in the *Alexandrian Quartet*, is seldom found in the poems, despite his curious simile for green coconuts:

> Broken, you think, from some great tree of breasts,
> Or the green skulls of savages trepanned[1]

and the morbid preciosity of the image which stands for his ideal of style:

> The dry bony blade of the
> Sword-grass might suit me
> Better: an assassin of polish.

> Such a bite of perfect temper
> As unwary fingers provoke,
> Not to be felt till later,
> Turning away, to notice the thread
> Of blood from its unfelt stroke.[2]

But the criticism levelled against his prose by Frank Kermode in his review of *Clea* applies to much of his poetry:

What one disliked about *Justine* was the over-perfumed manner, the insistence on exotic sin and fatigue, the Huysmans-like neurasthenias, the perpetual straining of the prose to produce dazzle and the consequent bathos.[3]

Nevertheless, in the poems, as in the novels, one admires the nervous vitality, the zest, the resilient energy, the courage, of the hedonist who soaks himself in the pleasures and pains of sensual experience and who accepts, without rancour or regret, whatever life may bring. Durrell acknowledges no need for the remission of sin, looks for no resurrection of the body, and believes only in the life everlasting of art:

> I, per se I, I sing on.
> Let flesh falter, or let bone break
> Break, yet the salt of a poem holds on,

---

[1] 'Green Coconuts: Rio'.   [2] 'Style'.
[3] *A Review of English Literature*, vol. I, No. 2 (April 1960), pp. 73–77.

Even in empty weather
When beak and feather have done.[1]

Although Bernard Spencer was born in 1909 his first volume, *Aegean Islands*, did not appear until 1946. Of the thirty-eight poems in it, twenty-two are dated 1940–1942, years when he was living in Greece and in Egypt, the remaining sixteen having been written before 1940. His only book since then, *The Twist in the Plotting* (1960), published in a limited edition by the University of Reading, contains twenty-five short poems.

During the nineteen-thirties few young poets were strong enough to resist the spell of Auden. It is typical of Spencer's aloof independence that scarcely any of his poems are in the least Auden-esque: the two apparent exceptions show a faint likeness to the Master but retain their own individuality. The penultimate stanza of 'Allotments: April' is reminiscent of Auden in his *Look, Stranger!* phase; yet the quiet lyricism, the firm delicacy, of the last stanza are entirely Spencer's own:

> Behind me, the town curves. Its parapeted edge,
> With its burnt look, guards towards the river.
> The worry about money, the eyeless work
> Of those who do not believe, real poverty,
> The sour doorways of the poor; April which
> Delights the trees and fills the roads to the South,
> Does not deny or conceal. Rather it adds
>
> What more I am; excites the deep glands
> And warms my animal bones as I go walking
> Past the allotments and the singing water-meadows
> Where hooves of cattle have plodded and cratered, and
> Watch today go up like a single breath
> Holding in its applause at masts of height
> Two elms and their balanced attitudes like dancers, their
> arms like dancers.

Even in 'Behaviour of Money', an attack on the economic system, Spencer is much more conscious than Auden of the relationships

[1] 'Carol on Corfu'.

between people, much less eager to trace an abstract intellectual pattern or to hazard a brilliant generalization. When describing how Money became a tyrant, he shows us its corrupting effect on the lives of decent men and women:

> And the town changed, and the mean and the little lovers
> of gain
> inflated like a dropsy, and gone were the courtesies
> that eased the market day;
> saying 'buyer' and 'seller' was saying 'enemies'.
>
> The poor were shunted nearer to beasts. The cops recruited.
> The rich became a foreign community. Up there leaped
> quiet folk gone nasty,
> quite strangely distorted, like a photograph that has slipped.

His most characteristic poems are those on Greece and on the Greek islands. He is not primarily interested in classical civilization, in the Alexandrian age, in Byzantium or in the struggle for independence against the Turk. What he cares for most of all is the hot sun, the blue sea, the wine and food, the rhythm of peasant life, the landscape of stony soil, and of olive trees growing among the ruins. The sight of excavated pottery, drinking vessels and jars for oil, awakens no thoughts of the glory that was Greece; it brings to mind the unheroic lives of the ordinary people who used these household goods:

> The minimum wish
> For the permanence of the basic things of a life,
> For children and friends and having enough to eat
> And the great key of a skill;
> The life the generals and the bankers cheat.[1]

Spencer can evoke the civilization of the past, when he chooses to do so, with an impressive authority and ease:

> Wealth came by water to this farmless island;
> Dolphins with backs like bows swim in mosaic
> Floors where the Greek sea-captains piled up money . . .

[1] 'Greek Excavations'.

Steps go down to the port. And in this area
You could buy corn and oil or men and women . . .

And it was here by the breakers
That strangers asked for truth.[1]

But he prefers to savour the present, drinking in all the whiteness
and the blueness that sparkle and dazzle in the Mediterranean sun.
He responds to all that is generous, carefree, and warm in human
relationships, unaffectedly admiring the frivolous, gay modes of
sophisticated life, enjoying the elegance which stimulates the mind
and sets the flesh tingling with pleasure:

Like air on skin, coolness of yachts at mooring,
a white, flung handful;
fresh as a girl at her rendezvous, and wearing
frou-frou names, Suzy, Yvette or Gaby.[2]

He can appreciate also with equal satisfaction the simple community
life of peasants as they camp after dark among piled fruit near the
mountain church, drinking wine, eating white cheese, singing and
treading their intricate dances to the cry of bagpipes.[3] Most poets
have a vision of Eden or of the just city; for Spencer, the Aegean
islands are no paradise lost, but a 'ribbed, lionish coast' where men
can still find a measure of happiness. Like so many poets of the north
he loves olive trees because they are:

first promise of the South to waking travellers:
of the peacock sea, and the islands and their
boulder-lumbered spurs.[4]

The poems in *The Twist in the Plotting*, though graver and more
melancholy than the verse of *Aegean Islands*, are no less crisp and
resilient. Now, grown older, he remembers in spring-time his
passion for Greece:

Alefkandra loved by winds,
luminous with foam and morning, Athens,

---

[1] 'Delos'.   [2] 'Yachts on the Nile'.
[3] See 'Peasant Festival' and 'Aegean Islands'.   [4] 'Olive Trees'.

P

> her blinded marble heads,
> her pepper-trees, the bare heels of her girls,
> old songs that bubble up from where thought starts,
> Greek music treading like the beat of hearts;
> haunted Seferis, smiling, playing with beads.[1]

Cities, mountains, and valleys recall one 'who for ever stayed behind'; your chest knocks in Athens when you meet a stranger, because 'someone you loved was like her'; barbed wire scars a city now breeding the fanatic and the duped:

> ... the once known and dear, once chosen
> city of our rendezvous.[2]

The generals and the bankers cheat us as they cheated those who lived in the long-shut house revealed by archaeologists when they dug for pots and shards. In England he remembers, in 'At "The Angler"',

> the great night crescent of the weir,
> swollen with rainfall, growling its white tons ...
> talking to our short from its long time.
>
> Lovers, we had our share of the ideal;
> again, next day, with end of storm
> how swans curved near as if to bring good news
> to us and — so love made it seem
> there and then certain — in their trance of calm
> blazed a white Always from that stream.

A cooler and more fastidious poet than Durrell, he resembles him in his pagan love of physical grace, his feeling for the fruits of the earth, his belief that art can reconcile us to our mortal condition. He is dazed, yet fortified, after a visit to the National Gallery where he gains 'what you might call a philosophy', and recalls

> the narrowed eyes and caught breath of the archers in
>   Pollaiuolo's 'San Sebastian',
> the smiling lips of Bronzino's 'Venus',

[1] 'A Spring Wind'.
[2] See 'At Courmaveur', 'In Athens', 'The Rendezvous'.

and in Piero di Cosimo's 'Florentine General'
the cold smite of the fluted armour my finger-tips had grazed.[1]

In his first volume there is a description of a dance by an Egyptian girl, 'Egyptian Dancer at Shubra'; a Spanish girl dancing is the theme of 'Castanets', printed in his second collection. For him, as for so many post-Romantics, the dance is a symbol of the body's unthinking perfection, the intuitive response of the flesh to the rhythm of life, an emblem of art itself.[2] He celebrates the tanned Sicilian peasant who answers metaphysical gaps and fears

> With a salty way of speech; with tasselled harness
> with a cart to match the sea and all the flowers;
> with Roger the Christian and Palermo towers;
> and in between the dusty wheels
> the Queen of Love in a yellow gown,
> featured like a peasant child,
> her three red horses rearing from the foam
> and their carved manes blown wild.[3]

Apart from an occasional sad, ironic reference, Spencer ignores the public world of politics and of social relationships in which we are all enmeshed. It may be argued that his resolve to linger in a private country, his evocation of Mediterranean landscapes where he once lived, his dwelling on sensuous impressions, his desire to recapture the exact flavour of the passing moment, limit his significance. But we are, first and foremost, human beings who respond to the weather, to food and drink, to the love of our families, to art, to pain, and to death more intimately and more fully than to the mingled dreariness and mania which characterize public affairs. Because Spencer traces 'the twist in the plotting of things'[4] as he has known it in his life and because, watching a stranger in the Underground, he feels pity for one 'condemned to sure death' and sees 'poetry roaring from him like a furnace',[5] he speaks across the frontiers to all men linked by a common humanity and by common

---

[1] 'Fluted Armour'.   [2] See Frank Kermode, *Romantic Image* (Routledge, 1957).
[3] 'On a Carved Axle-Piece from a Sicilian Cart'.
[4] 'In Athens'.   [5] 'Train to Work'.

human needs. And how refreshing it is, at a time when so many poems flaunt an emotional vulgarity and a crude exhibitionism, to read verse composed with deliberate skill by a man whose fineness of perception and clarity of intellect call to mind one of his recurrent images: sunlight on the Aegean islands.

Terence Tiller (b. 1916) gave proof of his poetic talents while still an undergraduate at Cambridge, where he won the Chancellor's Medal for English Verse. From the start his poems have often been bafflingly difficult, because of their elaborate texture, the subtlety of Tiller's emotional perceptions, the darting, elusive quality of his thought, and the wealth of scholarship with which he loads his verse, much of it not being in the current coin of the realm. He may give an unexpected twist to the legend of Eden, to the myth of Adam, Eve, and Lilith; he may invent a symbolic universe of his own; or weave astrological motifs into a rhapsodical meditation on the planets.

He was already a poet, with one volume[1] to his credit, when he reached Egypt, but the Foreword to his second collection, *The Inward Animal* (1943), makes it clear that the experience of war and of living in a strange land had shocked him into maturity — perhaps nobody writes verse of any depth until events have wounded him:

Now that the war has taken millions from their familiar environment and associates, its impact and the impact of strangeness must have shaken, and perhaps destroyed, many a customary self. There will have been a shocked and defensive rebellion; reconciliation must follow; the birth of some mutual thing in which the old and the new, the self and the alien, are combined after war.... The 'inward animal' is this child, so unwillingly conceived and carried, so hardly brought forth.[2]

His 'Examination Room' is worth comparing with Enright's poem on a similar theme. Enright, as we shall see, notes the grubby absurdity, the farcical aspects of the whole business; whereas Tiller remembers his responsibility for the students whom he teaches:

> I am to guide these futures, to approve
> their common copying of certain steps.

[1] *Poems* (1941).   [2] *The Inward Animal*, p. 8.

As so often with Tiller, his best poems in this volume are those in which the firm melodic line is uncluttered by ornate trills, the argument not smothered beneath a profusion of glittering images. His 'Egyptian Dancer', a far more lascivious creature than Bernard Spencer's 'Egyptian Dancer at Shubra', comes alive before us in the naked sensuality of her squirming act:

> The dance begins: she ripples like a curtain;
>   her arms are snakes
> — she is all serpent, she coils on her own loins
> and shakes the bell; her very breasts are alive
> and writhing, and around the emphatic sex
>   her thighs are gimlets of oil.

'The End of the Story', the last of *Four Love Songs*, is, in its sharp delicacy, an equally satisfying poem:

> Put out the candle, close the biting rose.
> For cock and cony are asleep; the sheep
> in her secretive hills, with fleece at peace,
> now lies enfolded.

Again, in *Unarm, Eros* (1947), he is most successful when he keeps his eye on the object, and restrains his fancy from adventuring into recondite fields of speculation or into labyrinths of brilliant imagery:

> As if a mask, a tattered blanket, should
> live for a little before falling, when
> the body leaves it: so briefly in his dead
> feathers of rag, and rags of body, and in
> his crumpled mind, the awful and afraid
>   stirs and pretends to be a man.[1]

> I see them swaying their strange heads like geese,
> nineteen camels in a string like geese in flight;
> as if approaching a problem, or in quest
> but baffled a little, a little unsure of their right.[2]

The longest and most ambitious poems in his latest volume, *Reading a Medal* (1957), are three complex meditations on literary

---

[1] 'Beggar'.   [2] 'Camels'.

history, grouped together under the general title 'Three Case Histories'. To appraise these discourses on the Arcadian Poets, the Metaphysicals, and the Shakespearean Tragic Heroes, one needs to have an insight into morbid psychology, to be a scholar versed in Elizabethan and Jacobean literature, and to enjoy dazzling conceits and tinkling symbols. If one lacks this faculty, this knowledge, and this taste, the coruscating images and the chromatic harmonies of the verse must seem a welter of bright confusion. Amid much that is subtle, intelligent, and finely-imagined, there are only two flawless poems in the book, each possessing a rare distinction. 'Street Performers, 1851' is ostensibly a straightforward portrayal of a scene in mid-nineteenth-century London, based on Mayhew's *London Labour and the London Poor*, 1851 (the source of Philip Larkin's 'Deceptions'). I know of few poems that convey with such a sombre richness the prosperous solid world of the Victorian bourgeois, the tattered clothes and existence of poor vagrants, the brevity of human life and the darkness of the shades into which the children of the big houses, the street performers, the puppets and (by implication) the readers of the poems all must move:

> The salamander and the swordsman, and
> the maypole-ribboned bear: from dark they pass
> to dark, through blazing islands — as if stained
> in mockery upon hot slips of glass.
> And the flame dies; the fingers are withdrawn;
> the puppets tumble; there are no more slides;
> the paints are in their boxes: they have gone,
> the fantoccini and the Chinese shades.

The title-poem is an even more remarkable achievement. Its circular reasoning, mimed by the syntax and by the poetic form, its concentrated imagery, cryptic hints and delight in playing with paradoxes, make it a difficult poem to analyse though not, I think, to accept imaginatively. If forced to paraphrase its meaning (and I am not one of those who hold that a poem is pure only when devoid of prose sense and drained of moral substance) I should offer the following summary of its argument: Pallas and Aphrodite symbolize respectively intellect, will, conscious reason, as opposed to intuition, emotion, and sexual desire. When the coin spins, the olives, which are the emblems of Pallas, fall to the ground, just as classical Greek civilization was destroyed, and as the intellect may become self-destructive. Aphrodite offers a relief from tension, by way of erotic pleasure, and suggests that the virtues of sympathy, understanding, and love will overcome the fiercer qualities of which Pallas is the emblem. The poet argues (in the italicized quatrain) that only in a synthesis of these opposing philosophies can there be rest. The debate between Pallas and Aphrodite circles endlessly: Pallas admits that the other side of the medal is true, whereas Aphrodite claims that everything spoken by Pallas is false, including her admission that there is truth in Aphrodite's words.

But how clumsy and obtuse my paraphrase sounds compared with the poem itself, which not only offers a sensuous delight entirely absent in my lumbering prose, but which is also far more intellectually precise and emotionally significant. Here, indeed, is language as dance and as gesture, as 'the outward and dramatic play of inward and imaged meaning':[1]

> who, minter of medallions,
> casting or striking, caused me so
> to speak with double voice in bronze,
> I may not help and cannot know.
> But I am Pallas, and I bear
> the mask of war by wisdom; you
> shall spin my olives to despair:
> all my reverse will say is true.
>
> *(Turn me, and read that other side;*
> *you must return: for, mask and coin,*
> *I give no rest unless you ride*
> *the felloe where my faces join.)*
>
> My face is Aphrodite's — she
> that rules by myrtle and by dove;
> I loose my zone to let you see

[1] R. P. Blackmur, *Language as Gesture*, p. 6.

the end of reasoning by love.
Nothing my obverse tells is true:
turn till you read me as it was;
turn till you know me, and renew
my helpless paradox — because

Despite my inability to enjoy or even to grasp the drift of much that Tiller has written, I have no doubt, on the strength of a dozen poems in his last three volumes, that he has a formidable talent. He has from time to time essayed long poems on large themes, and has worked in exacting stanzaic forms; the 'Prothalamion' from *Poems* and the 'Epithalamion' from *Unarm, Eros* may be signs that, when expressing a deep personal emotion, he naturally turns to a courtly, ceremonious form. Of all his poems which have appeared since the publication of *Reading a Medal*, the most splendid is 'Prothalamion', a long, stately celebration of love, distinguished by its refulgent imagery and by its subtle, yet lucid and unfaltering, melodic curve:

Light, fair Light infinitely springing, grace
all hours and seasons of these lovers, grown
by passionate mercy deeper than their own
                    each other's dwelling-place:
within them shine, and on this bed, the throne
and altar of their flesh; there flower and run,
rich Fountain, always; brightness, petal-fold
of spreading glory, break of pulsing gold,
adorn them: till, slow-lifted, endless one,
                    you rise, oh Unseen Sun.

As in Spenser's 'Prothalamion', the poetic learning and the rhythmical complexity derive from the Italian and the French elements in our culture and in our language, but the sensibility and the emotional temper are characteristically English. For, unlike Durrell and Spencer, Terence Tiller has returned from the shores of the Mediterranean to his native land.

D. J. Enright (b. 1920) has travelled and worked not only in the Mediterranean region but also in the Far East, having taught at universities in Egypt, Japan, Siam, and Malaya. He has published three volumes of poems[1] and several prose works, including a novel, *Academic Year*, set in Alexandria, a collection of critical essays, *The Apothecary's Shop*, and a book about Japan, *The World of Dew*, whose sub-title, *Aspects of Living Japan*, hints at Enright's desire to tell the truth at all costs, his concern with what is alive, his mistrust of dead conventions, of all that has become ossified or embalmed. His acute eye, his refusal to be hoodwinked, his satirical tongue, and his slightly malicious pleasure in pricking the bubble of academic and governmental cant have not endeared him to administrators, politicians, and diplomats. In his verse, as well as in his prose, he is a savage critic of evasion and of sham, uninhibited by good taste, determined to brush aside the comfortable pretences, the cosy self-deceptions, the half-lies which the prosperous, well-fed bureaucrats use to hush up scandal, hide the ugliness of human suffering, and throw a sop to their drowsy consciences. His eye has steadily grown more jaundiced, his mind more disenchanted, his irony more pervasive.

A few of the poems in his first big collection, *The Laughing Hyena* (1953), are light-hearted satires, the laughter being mocking but not bitter. 'University Examinations in Egypt' deftly evokes in a few lines the atmosphere of Middle Eastern academic life known to all western teachers who have sweated away with so little apparent success:

> Was it like this in my day, at my place? Memory boggles
> Between the aggressive fly and curious ant — but did I really
> Pause in my painful flight to light a cigarette or swallow drugs?
> The nervous eye, patrolling these hot unhappy victims,
> Flinches at the symptoms of a year's hard teaching —
> 'Falstaff indulged in drinking and sexcess', and then,
> 'Doolittle was a dusty man' and 'Dr. Jonson edited the
> Yellow Book'.

This is Egypt as seen by a sophisticated Englishman: in 'An Egyptian in Birmingham' Enright shows us the other side of the medal, the bewilderment and homesickness of a young man starved of his native sunlight, bored and dispirited by the damp Midland

[1] Since this chapter was written he has published a fourth volume, *Addictions* (1962).

dreariness. Not that he will ever confess his misery when he returns to his own country:

> But wait, when I go home, you too, Birmingham, you
> Shall be marvellous, your fame ripple through the bazaars
>   like a belly dancer —
> A city of peril, like the shark . . .

Enright, like Lawrence Durrell, writes poems about various aspects of Alexandrian life. In 'To Cavafy, of Alexandria', a far less accomplished and penetrating piece of work than Durrell's poem on a similar theme, Enright makes no attempt to convey the nature of Cavafy's art, or to sketch the character of the man. Instead, he gives us a neat but dull portrait of his old acquaintances, and then jots down a few observations about the changing face of Alexandria. The gossipy tone, the daubs of local colour, the general slackness of the writing, are more appropriate to smart journalism than to poetry. He seldom writes good verse unless he is genuinely angry at some example of official humbug, moved to pity by the uncomplaining courage of the oppressed, made uneasy by the sight of social injustice, or grieved at the spectacle of meaningless human pain.

'To an Alexandrian Poet' contains several elements which recur in his later verse. There is the ironical disparagement of art, occasioned by the fact that so many people with highly-refined aesthetic taste are often indifferent to the squalor and poverty of their fellow-men; there is also the self-mockery, the acknowledgement that his righteous indignation is only a means of quieting his uneasy conscience, a futile protest, designed to be no more than a gesture to allay his guilt, a hypocritical regret more contemptible than a frank hedonism. The Alexandrian poet pronounces his elegant dictum:

> 'Poetry is truth, but truth wrapped round with words.
> The wrappings matter more.'

Enright rejects this view of poetry:

>   For then I saw —
> Believe me, by no will of mine — the beggar's
>   red smashed leg,

He prying slowly at his filthy wrappings:
                    the wrappings matter —
And all the more along a public street.

But, as Enright asks himself, what has he gained, what has the
beggar profited, by this squeamish shrinking from the red smashed
leg?:

And so it seems I'm poorer, in the end, than you —
Have lost what you have found, and nothing gained beside
(The beggar fidgets at his rags and eyes me sullenly)
                    — neither a cure for beggars' legs
Nor your large graceful house and manners.

We find a similar juxtaposition of art and human suffering in 'The
Mosaics at Daphni'. Having conjured up the appearance of these
glowing, fierce mosaics, Enright casually passes on to another
observation:

Nearby is yet another amenity: an asylum
                    for the slightly insane,
Who roam the region in a kind of pyjamas, with
Shaved heads and a look of long and austere resentment.

Durrell might well have written poems on such themes, but he
would have found the contrast between the glory of art and the
filth of human degradation a source of excitement, an incompre-
hensible but stimulating paradox. Enright feels that hideous disease,
mass starvation, and inhumanity affront the image of man and
poison the sources of art.

Enright's second book of verse, *Bread Rather Than Blossoms*
(1956), is set against the background of post-war Japan. Most of the
poems are variations on one theme: millions of Japanese live just
above the survival line, crammed into city slums, victims of a brutal
society where the poor are systematically exploited and the ancient
Japanese customs, ceremonies, and religious beliefs are either
irrelevant, or pretty trappings designed to conceal human wretchedness. In such a civilization, art is a corrupt form of self-indulgence,
or a footling game played by men who do not care that their

brothers are dying of hunger in the street. His method of driving home this overriding truth is simple: he takes hallowed symbols of old Japan such as the cherry blossom, the geisha, the tea ceremony, and, like a film director, cuts to a shot of a beggar, a tired prostitute, an illiterate peasant cultivating rice, a down and out sleeping in the street. He surveys twentieth-century Japan with the same contempt for its traditional culture that Blake felt when he looked through the flimsy sham of polished eighteenth-century London society and saw the harlots crowding the Thames-side streets.

'The Short Life of Kazuo Yamamoto' illustrates Enright's characteristic technique of contrasting the big words of politicians, the noble ideals of culture, with the stark facts of life in a Japanese city. His tone of voice is quiet, ironical, unemphatic; the truth will speak for itself, even if nobody cares to listen:

> At the age of thirteen, you passed by the park
> Of Nakanoshima, you paused by the Public Library
> with its well-fed shelves . . .

> You swallowed the rat poison, all the easier
> for having a healthy appetite . . .

> Elsewhere the great ones have their headaches, too,
> As they grapple with those notable tongue-twisters
> Such as Liberation and Oppression.
> But they were not talking about you,
> Kazuo, who found rat poison cheaper than aspirin.

Again, in 'Yuki San and the Cherry Blossom', Enright strips prostitution of its glamour, of its literary wrappings, and shows it for the nasty thing that it is, whether in Durrell's Paris, Durrell's Alexandria, Dowson's London, Blake's London, or in geisha-land:

> —— And you?
> Desolate and sick of some old passion, did you cry
> For madder music and for stronger wine? Or call to
> Mind that at that moment, through that land, by
> Tens of thousands, faded *futon* were unrolled
> Across the sacred *tatami*, for couples such as you,

In countless shacks called 'houses', an endless scroll
Of acts called 'I-love-you', perhaps?

In 'The Interpreters (or, How to Bury Yourself in a Book)'
Enright attacks those who, when confronted by poems that reveal
the truth about hunger and prostitution, ingeniously gloss the text:

The poet mentions suffering and even starvation;
dead cats in the street and women slowly dying on
              the streets;
the lot of a sizeable part of a sizeable nation —
but dear me no! — that will not do for the critic,
              that connoisseur of words
who cannot abide the crude vulgarity of meaning —
his expertise, my dear, merits something richer
than these ancient histories of anguish and horror
              or an empty belly's tasteless keening . . .

But the scholars are chasing a glittering fragment
of Zen or the cracked semblance of an Emblem —
for it is not what a poem merely says that matters,
elsewhere than here it finds its true signification:
              whore, you may be sure,
refers to some mysterious metaphysical temptation;
hunger was his image for a broken dream; bread
an old religious symbol; his typhoons the wind of God.

The poems in his third volume, *Some Men Are Brothers* (1960)'
spring from his experiences in Siam and in Berlin, as well as from
his memories of Japan. The Japanese section follows the familiar
pattern of contrasting the traditional aspects of Japanese culture
with the sordid reality of the present day. 'The Popular Theatre'
shifts from the painted scene where

          someone's son was killed in battle, and a daughter
              sold into a brothel with a modest groan

to the world outside where

          A stone's throw off — though who would cast it,
              especially in so old and famed a city? —
          lies a dim lane of brothels.

We dab our eyes, moved to pity by the actors, but not much worried by the dim lane:

> Art's not so long, it seems, that its drawn tears
>   extend across the footlights to the same distresses:
> here in small rooms while actors doff their robes,
>   there in small rooms the daughters doff their dresses.

How much easier it is to take a photograph of a mother suckling her ragged children than to remove the causes of poverty:

> Make a picture of where your heart once bled,
> Move the world's conscience, or provoke an incident —
>   all simpler than to fill an empty mouth with bread.[1]

And how tempting to prove one's humanity by weaving poems round vagrant miners instead of round the moon, and flowers, and birds, and temples ('Changing the Subject').

Enright's observations on Siam and on Berlin are as sharply barbed and as well directed as his analysis of Japanese society. 'Spotted Deer', a fable about economic aid, cuts unpleasantly near the bone. The white-spotted deer, who had lots of everything, sent the poor black-spotted deer food, dishes, a professor to teach good table-manners and

>   artistic napkins, all embroidered,
> 'To the Black-spots: From their friends the White-spots'.

Unhappily, the presence of red-spots caused certain difficulties, but the real trouble began when

> A doctor white-spot arrived to instruct the black-spots
> In the construction of latrines to cope with the increased etc.

> Whereupon the black-spots invoked an ancient tradition
> Forbidding the digging of holes in the breast of Mother Earth.

> A white-spot cultural envoy was gored by black-spot students,
> And the red-spots were attracted by the smell of foodlessness.

> This coolness continued till low-level changes took place
> In both governments and some new traditions were uncovered.

[1] 'Where Charity Begins'.

He is no happier in Berlin, with its memorials of Stalinism and of Nazism, than in Japan, with its memorials of Hiroshima. One target of his satire is the efficiency of German dustbins, lavatories, ambulances, and burial facilities, just as in Japan it was the insanitary, brutalizing conditions of life that angered him. He pointedly refrains from observing that this same genius for organization facilitated the neat dispatch of several million Jews in gas-chambers, merely remarking that

> In no country
> Are the disposal services more efficient.[1]

I admire Enright for his dislike of cant, for his refusal to play the game of make-believe, and for declining to pretend that some reconciling metaphysical or aesthetic formula can subsume and heal the wounds inflicted on defenceless human beings all over the world:

> And now (in this one place, one time) to celebrate,
> One sound will serve.
> After the love-laced talk of art, philosophy and fate —
> Just, No.[2]

I admire also his determination to assert his independence, to keep clear of political propaganda, to maintain his integrity as a poet, committed only to the search for truth:

> And you, confused by fading rhythms,
> Otherworldly weathers, occult accords and schisms,
> Would prove for either side a slippery satellite.[3]

But his poetry, for all its wit, dexterity, and acidulous frankness, is both depressing and limited in scope. One may well feel guilty about writing poems while people die in the streets, but it becomes monotonous and unconvincing if one continues to write poems about feeling guilty about writing poems. Moreover, his carefully-cultivated informality, his studied colloquialisms, his casual, relaxed tone of voice, and his fondness for understatement rapidly harden

[1] 'No Offence'.   [2] 'Saying No'.   [3] 'Where Have You Been To?'

into mannerisms. Irony, his favourite device, used mechanically and predictably, becomes a means of evasion, a defensive weapon, enabling him to sidle away when a theme grows too painful to contemplate, a problem too hard to solve:

There should be no flight from irony and paradox in writing poetry, rather an insistence on them. ... But when irony and paradox are employed as a compositional *tic*, when they are used as a means to simultaneous assertion and retraction, when they produce only a brilliant surface of mock-logic, then what one has is the current version of 'pure poetry' — a highly camouflaged way of being *vox et praeterea nihil*.[1]

Finally, there is something glib and defeatist about the constant juxtaposition of art and life, with art presented always as an escape from or a denial of life. In his review of *Bread Rather Than Blossoms*, Donald Davie clings to the hope that

Enright has been composing poems more ambitious and deliberate than any here; and that he's not so out of patience with artiness and cultural window-dressing that he's forsworn for good the deeper reaches (and so the deeper humanity) of the art he practises.[2]

Davie's hope is only partially fulfilled by the poems in *Some Men Are Brothers*; and it would be a matter for regret if Enright's talents were to be stultified by a narrow concept of humanity, or dissolved by a corrosive scepticism and irony.

John Heath-Stubbs (b. 1918) is not, like Enright, a wandering scholar who moves from one academic post to another in various regions of the world. Apart from a three-year teaching spell at the University of Alexandria from 1955–1958, he has mainly resided in England, earning his living as a professional writer ever since he came down from Oxford. Although proud of his ancestry and conscious of his native roots, he is a man whose imagination leads him far away in space and in time from present-day England.

---

[1] Richard Wilbur, 'The Genie in the Bottle', in John Ciardi, *Mid-Century American Poets* (Twayne, New York, 1950), p. 5.
[2] Donald Davie, 'Common-Mannerism', in *Listen*, vol. 2, No. 2 (Spring 1957), pp. 20–22.

Ancient Greece, Rome, Alexandria, classical myth, Christian legend, works of art and of scholarship: these are the realms in which he is most at home. His volumes of poetry include two sets of translations, one from Hafiz, one from Leopardi; and scattered among his collections of original verse are poems adapted from Sappho, Anacreon, Alcaeus, Petrarch, de Nerval, and Mallarmé. He has published also a critical study of Victorian romantic poetry, *The Darkling Plain*, and edited in collaboration with David Wright two anthologies, *The Faber Book of Twentieth Century Verse* and *The Forsaken Garden*, which resurrects a number of forgotten Victorian poets from their darnelled tombs.

The poems in his first four volumes — *Wounded Thamnuz* (1942), *Beauty and the Beast* (1943), *The Divided Ways* (1946), and *The Swarming of the Bees* (1950) — are in every sense of the words literary and academic. Some of them depict episodes or characters from opera or from drama — 'Leporello', 'Mosca in the Galleys', 'Don Juan Muses', 'Tannhäuser's End'; some are reconstructions of classical or of Christian legends; 'Heroic Epistle' is an imaginary letter from William Congreve to Anne Bracegirdle; there are poems at the graves of Hart Crane, Mahler, and Gluck. All are written in an elaborate, learned, mannered diction, far removed from the colloquial language of our day and alien in spirit, as in rhythm, from any conceivable mode of current speech. Nobody wants to limit a poet's choice of subject-matter or of diction; but these early works, with their ornate craftsmanship and bejewelled richness, are more like the exercises of a university prizeman, the proficient Latin verses of public-schoolboys or of scholarly recluses, than poems drawing vitality and sap from living experience. Appropriately enough, one of these early pieces is a polished translation of Gray's Latin Ode to Richard West. Two examples of this Parnassian style may suffice:

> The memory of her lust
> Split open the rock-tombs, and buried kings
> Whose brown dead flesh was like dried dates, with eyes
> Of emerald glittering in a gilded mask,

Tripped forth, their grave-bands looped fantastically,
And made their court to her with antic bows.[1]

Her chariot is stopped; they pull her down; they drag her
To the Caesarium. They strip her; her virgin flesh
Is hacked and knacked by oyster-shells. Her blood
Is slippery upon the floor of the church.
Hypatia fell. She was lifted. She became Catherine.
A holy virgin in a bright dazzle of legend,
Hand-fasted to Christ, standing among the stars.[2]

One feels that in these volumes Heath-Stubbs has succumbed to the deleterious influence of the minor nineteenth-century Romantics, that he has lingered in the forsaken garden long after closing time.

In *A Charm Against the Toothache* (1954) the scholarship, the reveries about works of art, the verse on legendary themes are still much in evidence, but he has pared his language, discarded some of his opulent imagery, ceased to reproduce the rhythm and the sensibility of dead epochs and of antique modes. For the first time he looks directly at his own age and at himself, reporting his observations in a colloquial speech, an ironical tone. The Christian faith is no longer an affair of patristic theology, legends of the Saints, or mystical speculation, but a way of life, desired though not always followed. He has left the Oxford of Lionel Johnson for the dingier world of post-war London. In 'Address Not Known' there is sorrow at being betrayed by a friend; in 'Epitaph' the self-portrait reveals a man who has learned to face the possibility of loneliness and of failure, with mingled fortitude, scepticism, and hope:

Mr. Heath-Stubbs as you must understand
Came of a gentleman's family out of Staffordshire
Of as good blood as any in England
But he was wall-eyed and his legs too spare . . .

Orthodox in beliefs as following the English Church
Barring some heresies he would have for recreation

[1] 'Maria Aegyptiaca'.
[2] 'Alexandria'.

> Yet too often left these sound principles (as I am
> told) in the lurch
> Being troubled with idleness, lechery, pride and dissipation.

Not all the excursions into the present are entirely happy; the broad smoking-room humour of 'Good Night, Ireen' is forced and out of character; 'A Ballad of Good King Wenceslas', with its references to the People's Democracy in Czechoslovakia, is a bit too slick, though it has a neat ending:

> When Wenceslas knelt down at Mass,
> And sighed, 'Non nobis, Domine',
> His brother came and cut his throat
> For his unplanned economy.

He is still in some ways most at ease with traditional literary themes and devices; one salutes the sheer ingenuity and technical address of 'The Hundred and Thirty-seventh Psalm Paraphrased', to the tune of 'The Shandon Bells'; his ballad, 'The Death of Digenes Akritas', captures the heroic, extravagant quality of the long Greek struggle against heathen Turk and heretical Bulgar:

> You can take and break my rifle,
> Take my pipe and tinder-box;
> Lay me decent, light a candle,
> Keep the ritual orthodox.

The opening poem of his next volume, *The Triumph of the Muse* (1958), defines his attitude to poetic diction:

> Disdain, my verse, the language of the age:
> Be cold, be hard, impersonal as stone,
> Or only use that argot for your rage.[1]

In the long title-poem he satirizes many of his coevals: of the poets considered in this book the Muse admits to her Hall none but George Barker, whom she places near Villon; the *Personal Landscape* group and the new schoolmen who adopt a neutral tone are unceremoniously chased away. There is no major advance in this

---

[1] 'The Language of the Age'.

volume, although the practised ease and accomplishment of the best poems are more graceful than ever before. The prelude to the title-poem has an exquisitely-contrived melodic pattern:

> Tongueless the forest now,
> Under the arctic Plough;
> Where she with lucid brow
>   Walked in fine weather;
> Each bird of learned trill —
> Woodlark and whippoorwill —
> Sits, hunched, with tuneless bill
>   And drooping feather.

In the melancholy 'Quatrains', although the theme is commonplace and the metre that of FitzGerald's translation of Omar Khayyám, the note of weary resignation is personal and oddly affecting:

> Fate's discords have unharmonized those tunes,
> And blank abstractions blotted out the runes;
>   Each finds his loneliness: FitzGerald knew
> Like impotence among the Suffolk dunes.

> Time with unpitying and iron feet
> Bears down upon us all; we learn to greet,
>   Without despair, the inevitable void,
> Whether in Nishapur or Russell Street.

Some of the poems in his most recent collection, *The Blue-Fly in his Head* (1962), have a lean vigour, a decisive firmness, that may mark the beginning of a new phase in his development. The prefatory note to 'Titus and Berenice', the strongest and most trenchant poem he has ever written, explains that

according to a Jewish tradition Titus was afflicted with an insect in his brain as a punishment for his destruction of the Temple.

In this middle stanza of the poem it is Berenice who speaks:

> 'In darkness master me,
>   Rome with your seven hills,

Roads, rhetorical aqueducts,
  And ravaging eagles;
Worlds are at bitter odds, yet we
  Can find out love at least —
Not expedient to the Senate,
  Abominable to the priest.'
'Buzz!' said the blue-fly in his head.

John Heath-Stubbs is a curiously anachronistic figure in post-war England: a neo-Romantic with a keen satirical wit, a scholar who frequents Soho, a Christian haunted by guilt, remorse, and a fear of damnation. His affinities are with certain members of the Rhymers' Club, those friends and acquaintances of W. B. Yeats who met at the Cheshire Cheese in the eighteen-nineties and whom Yeats has recalled in a dozen poems as well as in his *Autobiographies*.[1] Certainly, Iain Fletcher's judgement on Lionel Johnson, one of the most gifted and most tragic of the Rhymers, is applicable to Heath-Stubbs:

... his eye ... stays for a moment only on the composition of the scene before him for, all too soon, the weight of the past, its learning, its many vivid associations, begin to blur the present.

But, as Fletcher points out, there are compensating virtues in such poetry, however unfashionable they may be:

A moral centre, a sense of style, a concern with human obligation at its noblest, these, where it is most typical, are the attributes of Johnson's verse. The sanctity of scholarship, the beauty of the past, the sense of piety towards institutions, now that the response to these things has faded, such Byzantine virtues have their place.[2]

An attentive reader of post-war poetry would notice the recurrence of certain themes, and the prevalence of a common philosophical temper, in the work of good poets who hold divergent

[1] W. B. Yeats, *Autobiographies*, pp. 164–71, 279–349.
[2] *The Complete Poems of Lionel Johnson*, ed. Iain Fletcher (Unicorn Press, 1953), pp. xxxviii–xl.

religious and political beliefs. The threat of nuclear warfare hangs over much verse composed since 1945, and even poems on traditional Christian themes may be overcast by this shadow. In Charles Causley's 'Innocent's Song' the identity of

> the smiling stranger
> With hair as white as gin

is at first left in doubt, and the purpose of his coming is unknown. Then, a sudden image evokes the glare of the bombs that burst over the cities of Japan:

> Why does the world before him
> Melt in a million suns?

and by the light of that glare, which distorts the Christmas flame, the stranger is revealed as both Herod and contemporary man who plots a new Massacre of the Innocents:

> Watch where he comes walking
> Out of the Christmas flame,
> Dancing, double-talking:
>
> Herod is his name.

Secondly, one observes in many good poets a quiet fortitude, an acceptance of sadness and of pain as inescapable modes of human life which must be borne with dignity. In Gascoyne's resolve to persevere, in R. S. Thomas's reverence for the uncomplaining toil of the muck farmers, and in Ted Hughes's admiration for men and beasts who endure the hostility of the elements, we may discern that Stoicism which, tempered by Christian ethics and softened by Christian sentiment, has been the true religion of most Englishmen since the Reformation.

Finally, in a world where, for all our talk about democracy and freedom, the individual is more dependent than ever before on the whims of bureaucrats and of politicians in our own and in other countries, poets have learned to recognize the fact that only in our private lives can we fruitfully exercise moral choice and practise virtue. To speak the truth, to maintain critical standards, to correct

the slovenly phrase and to prune the rank, luxuriant image: these
are the daily tasks of every man who lives by his pen. A poet who
vigilantly performs them may discover the principles of order and
of coherence that give life and meaning to a poem. There is, in post-
war verse, no more eloquent confession of this faith than the closing
lines of Thom Gunn's poem 'To Yvor Winters, 1955', from which
I have drawn the title and the dominant theme of this book:

> But sitting in the dusk — though shapes combine,
> Vague mass replacing edge and flickering line,
> You keep both Rule and Energy in view,
> Much power in each, most in the balanced two:
> Ferocity existing in the fence
> Built by an exercised intelligence.
> Though night is always close, complete negation
> Ready to drop on wisdom and emotion,
> Night from the air or the carnivorous breath,
> Still it is right to know the force of death,
> And, as you do, persistent, tough in will,
> Raise from the excellent the better still.

BIBLIOGRAPHY

The footnotes to the body of the text indicate the sources of my quotations and my specific debts to other authors. The following bibliography contains:

(i) A short list of anthologies.
(ii) A list of the main volumes published by the poets discussed in Chapters III–VII.
(iii) A short list of critical works.
(iv) A short list of surveys, articles, and reviews.

(i) ANTHOLOGIES

ALVAREZ, A. *The New Poets*. Penguin, 1962
BLACKBURN, T. *45–60: An Anthology of English Poetry 1945–60*. Putnam, 1960
CONQUEST, R. *New Lines*. Macmillan, 1956
ENRIGHT, D. J. *Poets of the 1950's*. Kenkyusha (Tokyo), 1956
FRASER, G. S. & FLETCHER, I. *Springtime*. Peter Owen, 1953
FRASER, G. S. *Poetry Now*. Faber, 1956
JENNINGS, E. *An Anthology of Modern Verse 1940–60*. Methuen, 1961
SERGEANT, H. & ABSE, D. *Mavericks*. Poetry and Poverty, 1957
P.E.N. NEW POEMS — Annually from 1952
THE GUINNESS BOOK OF POETRY 1–5 — Annually from 1956/7

(ii) BOOKS OF VERSE

AMIS, K. *A Frame of Mind*. Reading University, 1953
　　A Case of Samples. Gollancz, 1956
BARKER, G. *Calamiterror*. Faber, 1937
　　Lament and Triumph. Faber, 1940
　　Eros in Dogma. Faber, 1944
　　News of the World. Faber, 1950
　　The True Confession of George Barker. Staples, 1950; Parton, 1957
　　A Vision of Beasts and Gods. Faber, 1954

    Collected Poems. Faber, 1957

    The View from a Blind I. Faber, 1962

BLACKBURN, T. *The Outer Darkness.* Hand & Flower, 1951

    The Holy Stone. Hand & Flower, 1954

    In the Fire. Putnam, 1956

    The Next Word. Putnam, 1958

    A Smell of Burning. Putnam, 1961

CLEMO, J. *The Clay Verge.* Chatto, 1951

    The Map of Clay. Methuen, 1961

DAVIE, D. *Brides of Reason.* Fantasy, 1955

    A Winter Talent. Routledge, 1957

    The Forests of Lithuania. Marvell, 1959

    A Sequence for Francis Parkman. Marvell, 1961

DURRELL, L. *A Private Country.* Faber, 1943

    Cities, Plains and People. Faber, 1946

    On Seeming to Presume. Faber, 1948

    The Tree of Idleness. Faber, 1955

    Selected Poems. Faber, 1956

    Collected Poems. Faber, 1960

ENRIGHT, D. J. *The Laughing Hyena.* Routledge, 1953

    Bread Rather than Blossoms. Secker & Warburg, 1956

    Some Men Are Brothers. Chatto and Hogarth, 1961

    Addictions. Chatto and Hogarth, 1962

FULLER, R. *Poems.* Fortune, 1939

    The Middle of a War. Hogarth, 1942

    A Lost Season. Hogarth, 1944

    Epitaphs and Occasions. Lehmann, 1949

    Counterparts. Verschoyle, 1954

    Brutus's Orchard. Deutsch, 1957

    Collected Poems. Deutsch, 1962

GASCOYNE, D. *Man's Life is this Meat.* Parton, 1936

    Poems 1937–1942. Poetry London, 1943

    A Vagrant. Lehmann, 1950

    Night Thoughts. Deutsch, 1956

GUNN, T. *Fighting Terms.* Fantasy, 1954; Faber, 1962

    The Sense of Movement. Faber, 1957

    My Sad Captains. Faber, 1961

HEATH-STUBBS, J. *Wounded Thamnuz.* Routledge, 1942

HEATH-STUBBS, J. *Beauty and the Beast*. Routledge, 1943
    The Divided Ways. Routledge, 1946
    The Swarming of the Bees. Eyre & Spottiswoode, 1950
    A Charm Against the Toothache. Methuen, 1954
    The Triumph of the Muse. O.U.P., 1958
    The Blue-Fly in his Head. O.U.P., 1962
HUGHES, T. *The Hawk in the Rain*. Faber, 1957
    Lupercal. Faber, 1960
LARKIN, P. *The Less Deceived*. Marvell, 1955
MacCAIG, N. *Riding Lights*. Hogarth, 1955
    The Sinai Sort. Hogarth, 1957
    A Common Grace. Chatto and Hogarth, 1960
    A Round of Applause. Chatto and Hogarth, 1962
PRINCE, F. T. *Poems*. Faber, 1938
    Soldiers Bathing. Fortune, 1954
SPENCER, B. *Aegean Islands*. Poetry London, 1946
    The Twist in the Plotting. Reading University, 1960
THOMAS, R. S. *Song at the Year's Turning*. Hart-Davis, 1955
    Poetry for Supper. Hart-Davis, 1958
    Tares. Hart-Davis, 1961
TILLER, T. *Poems*. Hogarth, 1941
    The Inward Animal. Hogarth, 1943
    Unarm, Eros. Hogarth, 1947
    Reading a Medal. Hogarth, 1957
TOMLINSON, C. *The Necklace*. Fantasy, 1955
    Seeing is Believing. O.U.P., 1960
    Versions from Fyodor Tyutchev. O.U.P., 1960
WATKINS, V. *Ballad of the Mari Lwyd*. Faber, 1941
    The Lamp and the Veil. Faber, 1945
    The Lady with the Unicorn. Faber, 1948
    The Death Bell. Faber, 1954
    Cypress and Acacia. Faber, 1959
    Affinities. Faber, 1962

(iii) CRITICISM

ALVAREZ, A. *The Shaping Spirit*. Chatto, 1958
BLACKBURN, T. *The Price of an Eye*. Putnam, 1961

DAVIE, D. *Purity of Diction in English Verse.* Chatto, 1952
    Articulate Energy. Routledge, 1955
ENRIGHT, D. J. *The Apothecary's Shop.* Secker & Warburg, 1957
FRASER, G. S. *Vision and Rhetoric.* Faber, 1959
HOLLOWAY, J. *The Charted Map.* Routledge, 1960
JENNINGS, E. *Every Changing Shape.* Deutsch, 1961
MANDER, J. *The Writer and Commitment.* Secker & Warburg, 1961

(iv) SURVEYS, ARTICLES, REVIEWS

Surveys

Longmans have published for the British Council four surveys of English verse since 1939. Each survey contains brief discussions of individual poets, photographs of a number of these poets, and a bibliography. The following surveys have been published:

SPENDER, S. *Poetry Since 1939.* Longmans, 1946
ROSS, A. *Poetry 1945–1950.* Longmans, 1951
MOORE, G. *Poetry To-day.* Longmans, 1958
JENNINGS, E. *Poetry To-day.* Longmans, 1961

Articles

ALVAREZ, A. and DAVIE, D. 'A Discussion'. *The Review*, No. 1 (April/May 1962), 10–25.
DAVIE, D. 'Remembering the Movement'. *Prospect* (Summer 1959), 13–16.
DYSON, A. E. 'Ted Hughes'. *Critical Quarterly*, vol. 1, No. 3 (Autumn 1959), 219–36.
FRASER, G. S. 'The Poetry of Thom Gunn'. *Critical Quarterly*, vol. 3, No. 4 (Winter 1961), 359–67.
MERCHANT, W. MOELWYN. 'R. S. Thomas'. *Critical Quarterly*, vol. 3, No. 4 (Winter 1960), 341–51.
WAIN, J. 'English Poetry: The Immediate Situation'. *Sewanee Review*, LXV, No. 3 (1957), 353–74.
'English Poetry Since 1945'. *London Magazine*, vol. 6, No. 11 (November 1959), 11–36 — a symposium, with articles by G. S. Fraser, John Holloway, Roy Fuller, George MacBeth, Elizabeth Jennings, and A. Norman Jeffares.
'Context'. *London Magazine*, New Series vol. 1, No. 11 (February 1962), 27–53 — contains answers by twenty-six poets to a questionnaire

about poetry. Among these poets are Larkin, Durrell, Fuller, Blackburn, Enright, Gunn, Spencer, Watkins, and Hughes.

Reviews

BROWNJOHN, A. 'The Brutal Tone'. *Listen*, vol. 2, No. 4 (Spring 1958), 20–23 — contains a review of Ted Hughes, *The Hawk in the Rain*.

CARR, W. I. Review of Ted Hughes, *The Hawk in the Rain*. *Delta*, No. 14 (Spring 1958), 25–27.

GUNN, T. 'Three Poets'. *Listen*, vol. 3, No. 1 (Winter 1958), 12–14, 19–22 — contains a review of Donald Davie, *A Winter Talent*.

KERMODE, F. 'The Problem of Pleasure'. *Listen*, vol. 2, No. 4 (Spring 1958), 14–19 — contains a review of Thom Gunn, *The Sense of Movement*.

TOMLINSON, C. 'The Middlebrow Muse'. *Essays in Criticism*, vol. VIII, No. 2 (April 1957), 208–17 — review of *New Lines*, ed. Robert Conquest.

INDEX

PRINTED BY ROBERT MACLEHOSE AND CO. LTD
THE UNIVERSITY PRESS,
GLASGOW